St JEAN

Chemin de la Métairie

Ancien Chemin du Lac

Chemin du Lac Pontchartrain

GATEWAY TO NEW ORLEANS

BAYOU ST. JOHN
1708-2018

GATEWAY TO NEW ORLEANS

BAYOU ST. JOHN
1708-2018

Edited by

Mary Louise Mossy Christovich
Florence M. Jumonville
Heather Veneziano

Written by

Hilary Somerville Irvin
R. Stephanie Bruno
Heather Veneziano
S. Frederick Starr

Photography by

Robert S. Brantley and Jan White Brantley

LOUISIANA LANDMARKS SOCIETY

UNIVERSITY OF LOUISIANA AT LAFAYETTE PRESS

2018

Book design: Heather Veneziano

ISBN 13 (paper): 978-1-946160-24-9

http://ulpress.org
University of Louisiana at Lafayette Press
P.O. Box 43558
Lafayette, LA 70504-3558

Printed on acid-free paper in Canada.

Library of Congress Cataloging-in-Publication Data

Names: Christovich, Mary Louise, editor. | Jumonville, Florence M., editor.
| Veneziano, Heather, editor. |
   Louisiana Landmarks Society, issuing body.
Title: Gateway to New Orleans : Bayou St. John, 1708-2018 / edited by Mary
   Louise Mossy Christovich, Florence M. Jumonville, Heather Veneziano ;
   written by Hilary S. Irvin, R. Stephanie Bruno, Heather Veneziano, S. Frederick Starr ;
   photography by Robert S. Brantley and Jan White Brantley.
Description: Lafayette : Louisiana Landmarks Society, Center For Louisiana
   Studies, University of Louisiana At Lafayette Press, 2018. | Includes
   bibliographical references and index.
Identifiers: LCCN 2018006720 | ISBN 9781946160249 (alk. paper)
Subjects: LCSH: Bayou St. John (New Orleans, La.)--History. | Bayou St. John
   (New Orleans, La.)--Buildings, structures, etc. | Historic
   districts--Louisiana--New Orleans. | Architecture--Louisiana--New Orleans.
   | New Orleans (La.)--History. | New Orleans (La.)--Buildings, structures,
   etc.
Classification: LCC F379.N56 B394 2018 | DDC 976.3/35--dc23

LC record available at https://lccn.loc.gov/2018006720

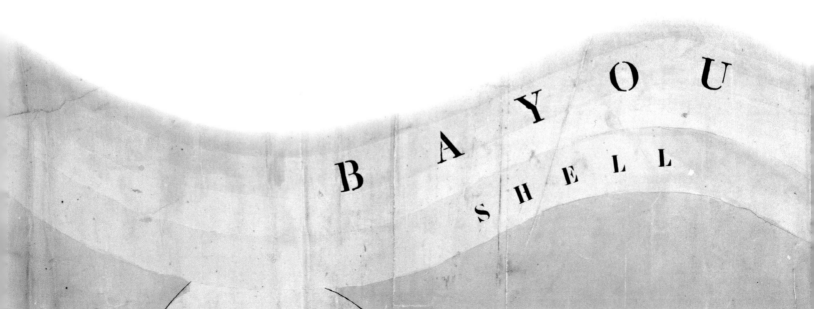

To our dear friend and mentor,
Mary Louise Mossy Christovich
(1928-2017)

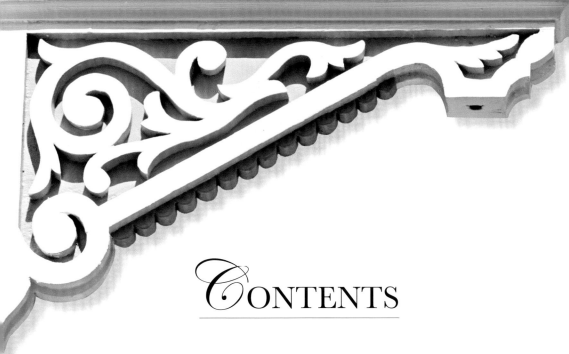

CONTENTS

$\mathscr{L}$OUISIANA LANDMARKS SOCIETY

Sandra L. Stokes, President

Founded in 1950, Louisiana Landmarks Society is the oldest statewide preservation association in Louisiana. The society was officially organized in response to futile efforts the year before to save the nineteenth-century David Olivier House on Chartres Street from demolition. The founders included nationally recognized stalwarts of preservation, such as Harnett T. Kane, Martha Robinson, Samuel Wilson Jr., Mrs. S. Walter Stern, Ray Samuel, Charles "Pie" Dufour, and Buford L. Pickens.

Subsequent preservation initiatives by the Landmarks Society met with great success, beginning with the preservation of the 1845 Gallier Hall designed by James Gallier Sr., which served as the original city hall of New Orleans for more than one hundred years and now is the center stage for the city's Mardi Gras royalty. The 1855 Carrollton Courthouse, which had been designed by architect Henry Howard to house the seat of Jefferson Parish government until New Orleans annexed the City of Carrollton in 1874, had been slated for demolition for a grocery store and parking lot prior to the campaign to save it. Louisiana Landmarks Society was crucial in saving portions of the Chalmette Battlefield and instrumental in stopping the Riverfront Expressway, a proposed elevated expressway in front of Jackson Square that would have destroyed the ambience of the French Quarter and created a barrier precluding residents' access to the Mississippi River.

The circa 1799 French colonial plantation-style Pitot House graces the banks of beautiful Bayou St. John as a tangible legacy of the dogged determination and ability of Louisiana Landmarks Society to fulfill its mission. Saved from demolition in 1964, the Pitot House was moved several blocks to its current site on Moss Street. After suffering a major setback from the wrath of Hurricane Betsy in 1965, the house was fully restored by 1972. Following the acquisition of a collection of period furnishings, Louisiana Landmarks Society opened the Pitot House Museum to the public in 1973. Today the house museum and gardens remain open for tours for the public and school groups, hosts rotating special exhibits and events, and serves as offices and headquarters for the organization.

From its inception, Louisiana Landmarks Society objectives have been:

- To focus attention on Louisiana's historic buildings as living remains of our history and physical reminders of the rich heritage bequeathed to us.

- To promote the preservation of important landmarks and to encourage public appreciation and support when their loss or destruction is threatened.

- To foster a more general interest in the architectural traditions of this region and to encourage research and aid in publishing results.

- To provide a forum for those who have an interest in Louisiana's landmarks and cooperate with other organizations whose activities touch upon these aims.

These purposes still guide the organization as Landmarks Society continues to lead various advocacy efforts: working tirelessly to stop demolition of historic buildings; to protect the quaint and distinctive character of historic neighborhoods of New Orleans; and to promote proper land use and the strengthening of the city's Master Plan and Comprehensive Zoning Ordinance.

Each year Louisiana Landmarks Society designates "New Orleans' Nine Most Endangered Sites" to focus attention on the most at-risk buildings or issues threatening our city's cultural and architectural resources. Additionally, by hosting the annual "Awards for Excellence in Historic Preservation," the organization recognizes outstanding achievements in historic restoration, renovation, and new construction. Louisiana Landmarks Society also serves the community by providing numerous educational opportunities for all ages, including lectures, panel discussions, exhibits, school field trips, tours, and heritage programs.

New Orleans is truly a unique city. The preservationists who founded Louisiana Landmarks Society understood this and laid down a solid foundation for the future. The organization remains true to its mission—promoting historic preservation through effective advocacy, education, and operation of the Pitot House.

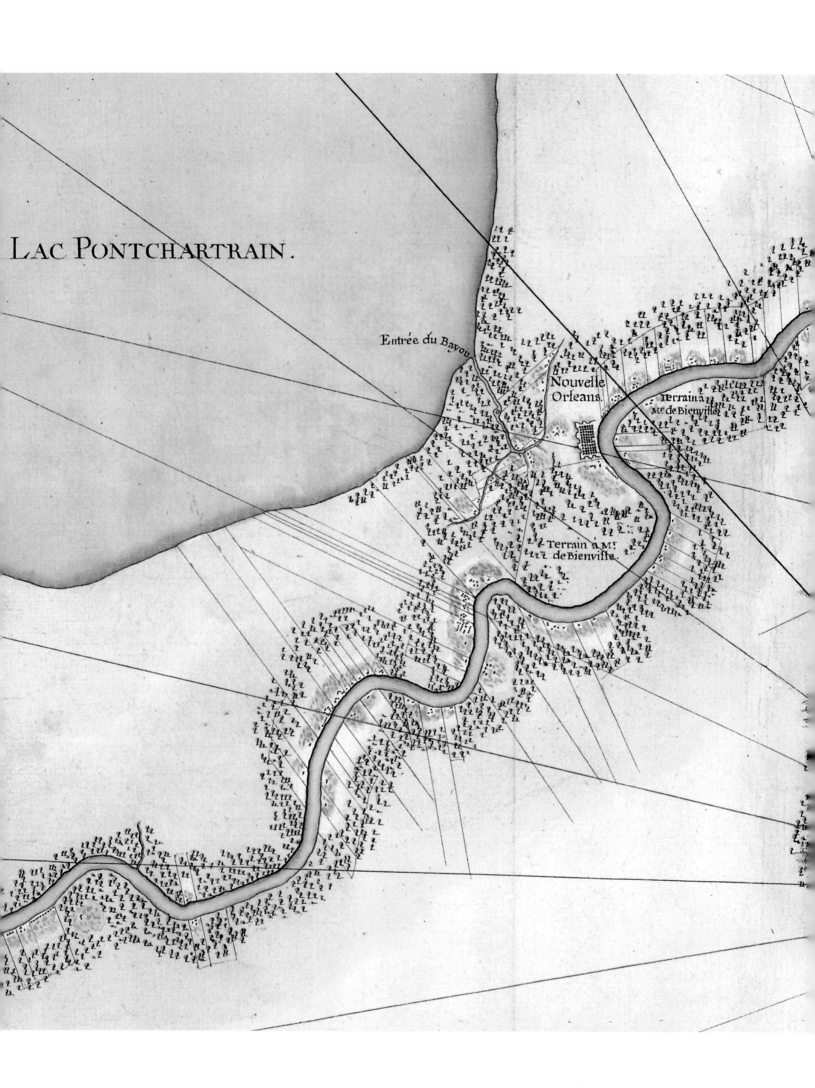

LAC PONTCHARTRAIN.

Entrée du Bayou

Nouvelle
Orleans.

Terrain à
M. de Bienville

Terrain à M.
de Bienville.

REFACE

Richard Campanella

The natives called it *Bayouk Choupic*. The French renamed it *St. Jean*, which the Spanish translated as *San Juan* and Anglophones as *St. John's Creek*. Today we call it Bayou St. John, and were it not for this sluggish rivulet, we would not have New Orleans today—at least, not in this location.

For over three hundred years, placid, scenic Bayou St. John has played an outsized role in the history and geography of greater New Orleans, and it is fitting that a volume be devoted to its dazzling inventory of historical architecture.

That role was all about *access*, or, more specifically, *alternative* access: a way for French colonials to get to the banks of the Mississippi, even when treacherous shoals impeded the river's mouth. The route entailed sailing westward from Mobile or Biloxi, across the

Above: View of Bayou St. John *by William Henry Buck, 1880. Courtesy of Neal Auction Company.*

Left: Detail of Carte du cours du fleuve St. Louis depuis dix lieues audessus de la Nouvelle Orleans jusqu'à son embouchure ou sont marquées les habitations formées, et les terrains concedez *[i.e.* concédés*], auxquels on n'a pas travaille, ca. 1732, showing Bayou St. John and its entrance on Lake Pontchartrain and New Orleans on the Mississippi River. Library of Congress, Geography and Map Division.*

Mississippi Sound and into Lake Borgne, through the Rigolets Pass, and to the southern shore of Lake Pontchartrain, where Bayou St. John beckoned amid the dense, dark *ciprière*.

Twisted and debris-strewn as the channel was, the two-mile bayou nevertheless allowed navigable

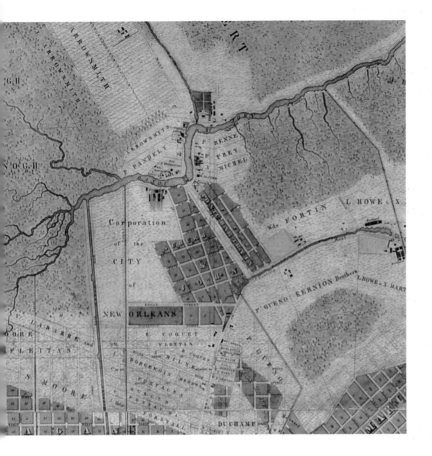

passage to a ridge (today's Bayou Road), which thence enabled terrestrial portage through the swamps to the upraised banks of the Mississippi—and the site that Bienville, in 1718, selected for New Orleans. "The capital city is advantageously situated," wrote Bienville eight years later. "Bayou St. John which is behind the city is of such great convenience because of the communication . . . it affords with Lake Pontchartrain and consequently with the sea. . . . It cannot be esteemed too highly."

Two adjacent bayous, Metairie and Gentilly, now mostly extinct, help explain how Bayou St. John formed. Around 2,600 years ago, the Mississippi River partially lunged eastward, disemboguing in what is now eastern St. Bernard Parish. While flowing in this channel, the river deposited sediment and began forming the Metairie-Gentilly Ridge (today's Metairie Road, City Park Avenue, and Gentilly Boulevard). Over the next 1,200 years, the river would jump twice more and eventually settle into its current channel, turning the Metairie-Gentilly channel into an "abandoned distributary"—that is, a long, narrow stream broken off from the river, paralleled by upraised banks.

Sometime later, possibly on account of a sedimentary fault, a break opened along its banks, allowing water to flow northward into Lake Pontchartrain, forming Bayou St. John. Another theory holds that the bayou originated as a distributary of the Mississippi itself, during the time when it wended along the Metairie-Gentilly route.

By the dawn of the colonial era, Bayou St. John intercepted the Metairie-Gentilly Ridge, with Bayou Metairie on the west side and Bayou Gentilly on the east, while its own hydrology intermixed tide-influenced waters from Lake Pontchartrain with run-off from as far inland as today's Broadmoor. Bayou St. John was thus an ecologically rich mini-estuary, with brackish water at one end, fresh water at the other, hardwood forests all along, and dense cypress swamps all around.

What makes the area covered in this volume so historic, and so geographically critical to the larger

New Orleans story, is that it brought together four vital elements for colonial settlement: navigable access, passable roads, developable high ground, and arable soils. No surprise, then, that Bayou St. John, at its intersection with the Metairie and Gentilly ridges, witnessed the region's first French settlement, in 1708, fully ten years before the founding of New Orleans. Bienville selected a small group of Mobile colonists from the Gulf Coast to attempt to meet the King's mandate to grow wheat and tobacco. Those Mobile colonists' wheat and tobacco crops failed, but small farms and dairies would later prosper around Bayou St. John in the French era, helping feed early New Orleans.

In the Spanish colonial era, Governor Hector de Carondelet deemed *Bayou San Juan* so vital that in 1794 he had a channel excavated to extend its navigable waters to the rear of the city. "This canal rises in a basin sufficiently capacious to accommodate several small vessels," wrote Amos Stoddard of the Carondelet Canal in 1812. "It extends . . . two miles to St. John's creek, and is [a] great advantage to the city, particularly as the products of the lake and back country, such as fish, lime, tar, pitch, and various other articles, find an easy water access to the inhabitants. . . ." The Carondelet Canal is today's Lafitte Greenway, and the canal's old turning basin gave Basin Street its name.

Commercial access plus adjacent high ground attracted the forces of urbanization to Bayou St. John in the opening years of the American era. Initial platting as Faubourg Pontchartrain occurred as early as 1809, but development stalled as a prolonged lawsuit involving land ownership played out. The suit by Myra Clark Gaines to recover her inheritance from her father, Daniel Clark, from the City of New Orleans lasted for more than fifty years (1834-1891) and is known as the longest-running lawsuit in U.S. history. After its settlement, the disputed area became accessible for development.

By the 1830s, street grids for both Faubourg Pontchartrain and Faubourg St. John were laid out on either side of Grand Route St. John, with Bayou St. John at one end, the remnants of Bayou Gentilly on the other, and both Bayou Road and the Carondelet (Old Basin) Canal connecting them with downtown New Orleans. Shortly thereafter, Esplanade Avenue would be cut through as a grand avenue between city and bayou, almost literally paving the way for this bucolic landscape of farms, dairies, drawbridges, and pirogues finally to be subsumed into urban New Orleans.

Bayou St. John as a waterway would change radically in the early twentieth century, as its navigation days came to pass, the swamps were drained, City Park and Gentilly came into being along its flanks, and its channel was straightened and banks stabilized. But Bayou St. John as a neighborhood would remain remarkably stable, its hundreds of historical structures and intimate streetscapes retaining their secluded, village-like ambience.

This book tells their stories, and those of the people behind them. It is a story older than the city itself; indeed, it is a story of the very provenance of New Orleans.

Left: 1920s aerial view of the Faubourg St. John area and Bayou St. John looking toward the lake, with City Park at upper left and Gentilly, still mostly undeveloped at upper right, beyond the New Orleans Fair Grounds Race Course. The Charles L. Franck Studio Collection at The Historic New Orleans Collection, 1979.325.6430.

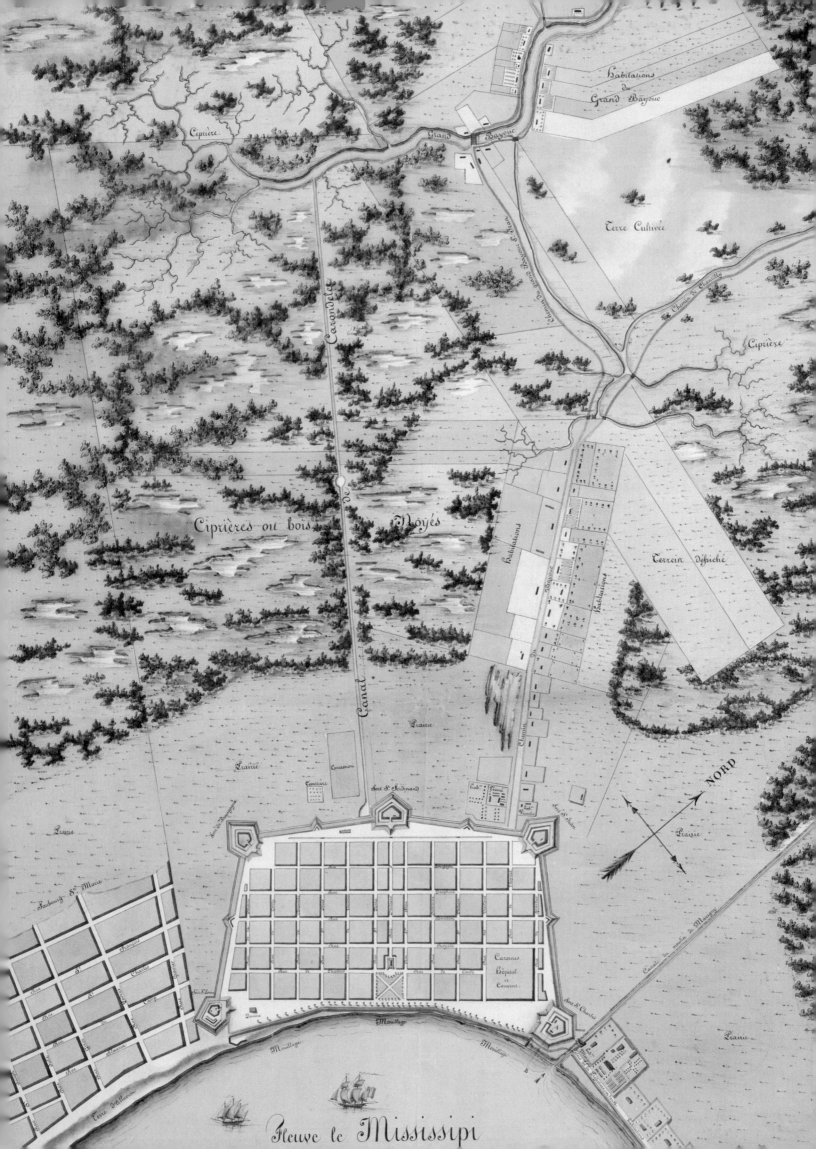

Fleuve le Mississipi

Historical Overview

BAYOU ST. JOHN: THE SETTLEMENT
THAT GAVE BIRTH TO NEW ORLEANS

S. Frederick Starr

The Bayou St. John neighborhood occupies a singular place in the history of New Orleans and the lower Mississippi valley. Settled in 1708, at the very beginning of the eighteenth century, it is a decade older than New Orleans itself, founded in 1718, and also predates the establishment of Natchitoches, founded in 1714. It is Louisiana's oldest settlement, and would be acknowledged as such were it to be considered a city rather than, today, as a neighborhood of some 4,500 inhabitants. Indeed, it was the existence of Bayou St. John and the settlement that arose along its banks that led to the founding of New Orleans.

Like the city itself, but unlike many other areas that became faubourgs, the existence of the Bayou St. John's district resulted from specific economic benefits that arose from its location astride a key transport route. Like the city as a whole, but unlike any other neighborhood, Bayou St. John briefly enjoyed geostrategic importance to all three of the great global empires whose armies contended for control of the Mississippi valley during the eighteenth century, as well as to the United States. And to a significant degree, both the rise and fall of Bayou St. John as an economic force in the city of New Orleans traced directly to technological innovation, which deeply impacted the area twice in the nineteenth century.

Geography determined the location and character of the Bayou St. John neighborhood. From the late seventeenth century, French explorers and settlers sought a way to transport people and goods up the

Mississippi. The river's powerful and relentless current made sailing upstream an arduous and uncertain task. Prevailing winds required ships to tack endlessly in order to sail upstream, a formidable challenge for even the best sailors. What is known today as English Turn presented a nearly impassable obstacle to sailing vessels, which had to wait days or weeks for the right combination of wind and currents. It was one thing for France to have claimed the Mississippi valley but quite another matter to settle it.

Fortunately, the French explorers quickly discovered a shortcut. By crossing Lake Borgne, sailing through the narrow straits at the Rigolets, and then traversing Lake Pontchartrain, they could reach Bayou St. John, which offered a (barely) navigable route that brought vessels to a point less than two miles from the Mississippi. A short portage that Native Americans had used since time immemorial connected the bayou to the Mississippi. This route saved vessels seeking to ascend the Mississippi nearly fifty miles of slow and uncertain upstream struggle against currents and wind.

This shortcut—defined by Bayou St. John—led directly to the founding of New Orleans at what was otherwise a very unlikely and unwelcoming location. Ascending the river from its mouth, the first site that is truly suitable for settlement is Baton Rouge. But once they had discovered the route through Bayou St. John and begun using it, the French recognized the need to establish a depot and defense point on the banks of the Mississippi at the southern end of the short portage— in other words, at what became New Orleans. Thus, Bayou St. John was the key to both the establishment and siting of New Orleans. Without Bayou St. John, it is doubtful that New Orleans would have existed where it currently stands.

Left: Plan de la Nouvelle Orléans et des environs. Dédié au Citoyen Laussat Préfet Colonial et Commissaire de la République Française. *By Joseph Antoine Vinache, 1803. The Historic New Orleans Collection, 1987.65 i-iii.*

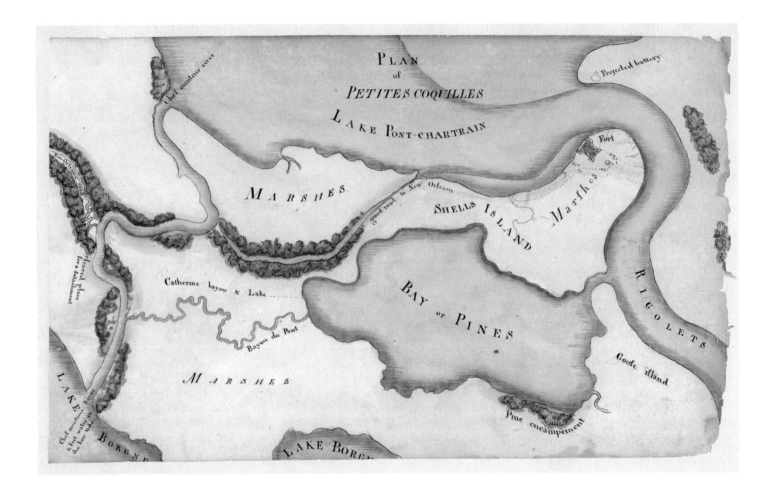

Above: Plan of Petites Coquilles *(Small Shells). Hand-drawn plan showing Lake Pontchartrain, Shells Island, Bayou Catherine, Lake Borgne, Bay of Pines, Goose Island, the Rigolets, Fort Petites Coquilles, and a projected supporting battery opposite the fort. Produced by Barthélémy Lafon, 1814. The Historic New Orleans Collection, 1970.2.14.*

But the bayou presented many impediments of its own. It was of such slight depth that only vessels with a very shallow draft could navigate it. Worse, tall trees along its soggy banks often collapsed into the water, cutting off navigation until sailors could remove them. Nonetheless, the French persisted, for they knew that this obscure shortcut greatly simplified transport from Spanish-held Pensacola and Mobile, where France had planted its flag. Most of the French vessels that traversed this route were small, coastal ships with far less draft than the grand ocean-going ships. This enabled them not only to pass safely through the narrow, eight-mile-long Rigolets strait, but even to sail up the bayou itself. If the wind failed them, these boats could be towed by mules plodding along the banks of the bayou.

As a result, Bayou St. John—or "Grand Bayou de St. Jean," as Jean Baptiste le Moyne, Sieur de Bienville named it—from the end of the seventeenth century was recognized as the essential route for transporting goods to the Mississippi River and thence to the Mississippi valley. Correspondence and legal transactions confirm the presence of early settlers along the upper reaches of the bayou as early

as 1708, a full decade before Bienville established a few huts in the front of his majestic river crescent. Wharfs and more warehouses were constructed at the bayou's mouth at Lake Pontchartrain and at its inland terminus, approximately where Bell Street is today.

Early on, warehouses and nautical supply houses, not grand residences, became the most common building types in the area, providing the earliest evidence of these nautical- and transport-related industries near the mouth of the bayou. Other warehouses were built near the Bell Street end of the bayou from an early date. Related facilities quickly arose near the Mississippi to store goods that had either been transported along the narrow ditch that headed off from the bayou toward the city or had been carried by wagon along the two-mile portage trail from the bayou's terminus.

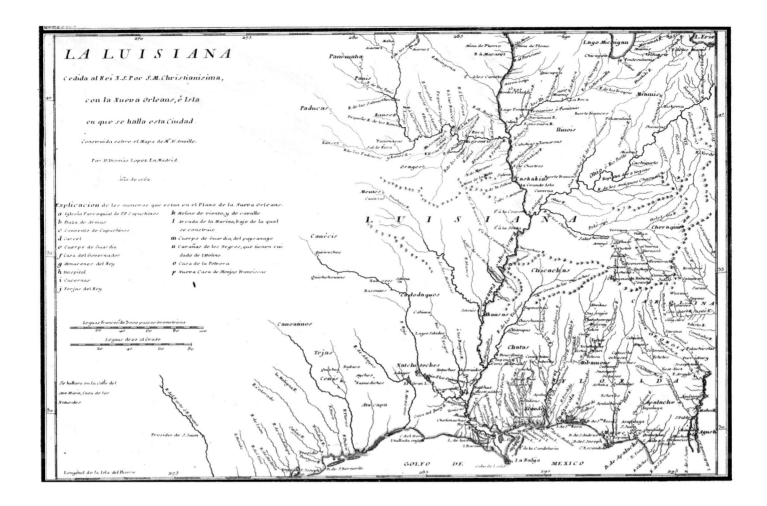

Above: La Luisiana *depicts the territory of Colonial Louisiana, extending from Florida to Texas and north to the southernmost shore of Lake Michigan. By Tomás López de Vargas Machuca. Madrid, 1762. The Historic New Orleans Collection, 1955.20 i-iii.*

Down to 1762, the French settlements at Bayou St. John and New Orleans were relatively secure, not only from Native American raids but also from incursions by rival colonial powers. Nor did that really change thereafter. But over the preceding three years, the British army (which included George Washington as a junior officer) achieved a momentous victory over French forces in the New World. Soon, events occurring as far away as Quebec City, Detroit, Florida, and Pittsburgh impacted Bayou St. John and New Orleans itself. A secret provision of the treaty that settled the conflict forced the French to cede all lands west of the Mississippi, and New Orleans itself, to Spain. This compensated the Spanish for their loss to Britain of Florida, and its capital, Pensacola. With little to say in the matter, French residents of the scraggly settlements at New Orleans and Bayou St. John suddenly found themselves part of Spain's vast empire. Overnight, they ceased to be a remote backwater and became entangled in a major geostrategic struggle between the two greatest empires on earth, Spain and Britain.

It took Spain several years to appoint a commandant for these territories and to install him within the governing body—the Cabildo in New Orleans. Despite two devastating fires in 1788 and 1794, New Orleans was to expand under Spanish rule, with the addition of handsome public buildings and private residences with flat roofs (*azoteas*). But the route through Bayou St. John languished, since Spain had been forced to cede its lands to the east to Britain.

This did not mean, however, that Bayou St. John was forgotten. Far from it! From the moment Spain gained control of Louisiana, it began maneuvering to capture the entire Gulf Coast, clear to Pensacola. Britain, for its part, immediately perceived the new threat from Spain, which was made more ominous by the proximity of the large Spanish garrison and naval base at Havana. Bayou St. John, like New Orleans itself, now found itself as a pawn in this European Game of Thrones.

Tension between Britain and Spain had boiled for decades, but came to a head when Britain's American colonies declared their independence in 1776. This drove both Britain and Spain into head-to-head conflict over the Gulf Coast, which each empire rightly perceived as crucial to its interests in North America and the Caribbean. The appointment in 1777 of Bernardo de Gálvez as the Spanish governor of Louisiana brought to power a man known for his staunchly anti-British stance. When Spain declared war on Britain in 1779, Lake Pontchartrain and Bayou St. John were suddenly thrust into the front line of imperial conflict. Only with the Treaty of Paris in 1783 did Britain and Spain come to terms, with Spain holding on to West Florida but gaining East Florida as well, in exchange for Bermuda. A tense truce resulted.

In 1791 the Spanish King Carlos IV appointed forty-three-year-old Baron Francisco Luis Hector de Carondelet as governor of Louisiana and West Florida. Of Burgundian descent and a fluent French-speaker, Carondelet was well versed in the geopolitics of the day. In a classic case of "refighting the last war," Carondelet continued to view New Orleans as a besieged city. Anticipating a British attack either from the Mississippi or from Lake Pontchartrain, he constructed a major fort on the Mississippi below New Orleans, as well as forts at the Rigolets and improved defenses at Fort St. John at the mouth of the bayou on Lake Pontchartrain.

However, many of Carondelet's fortification plans were never fully carried out during his term in office. The Treaty of San Ildefonso in 1800 returned Louisiana to France, thus eliminating the need for such strong defenses in the area. Future mayor of New Orleans James (Jacques) Pitot, who arrived in the city in 1797 and eventually took up residence on Bayou St. John ("Pitot House"), considered all of Carondelet's fortifications, including his improvements to Fort St. John, as a useless waste of money. In a report to the French government that he penned in 1802, he objected to the "costly fortifications with which Carondelet needlessly surrounded New Orleans."[1]

Above: Don Bernardo de Gálvez (1746–1786). *Lithograph, Goupil and Company, 1903. The Historic New Orleans Collection, Gift of Mr. Thomas N. Lennox, 1991.34.15.*

Below: Francisco Luis Hector, Baron de Carondelet (1748–1807). *Unknown artist, twentieth century. Courtesy of the Collections of the Louisiana State Museum, Accession #T0001.1967.*

A Map of the State of Louisiana with Part of the State of Mississippi and Alabama Territory. *Insert:* Map showing the landing of the British Army, 1815, at the Battle of New Orleans. *Maxwell Ludlow, ca. 1820. The Historic New Orleans Collection, 1939.2 i,ii.*

Pitot had a point. By the time Carondelet arrived, little military need remained for a fort on the Mississippi and none for the forts protecting Bayou St. John. From what quarter did Carondelet anticipate an attack? Britain was nearly out of the picture and was to remain so down to its last-ditch and ill-fated attempt to seize New Orleans in 1815. Even then, General Pakenham chose neither the Mississippi nor the Rigolets-Bayou St. John approach to the city, using instead a convoluted route that brought him overland to present-day Chalmette. The United States, if it were to covet New Orleans, would surely get there by sailing down the Mississippi, not up it. Only much later did the American military planners decide to refortify the Rigolets, but then the officer in charge, locally born Pierre Gustave Toutant Beauregard, made no effort to refortify the mouth of Bayou St. John.

Carondelet's over-reaction to geopolitical events may be excused in light of his full appreciation of the commercial importance of Bayou St. John, for it was this Spanish governor who undertook to widen the mere ditch that had headed from the bayou toward the city and turned it into a navigable waterway. The Carondelet Canal (1794-1938), which was initially dug under his governorship, enabled merchants with small vessels to sail from the Gulf of Mexico directly to a basin just outside the fortifications of New Orleans itself, without reloading their goods onto smaller vessels or canal boats. This opened a new era for Bayou St. John, both as a commercial center and as a place of residence. Carondelet's canal is remembered today only in the name of Basin Street and has been reconfigured into a bicycle path, the Lafitte Greenway.

It has long been assumed that the house still standing at 1300 Moss Street was originally a Spanish custom house. This may indeed have been the case, but currently there is no documentary evidence to confirm it. An equally likely spot to situate a customs point would have been the small settlement of wharfs and warehouses that grew up at the mouth of the bayou near Fort St. John.

James Pitot gave Governor Carondelet high marks for initiating the canal project but had only abuse for the city fathers at the Cabildo who failed to maintain

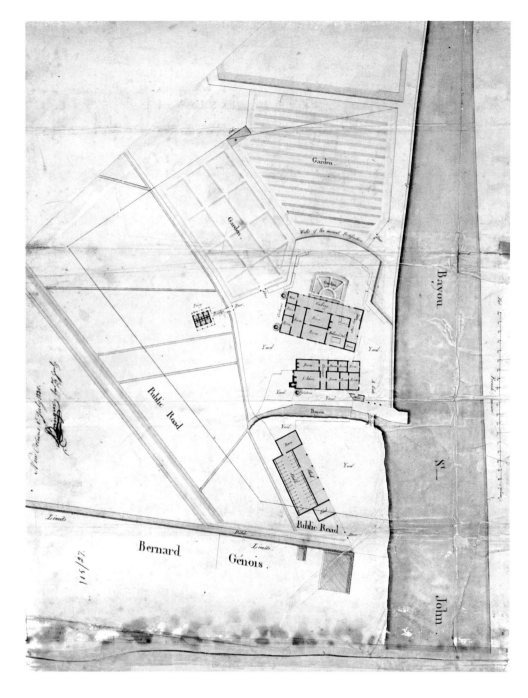

it. In his *Observations*, Pitot complained that by 1802 the canal was in serious need of repair and that Bayou St. John itself was barely navigable, being "more and more blocked by debris and old trees that have fallen from its banks." So badly was it silted up that a pirogue could barely pass along it. This, he charged, was "due to the culpable indifference and the lack of maintenance."[2] In a telling conclusion, he noted that this hurt not only the economy of New Orleans but all the farmers of the Florida parishes.

Later, when Pitot served briefly as mayor, he tried to rectify these problems. He and other New Orleanians concluded, however, that the only way to assure that the bayou and Carondelet Canal would

function effectively was for the canal to be run by the private sector. Accordingly, he helped organize the New Orleans Navigation Company, of which he then served as president. Pitot's clever plan was to turn the waterway into a toll canal. Thanks to his political connections, he and his partners gained the right to set up this business, which proved lucrative for many decades thereafter while at the same time greatly benefiting the regional economy.

The construction of the Carondelet Canal in 1794 marked the completion of a transport system that was regional in scope. It opened supply chains from the entire Gulf Coast region, from Louisiana's Florida parishes, and from the southern half of Mississippi.

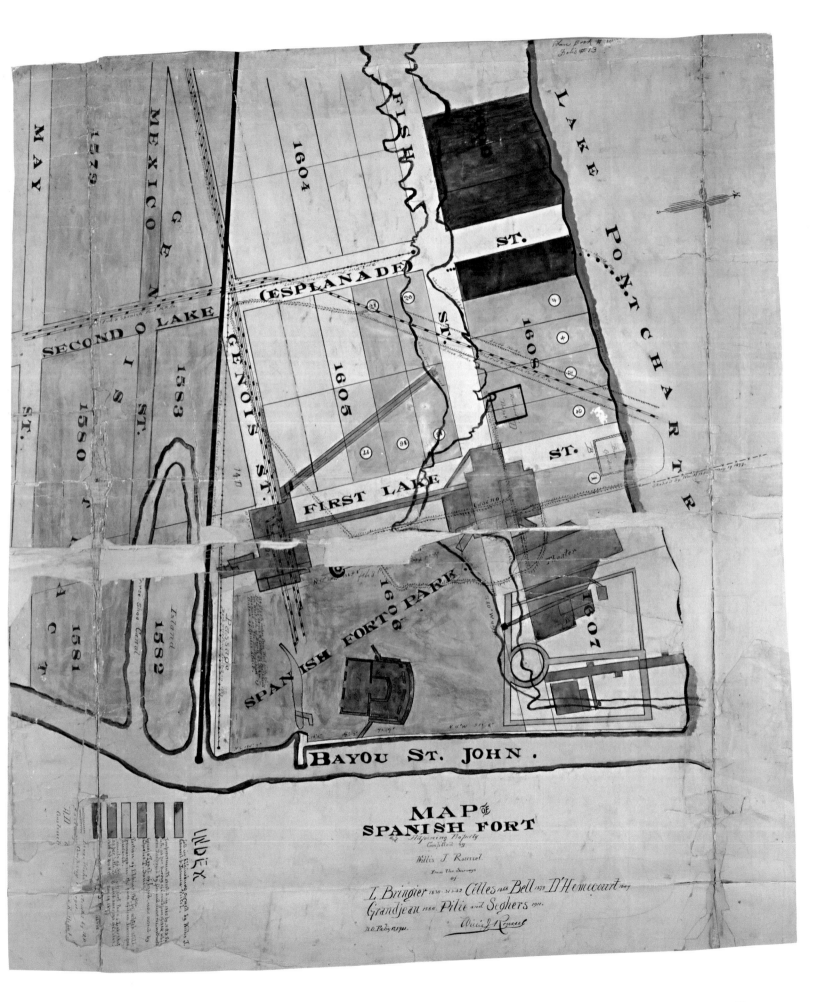

MAP OF
SPANISH FORT

Left: Theodore Lilienthal's 1867 photograph of the Old Basin illustrates the heavy commercial use of the Carondelet Canal. The basin is lined with skiffs and coast schooners that have delivered their cargo of lumber, cordwood, oysters, produce, and other materials. The yard seen on the left belonged to Joseph Jouet. One year later it was acquired by C. L. Hote & Co. and remained active into the twentieth century. The well-designed two-story brick building on the right was the Masonic Temple, meeting place of over ten separate lodges. By the 1890s it had become a dance hall. The Historic New Orleans Collection, Courtesy of Fritz A. Grobien.

Once Pitot's New Orleans Navigation Company gained the right to charge for its use, the canal's maintenance was assured. This event marked the beginning of the second phase in the history of Bayou St. John. The U.S. government still thought it prudent to fortify the entrance to the Rigolets, but military concerns were now a thing of the past.

These conditions greatly fostered the development of the neighborhood adjoining the bayou. Pitot, as head of the company that managed the canal, found it convenient to reside there. As Hilary Irvin documents in this volume, more than a few wealthy New Orleanians found it an attractive place to live, even if it was somewhat remote from town. But there were factors that would surely have made the area less attractive to well-heeled prospective residents. For one thing, warehouses were everywhere, along with an uncared-for waterway with unmanned skiffs and flatboats. These structures of two or even three stories lacked all architectural refinement. Built of beams and boards shipped across the lake, they were windowless and inaccessible, so as to discourage thieves. In addition to warehouses were facilities to repair boats, fashion sails, and sell

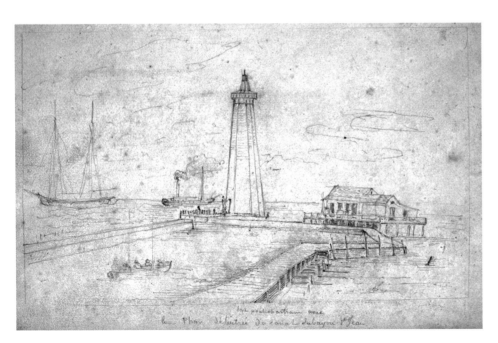

Le lac Pontchartrain avec ce phare de l'entrée du canal du Bayou St. Jean, Charles Alexandre Lesueur, 1830. The octagonal wooden lighthouse, built in 1811 on an artificial island, was the first lighthouse constructed by the United States outside the original thirteen colonies. An eight-foot storm surge in the hurricane of October 5-6, 1837, now known as "Racer's Storm," destroyed it. A replacement was built in 1838 and the site deactivated in 1878. The drawing depicts an outbound coast schooner and a single-mast, rear-paddlewheel steamboat entering the bayou; also included is a rowboat with five individuals who appear to be fishing. Muséum d'Histoire Naturelle du Havre, Le Havre, France.

Above: Then-and-now views of the bayou, looking toward the Magnolia Bridge from near Carrollton Avenue. The detail of the 1867 photograph by Theodore Lilienthal shows a "lumber float" awaiting transport, and on the far left is the office and car barn of the New Orleans City & Lake Railroad, followed by the Tissot and Pitot houses. Streetcar tracks run along the levee on the right. The Historic New Orleans Collection, Courtesy of Fritz A. Grobien.

Left: The Old Basin of the Carondelet Canal. The boat in the foreground is a coast schooner, inspired by the schooners on the Chesapeake Bay. These workhorse vessels carried supplies along the Gulf Coast to and from New Orleans. Their shallow draft and two masts made them ideal for transport of materials on Bayou St. John and the Carondelet Canal. Stereograph by S. T. Blessing, ca. 1868. The Historic New Orleans Collection, 1998.93.2 i,ii.

rope. The absence of zoning in New Orleans, combined with the eccentric mix of small and large lots, meant that a warehouse or naval outfitter might stand cheek-by-jowl with an elegant plantation-type residence. In Bayou St. John, this situation resulted in what today would be considered a bizarre mixture of high and low architecture.

Since the neighborhood lived off bayou-borne trade, boatmen and warehousemen also needed homes. These were scattered randomly throughout the area. Like the warehouses, these modest, carpenter-built wooden dwellings stretched far down the bayou, where cheaper lots were available. Warehouses, grand residences, and modest shacks were intermingled in a seemingly random fashion. Ubiquitous cisterns, which ranged up to two stories in height, gave the entire area a semi-industrial quality.

We are fortunate to have a series of sketches of the banks of the bayou, done by one Charles-Alexandre Lesueur in 1830. These, along with other paintings and early photographs, reveal a built-up and active neighborhood. Indeed, they show both multi-story warehouses or commercial buildings and grand houses that no longer exist. At the same time, they confirm that the Bayou St. John neighborhood remained relatively detached from the city as a whole until the late nineteenth century. Where today one sees nicely restored shotgun houses and other buildings, land remained open for most of the era launched by the opening of Carondelet's canal.

The Lesueur sketches also present a picture of active life along the bayou. Besides a proliferation of skiffs and pirogues, one sees a sailboat with a beam of approximately five feet, again with a canopy. One of the drawings even presents what looks like a pleasure boat that might have seated six or eight people beneath a canopy to afford protection from the sun or rain. Of particular interest is Lesueur's depiction of the bridge that probably connected the end of Grand Route St. Jean to the north side of the bayou. So as not to impede aquatic traffic along the bayou, the middle section of the bridge could be opened.

Despite the hodgepodge of building types in the Bayou St. John neighborhood during the golden age of the Carondelet Canal, many wealthier New Orleanians still considered it an attractive place to live and brought a stretch of order along the water's shore. The bayou itself offered (and still offers) attractive semi-rural vistas, and the neighborhood was considered to have "better air" than the more densely built-up downtown faubourgs.

If the earliest phase of Bayou St. John's history was shaped by geography, the second phase determined by geopolitics and great-power rivalries, and the third phase shaped by mercantile energies unleashed by Carondelet's canal, the fourth phase was defined, above all, by new technology. The first steam-powered boat, the *New Orleans*, descended the Ohio and Mississippi in 1811. It took several more decades for engineers to perfect the art of constructing large

Opposite: This pencil sketch by Charles Alexandre Lesueur from May 16, 1830, presents a vision of active life on Bayou St. John. Utilitarian and pleasure boats can be seen docked on the banks of the bayou alongside a proliferation of homes and industrial buildings. Muséum d'Histoire Naturelle du Havre, Le Havre, France.

steam-powered ocean-going vessels. Many technical problems had to be overcome. But well before the Civil War, when Farragut's steam-powered fleet sailed up the Mississippi and conquered New Orleans, steam-powered ocean vessels were plying the deep waters of the lower Mississippi. This greatly sped the export of cotton and other goods and facilitated the mass import of everything from roof tiles to porcelain china. But it destroyed in a stroke part of the rationale for the Bayou St. John route and the Carondelet Canal. If cargo could be shipped directly from Europe or the Caribbean to New Orleans by steamer, what need was there for a route whose main virtue was to save sailing ships the need to plow slowly upstream for some fifty miles?

This logic might lead one to expect that Bayou St. John's days were numbered, both as an entrepôt and as a residential area connected with commerce along the bayou and the Carondelet Canal. But, surprisingly, this did not happen. In fact, the rise of steam-powered ocean-going ships that could ascend clear to New Orleans had only a marginal impact on Bayou St. John, for even when sailing ships still prevailed on the Atlantic and Gulf, river steamboats could sail down to the mouth of the Mississippi to pick up goods from them directly. This meant that barely three decades after Carondelet dug his canal, goods could be brought directly up the Mississippi, without resorting to the Rigolets-Pontchartrain-Bayou St. John route.

But other technological changes proved favorable to Bayou St. John and more than compensated for the losses imposed by the ability of steam-driven ocean ships to ascend the Mississippi. By the

Below: Charles Alexandre Lesueur's 1830 pencil sketch, View of the Port on Bayou St. John, *shows the old bridge that was located at the terminus of Grand Route St. John. An excursion boat loaded with passengers drifts in the bayou. Muséum d'Histoire Naturelle du Havre, Le Havre, France.*

1850s, machine shops and shipyards in Cincinnati and elsewhere were turning out large numbers of inexpensive, low-displacement boats powered by small steam engines. Soon Lake Pontchartrain and the adjoining bayous were alive with steamboats. Smaller steam-powered lighters based in Bayou St. John carried goods back and forth along the Carondelet Canal. Thus, in its second phase, the revolution unleashed by steam power enhanced the economy of Bayou St. John.

The mid-nineteenth-century rise of New Orleans as a metropolis and regional economic center created an insatiable demand for just about everything. Above all, the rapidly expanding city needed construction materials, including bricks, sawn pinewood, resins, and tar. It was to the good fortune of Bayou St. John that it enjoyed a near monopoly as a supplier of these resources. Though a few brickyards were located within the city limits, the bricks produced were of inferior quality to those made in kilns on Lake Pontchartrain's north shore, where the local clay could be used to turn out vast quantities of cheap but sturdy bricks, beginning toward the latter half of the nineteenth century. As to pinewood and related products, virgin forests of longleaf pine stretched from Lake Pontchartrain clear to Florida. Bayou St. John offered the cheapest route for getting these and other local products to New Orleans.

The development of smaller and more efficient steam engines brought about the partial motorization of Bayou St. John and the Carondelet Canal. By mid-century, small steamboats and narrow, steam-powered crafts, including luggers, dinghies, and scows, were to be seen everywhere. Local operators used them to ply the navigable bayous on the North Shore and deliver goods from there to Bayou St. John. Many of

their vessels, most powered by steam but many still being wind-powered, are shown in photographs and paintings of the Carondelet Canal from the turn of the last century.

Ready access to inexpensive wood and bricks arriving from Bayou St. John and the Carondelet Canal enabled New Orleans builders to erect thousands of residential and business buildings and sell them at reasonable prices. Stimulated by a booming economy and the arrival of hundreds of thousands of Irish, German, and Italian immigrants, New Orleans burgeoned during the decade after the Civil War. The prevailing prosperity brought new construction along Esplanade Avenue clear to Bayou St. John, transforming what had only recently been open land into new suburbs. Amidst the houses

Opposite, above: New Orleans, La and Its Vicinity. *An aerial view of the city of New Orleans and area to the Gulf of Mexico. Engraving by W. Ridgway. Published by Virtue & Co., 1863. The Historic New Orleans Collection, 1953.20.*

Opposite, below: Plan du Fauxbourg St. Jean executé sur la propriete de Mr. D. Clark. *Copy made by C. J. A. d'Hémécourt of a plan by Barthélémy Lafon, dated June 1, 1809, showing a portion of Faubourg St. John containing Daniel Clark's land holding, June 19, 1875. The Historic New Orleans Collection, 1966.34.1.*

Four Biloxi schooners under tow, leaving the mouth of Bayou St. John and entering Lake Pontchartrain. The boats are laden with cargo, and the sailors are beginning to hoist sails. "Atlantic & Bay St. Louis" is painted on the stern of the second boat. Photograph by Alexander Allison, ca. 1899–1910. Louisiana Division/City Archives, New Orleans Public Library.

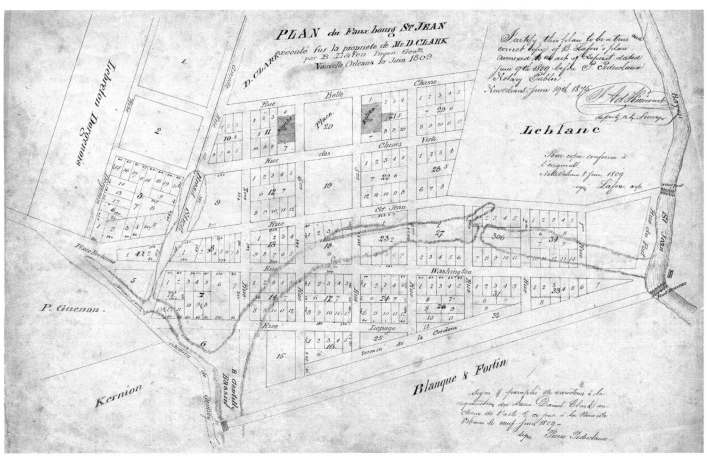

arose handsome churches and schools, as well. New Orleans's post-Civil War construction boom gave the Bayou St. John neighborhood much the appearance that it retains to the present day. In 1873 the post-war building boom came to an abrupt halt. For many years thereafter, the pace of new construction slowed to a snail's pace. The cause of this turnabout was the national and international Panic of 1873. This financial crisis impacted New Orleans profoundly. For several generations, the city had viewed itself much the way Houstonians view their city today. This was the place where fortunes could be amassed in the wink of an eye, and where bumptious, self-made businessmen set the tone of local life. In the wake of the prolonged panic, however, many New Orleanians came to view their city in an entirely different light, as a somewhat quaint repository of the past, where old ways and old buildings prevailed.

To be sure, there was still justification for Mark Twain's observation in 1881 that the city could boast a solid group of forward-thinking business and civic leaders. But the Panic of 1873 gave rise to another view of the place, namely, as a backward-looking but supremely comfortable community where living well might have taken precedence over doing well and where a colorful local culture held at bay the spreading generic monoculture. During the 1870s and 1880s, the writers George Washington Cable and Lafcadio Hearn crystalized this perspective in newspaper articles and books that gained a national audience and, at the same time, fixed the image in the local imagination.

How did this change affect Bayou St. John? The post-Civil War building boom had transformed the village from a trade-based agglomeration of warehouses, small businesses, and homes, both large and small, to a respected New Orleans neighborhood. The eventual slowing of the pace of development allowed the emerging neighborhood to settle in and its inhabitants to take root there. By the beginning of the twentieth century, most of the better potential building sites had been developed. The main exception was a large space nearby at 3700 Orleans Street that remained open until 1907, when the American Can Company purchased it and opened a factory there to provide tin cans for the cane sugar industry. Many of its five hundred employees chose to live in the village of Bayou St. John, and the few empty lots that remained were quickly developed. But far from taking the neighborhood in a new direction architecturally, this fresh wave of construction consisted mainly of single and double shotguns of a type that had been well known locally for a generation.

Evening on Bayou St. John, New Orleans, La., *ca. 1900–6. Photographer unknown. Library of Congress, Prints and Photographs Division.*

Bayou St. John: Reflections, November 3, 2017.

The in-filling of unoccupied lots had the further effect of warding off newcomers who might have added large numbers of Arts and Crafts residences, Sears's prefabricated bungalows, or early Modern residences in the International Style to the mix. This capped the further development of the neighborhood and helped preserve what was already there. Indeed, by far the biggest nearby development in recent years was the adaptive re-use as apartments of the old American Can building on Orleans Avenue. At a time when old neighborhoods in many American cities are stagnating or dying, the blocks adjoining Bayou St. John are protected by the presence of several good schools on broad avenues, both Catholic and Protestant churches, and a prevailing civic sense among large numbers of its residents.

In this volume, Richard Campanella outlines the geophysical conditions that created the bayou and its borders, while Heather Veneziano clarifies and reveals intricacies of the earliest settlement in 1708. Hilary Irvin details not only those more impressive residences that are still standing but others, like the noble, circa 1800 Fernandez-Tissot house, that have been demolished over the years. Stephanie Bruno lists and illustrates approximately a hundred houses in the "Photo Index" to exemplify house types that currently proliferate and offers, as well, a timeline of harmonious architectural similarities and plant vistas that unify street after street. This glorious village and its bordering Bayou St. John waterway retain the civic spirit embodied in the development of a rhythmical, unified neighborhood, alive and well, that thrives down to the present.

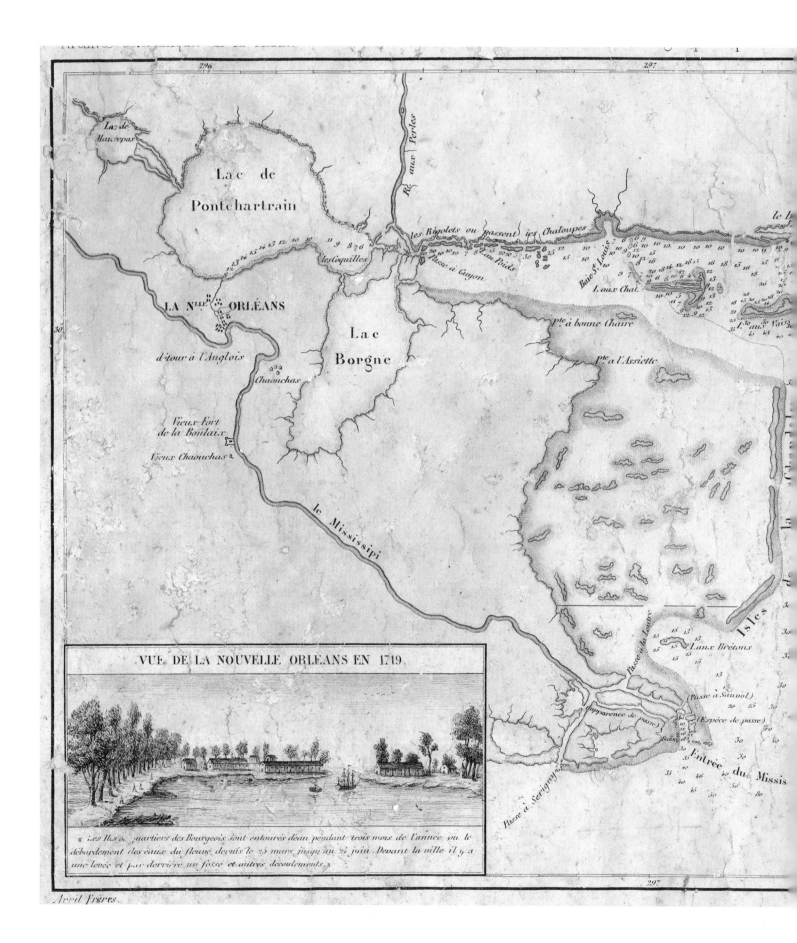

Lac de
Maurepas

Lac de
Pontchartrain

Les Rigolets ou passent les Chaloupes

les Coquilles

au Poids

Baie St. Louis

Passe à Gayon

LA N.LLE ORLEANS

d'tour à l'Anglois

Pte. à bonne Chaire

Chaouchas

Lac
Borgne

Pte. a l'Assiette

Vieux Fort
de la Boulaix

Vieux Chaouchas

le Mississipi

Isles

I. aux Brétons

Passe à la Loutre

Passe à Sauvol

Apparence de passe

Espéce de passe

Entrée du Missis

Passe à Serigny

VUE DE LA NOUVELLE ORLEANS EN 1719.

« Les Ilts ou quartiers des Bourgeois sont entourés d'eau pendant trois mois de l'année ou le
débordement des eaux du fleuve, depuis le 25 mars jusqu'au 24 juin. Devant la ville il y a
une levée et par derrière un fossé et autres découlements. »

Avril Frères.

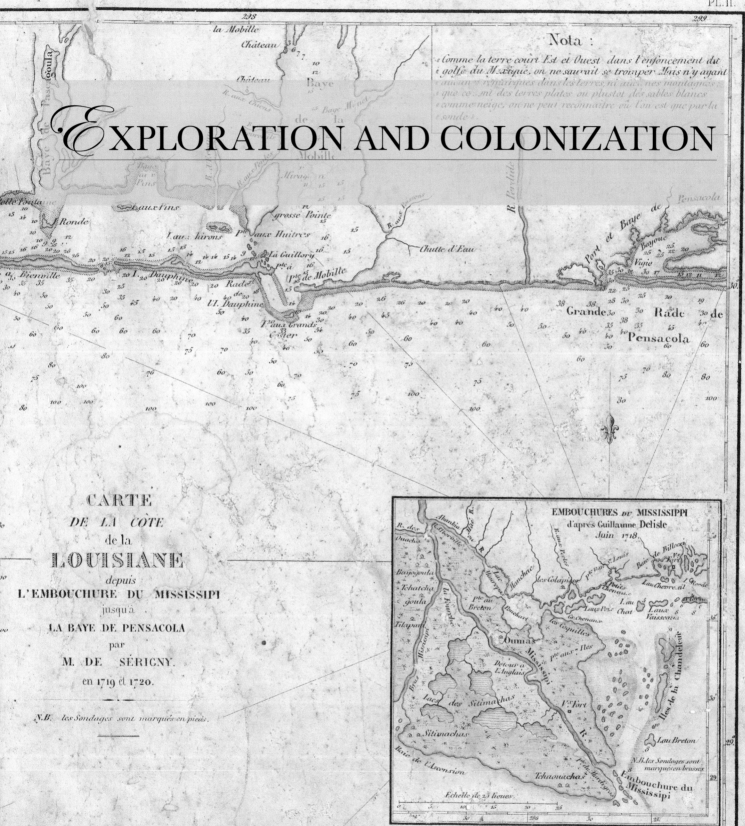

EXPLORATION AND COLONIZATION

EXPLORATION AND COLONIZATION

EARLY HISTORY OF BAYOU ST. JOHN

Heather Veneziano

All major historical events result not from a straight linear timeline of cause-and-effect occurrences or happenstance, but rather from a complicated web of relationships, timing, manipulations, and intricacies. One cannot claim that New Orleans exists today in its current location because of any singular event or person. However, the city, now known worldwide as a center of culture, of trade, and of industry, most certainly would not be located where it is if not for Bayou St. John and its first colonists. Many early key figures and transactions set into motion the framework for the establishment of the city. The story begins on the banks of Lake Pontchartrain and Bayou St. John.

Early in 1699, French Canadian soldier, explorer, and trader Pierre Le Moyne, Sieur d'Iberville (1661-1706) set out to locate the mouth of the Mississippi River and claim it for France. After a successful first journey and the establishment of Fort Maurepas at present-day Ocean Springs, Mississippi, Iberville returned to France to report upon his accomplishments. In January of the following year, he began his second exploratory journey through the area that the indigenous inhabitants had described to him during his first voyage. In his journal, he marked his plan "to go to the portage from Lake Pontchartrain to the Mississippi, to see whether the barques could get in there."[1] His

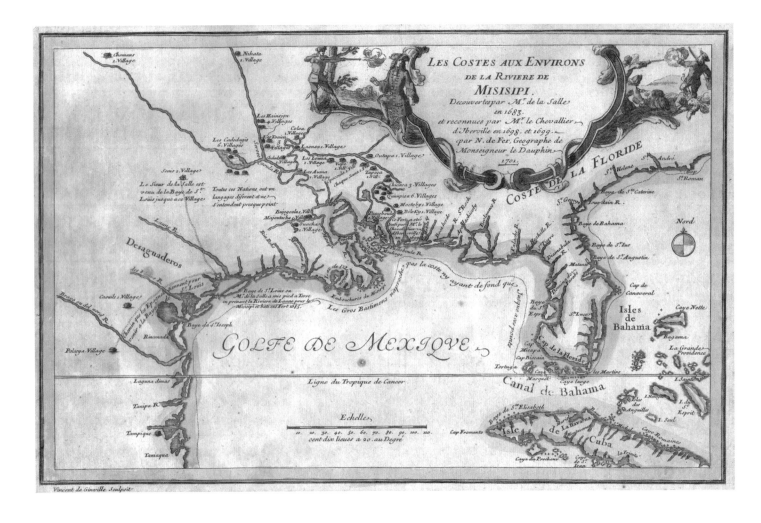

Opposite: Les Costes aux Environs de la Riviere de Misisipi. *Hand-colored engraving of areas of French exploration in America east of the Mississippi River, Cuba, and the Bahamas from 1683 to 1698. Drawn by Nicholas de Fer; engraved by Vincent de Ginville, 1701. The Historic New Orleans Collection, bequest of Richard Koch, 1971.34.*

Right: Jean-Baptiste le Moyne, sieur de Bienville (1680-1767), *oil on canvas, unknown artist, ca. 1743-53. The Historic New Orleans Collection, acquisition made possible by the Clarisse Claiborne Grima Fund, 1990.49.*

younger brother, Jean-Baptiste Le Moyne, Sieur de Bienville (1680-1767), who had remained at Fort Maurepas as lieutenant during Iberville's sojourn to France, accompanied him on his second expedition.

This journey would take the men to the south shore of Lake Pontchartrain and into the muddy, cypress-strewn waters of Bayou St. John. After disembarking from their vessels, they trekked from the bayou to the Mississippi by traversing the portage trail used by the Annocchy, Acolapissas, and doubtlessly many other indigenous peoples who had called the water-filled terrain home throughout the centuries. It may be surmised that Iberville held high hopes for the colonization of the area. While there, he had his men clear a small field and plant sugar cane that he had brought with him from Saint Domingue. In his journal, Iberville noted, "The south side of the lake is bordered by a prairie half a league to one league wide, after which one comes to the tall trees. This looks like a fine country to live in."[2]

Iberville's view of the landscape rang true to his younger brother, as well. The 1700 visit to Bayou St. John and the bank of the Mississippi River, in what is now New Orleans, proved to be a pivotal event that would inform Bienville's future choice of locations for a settlement. This alternate route to the river, from the Gulf coast through the more navigable waterways of Lake Borgne, the Rigolets, and Lake Pontchartrain, allowed for an ease of transport and a more secure fortification against other nations seeking to claim the river as their own.

Bienville returned to Fort Maurepas after the journey and took over the role of commander when the initial commandant, Sieur de Sauvole, passed away on August 22, 1701. Iberville directed his brother to construct an additional fort on the Gulf Coast and to begin a settlement at *La Mobile,* now referred to as "Old Mobile," which was established as the capital of French Louisiana. The young Bienville found himself in charge of a colony without adequate supplies and practically cut off from all French aid by the War of the Spanish Succession (1701-14). Soldiers and Canadian explorers and trappers initially comprised this settlement's population; later, French craftsmen and women would arrive, at Bienville's request, to help solidify and stabilize the colony. The inhabitants existed on meager rations from France, but years passed between the arrival of shipments, forcing the settlers to rely almost exclusively on the neighboring Native Americans for their subsistence. During times of near famine, Bienville instructed young men of the colony to seek refuge beyond the settlement in the villages of the surrounding indigenous peoples.

Bienville's relationship with the Chickasaw and Choctaw tribes, the two largest and most powerful na-

Crocodil/Serpent a Sonette/Serpent Verd [sic]. *Illustration from Vol. II of* Histoire de la Louisiane *by Antoine Simon Le Page du Pratz, 1758. The Historic New Orleans Collection, The L. Kemper and Leila Moore Williams Founders Collection, 73-16-L.*

tions in the region, was perhaps his greatest strength as a leader. Without their support, the survival chances of the settlement and its inhabitants would have been slim to none. Though records indicate time and again that Bienville was consistently at odds with his fellow French settlers, it seems that his relationships with tribal leaders made up for what he lacked in his countrymen's esteem.

Before his death in 1704, explorer Henri de Tonti wrote, "An officer, a man of breeding whose name you would recognize, who, as well as an image of the Virgin and the baby Jesus, a large cross on his stomach with the miraculous words which appeared to Constantine and an infinity of marks in the savage style, had a serpent which passed around his body and whose tongue pointed toward an extremity which I will leave you to guess."[3] The words that appeared to Constantine, to which Tonti referred, were "*in hoc signo vinces*" (in this sign, you will conquer) or "*hoc vince*" (in this, conquer). Bienville had served as interpreter during Tonti's negotiations between the Choctaw and Chickasaw in 1702 and was, therefore, already well versed in the culture and language of the two tribes. Could this tattooed soldier, with the ambitions of a great conqueror, be the young Bienville?

In 1720 Jean-François de la Clue-Sabran helped confirm the identity of the officer by noting that members of the indigenous tribes "have their skins covered with figures of snakes which they make with the point of a needle. Mr. de Bienville who is the general of the country has all of his body covered in this way and when obliged to march with them he makes himself nude like them. They like him very much but they also fear him."[4]

This assimilation into native tribal culture, while still defining himself as an outsider and a leader who should be feared, was key to Bienville's success in managing the territory of French Louisiana and to expanding the holdings of the crown beyond Mobile Bay.

As the War of the Spanish Succession dragged on, the situation within the colony continued to deteriorate. Soldiers were cut from the payroll and ordered to settle the land and begin farming—a directive from France that was met with much resistance. Eventually a number of Canadians took up the offer of land outside of the settlement, supplemented with farming supplies and other provisions. In spring 1708, a handful of these men agreed to provisional land grants from Bienville and Jean-Baptiste-Martin Dartaguette d'Iron, acting agent of the Crown, with the understanding that the concessions would have to be approved by the new governor once one was appointed. These concessions, measuring roughly four arpents frontage by thirty-six

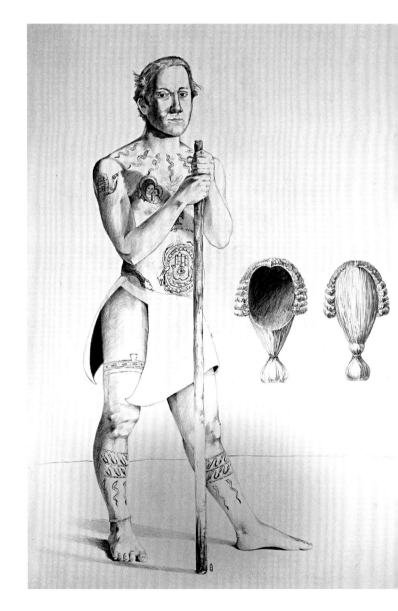

arpents in depth, were located on the land first viewed eight years prior by the Le Moyne brothers and others on the expedition, past Lake Pontchartrain, on the banks of Bayou St. John.

These first Canadian settlers were not alone in their new habitation. The Houma people had been occupying the general area since around 1706 and the Biloxi had been relocated to near the portage trail by order of Bienville and the commander of Fort de la Boulaye in 1700, in the hope that they would assist in provisioning the post.[5] There is no doubt that these two groups provided somewhat of a safety net to the new inhabitants, allowing for an easier transition to this new land. The Canadians' concessions were located close to the high ground of Esplanade Ridge, roughly where the Pitot House stands today, and followed up along the curve of the bayou, stretching over the land now occupied by the Fair Grounds Race Course, on the east bank—allowing for direct access to the portage trail, today's Bayou Road, traversed by the Le Moyne brothers and their exploratory group in 1700.

Documentation identifies five of the Canadians grantees of these earliest concessions: Antoine Rivard *dit* Lavigne, François Dugué, Jean-Baptiste Poitié, Maturino Derbon, and Nicolas Delon.[6] Tasked with growing wheat to supply food for the colony at Mobile, they celebrated the height and health of the first crop, which spanned roughly an acre on each concession.[7] Unfortunately, days before the harvest date, the late spring heat claimed the plants, and the hope for the salvation of the colony withered with them in the hot Louisiana sun. Just seven bushels were salvaged from the first crop. The settlers tried a second time but experienced the same results; a different crop would have to be chosen if the colony was to survive.

After the wheat crop failed, the settlers refocused their energy into the cultivation of maize, tobacco, and plants like them that were more suitable for the subtropical climate and did not require a large labor force. Though their families and some enslaved indigenous people that the settlers had brought with them from Mobile aided their work, successful mid- to large-scale farming would not be seen in the area until the slave trade imported thousands of Africans.

Opposite: Contemporary portrait of Jean-Baptiste le Moyne, sieur de Bienville, illustrating his tattoos; based upon the description provided by Henri de Tonti. By Adam Montegut, 2017. Courtesy of Adam Montegut, New Orleans Tattoo Museum.

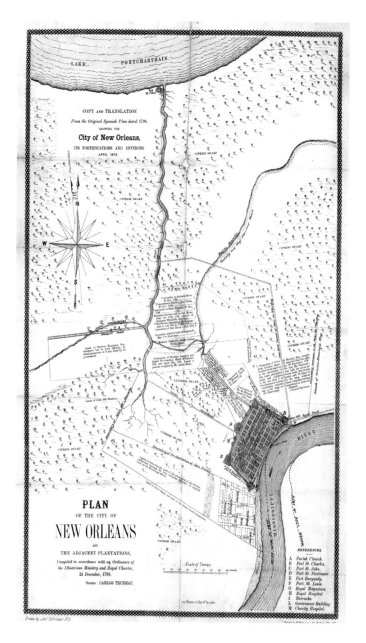

Hand-colored lithographic reproduction of Carlos Laveau Trudeau's 1798 Plan of the City of New Orleans and Adjacent Plantations, April 1875. Some of the earliest land concessions on Bayou St. John can be seen toward the center of the map. The Historic New Orleans Collection, Gift of Irving Saal, 1959.81.2.

In addition to the aforementioned concessions granted in 1708, one more was conceded in that year, in October, to Louis Juchereau de Saint-Denis, "volunteer" officer in the Louisiana troops and a nephew by marriage to Iberville. Saint-Denis had accompanied the Le Moynes on the exploratory journey in 1700 and had been made commandant of Fort de la Boulaye, roughly twenty kilometers south of New Orleans. While serving as commandant, he was in direct communication with the Biloxi people, whom he had relocated to Bayou St. John to provide provisional support for his garrison. During this time, he reported to Bienville and Dartaguette on the quality of the land surrounding the bayou, noting that based upon the Biloxi's success in farming, the land was "the finest in the world for raising crops."[8] It can be assumed that the first concessions on Bayou St. John came about as a direct result of these recommendations.

Fort de la Boulaye was eventually abandoned in early 1707 because of staff shortages, resulting in a need to concentrate fortification efforts in Mobile Bay.[9] After the decommissioning of the garrison, Bienville ordered Saint-Denis to return to Mobile. Being a "volunteer" officer and not bound to obey, he refused the order because of a lack of monetary compensation for his work. Instead he agreed to take up command of the "territory of Saint John"[10] close to the area where he had resettled the Biloxi tribe in 1700. The concession granted to Saint-Denis stood on the west bank of the bayou, away from the recently established farming village. He and a few of his men occupied the site, measuring four arpents fronting the bayou by forty or so expanding westward on the cusp of land now bordered by City Park Avenue. Saint-Denis would not remain long on his concession. In 1713 he sold his land to Canadian Jean Baptiste Gravelines *dit* Baudreau and François Desbonnes[11] in order to carry out a mission authorized by acting Governor Antoine Laumet *dit* Lamothe, Sieur de Cadillac (1658-1730), to explore the Red River and establish an outpost. This mission resulted in the founding of Natchitoches.

As the first landowners struggled to tame the wilderness bordering the bayou and to secure it as habitable and productive farmland, changes were occurring in France and beyond that would have far-reaching effects upon the success of their developing village. Suffering financially because of the War of Spanish Succession, France saw the need to unburden itself of responsibility in the New World without entirely giving up a claim on it, so as to safeguard its profits from the colony if circumstances improved and the project became successful rather than teetering consistently on the brink of failure. The Crown found its answer in the king's counselor and financial secretary, Antoine Crozat (ca. 1655–1738), to whom the King offered a fifteen-year trade monopoly in Louisiana if he would take over its administration. Governor Lamothe helped to convince Crozat to take the offer by boasting of the mining potential he claimed existed in the territory.[12] After two months,

Crozat finally agreed to the offer. The deal lasted from 1712 until 1717, when he requested an early end to the agreement; the colony was too much of a drain on him as an individual, and the expense—as he had feared—far outweighed the profit.

During Crozat's administration of the colony, the construction of what would later become Fort St. John (Spanish Fort) took place. Built upon high ground formed by a Native American midden,[13] the garrison was set up by ten men in 1716 "at the spot where a small branch of water runs . . . from the Micisispy [*sic*] to Lake Pontchartrain."[14] The positioning of an outpost in this key location protected not only the young, bayou-based settlement but also this alternative access point to the river. Acting in his dual role as administrator and as one who stood to profit greatly through the growth of the colony, it was advantageous for Crozat to protect his interests from all sides. It may be assumed that after he ended his contract with the Crown, funding for the garrison became limited. By 1719 the site was noted as a redoubt with only one guard.[15]

Following on the heels of Crozat's financial failure, New France came to the attention of Scottish economist John Law (1671-1729). Law, who had been actively setting up banking systems in France for many years, saw the opportunity for the colony to turn a large profit through the speculative sale of shares held in a management company. In 1717 he established the Company of the West (later evolving into the Company of the Indies) and received a charter from the Crown that granted it a twenty-five-year trade monopoly in Louisiana. In turn, the company was expected to populate the colony with six thousand settlers and three thousand enslaved people over the following ten years.[16]

With Law at the reins, the colony across the Atlantic became a sensation, and the myth of Louisiana's wealth grew with each new share purchased. A capital city of Louisiana, New Orleans, was named in honor of the Regent of France, Philippe II, duc d'Orléans (1674–1723). Where that city was located exactly was unclear for some time. Fortunately for the early settlers of Bayou St. John who had remained there toiling the land, a twist of fate left the decision to Bienville.

In the early spring of 1718, Bienville instructed some men under his command to clear an area of land near the Mississippi River close to the portage trail that linked the site to Bayou St. John. This clear-

LE COMMERCE QUE LES INDIENS DU MEXIQUE FON   AVEC LES FRANÇOIS AU PORT DE MISSISIPI

Above: The Company of the Indies produced this ca. 1720 engraving as a form of propaganda to draw settlers to Louisiana. Highly inaccurate in its representation of the colony, it shows New Orleans as a well-constructed and well-fortified town built upon rolling hills. The Historic New Orleans Collection, 1952.3.

ing and the few simple structures first built upon it marked the site of New Orleans. Concurrently, first engineer Paul de Perrier was en route to the territory with a letter from the Company of the West recommending Manchac as the location for the new city.[17] Perrier died during the journey, so, to Bienville's advantage, there was no immediate need to defend his choice of location. The decision had been reached, a decision close to twenty years in the making. Everything up to that point had been mere speculation, and if not for the brief periods in which Bienville administered the colony, things would have developed much differently.

By 1718 many of the original landholders along the bayou had moved on. Between 1718 and 1721, Antoine Rivard *dit* Lavigne had acquired all land granted within the initial concessions and three additional arpents of bayou frontage conceded to him by Bienville. His neighbors, perhaps put off by the difficulty of farming unfamiliar soil, had by that time relocated out of the area. In addition, Lavigne obtained land across the bayou from his original concession, which included structures remaining from an abandoned Acolapissa village. He now stood as the largest individual landowner at the gateway to a new, well-funded capital city.

A year later, in 1719, a company warehouse had been constructed on the bayou, and at least three Canadian houses existed.[18] Bayou St. John and the small village established upon its banks were positioned to become the entrance to New Orleans. Supply ships from Dauphin Island and beyond began arriving on

VUE DE LA NOUVELLE ORLEANS EN 1719.

« Les Iles o... quartiers des Bourgeois sont entourés d'eau pendant trois mois de l'année vu le debordement des eaux du fleuve, depuis le 25 mars jusqu'au 24 juin. Devant la ville il y a une levée et par derrière un fossé et autres decoulements. »

Left: Vue de la Nouvelle Orléans en 1719. *Watercolor engraving, delineated by Joseph Le Moyne, sieur de Sérigny, detail of a map from* Géologie pratique de la Louisiane *by Raymond Thomassy, 1860. The Historic New Orleans Collection, The L. Kemper and Leila Moore Williams Founders Collection, 00.12 i-iii.*

the bayou, loaded with materials to be hauled down the portage trail to begin the construction of New Orleans. The Company of the Indies kept its part of the agreement to populate the new city, and in the spring of 1718, the first boatload of sixty-eight settlers set out from France to reside within the limits of the newly christened capital. This group included Antoine Simon Le Page du Pratz (ca. 1695–1775), who would spend two years living on Bayou St. John, first in the abandoned Acolapissa village owned by Lavigne and later on a concession of land he acquired from the company.[19] Le Page's memoirs, which detailed his experiences in Louisiana, were published in France in installments between 1751 and 1753 and as the three-volume *Histoire de la Louisiane* in 1758. It provides colorful accounts of life in the colony during the time of his habitation.

In addition to dispatching white settlers from Europe to the colony, the company sent over the first ship containing enslaved Africans, 250 of them, in 1719. Between that date and 1731, the company transported more than six thousand persons from multiple areas of Africa to Louisiana through the slave trade.[20] This new influx of Africans into the population allowed for the mass development of the land by those forced into servitude. A handful of enslaved Africans had arrived in the territory

Right: Illustration from Vol. II of Histoire de la Louisiane *by Antoine Simon Le Page du Pratz, 1758. Le Page du Pratz wrote extensively about the native tribes he encountered during his stay in Louisiana. Shown here, his depiction of a Native American woman in winter attire. The Historic New Orleans Collection, 1980.205.31.*

T. 2 p. 309.

Naturels en Hyver

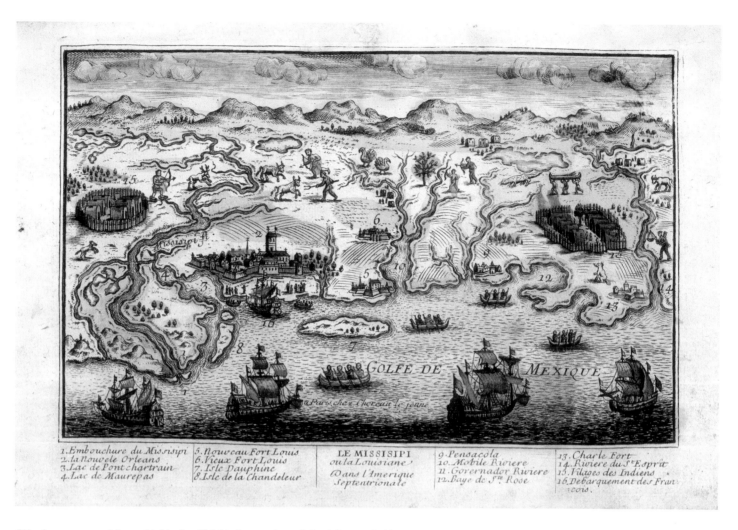

Woodcut map providing a highly fanciful bird's-eye view of Louisiana's Gulf coast. New Orleans is prominent, though on the wrong side of Lake Pontchartrain and very close to the Gulf of Mexico. Produced for a European audience by printmaker François Chéreau, ca. 1720. The Historic New Orleans Collection, 1959.210.

as early as 1708 or 1710, most traveling by way of the West Indies. The majority of those enslaved in Louisiana prior to 1719, however, were members of the area's indigenous tribes, captured during tribal warfare or sold or traded to the French Canadian settlers by other tribesmen.

With an established workforce, eager investors, curious newcomers from Europe, and a designated location, New Orleans began to take shape. Its growth brought prosperity to those dwelling along the bayou. As established residents of the land and as acting gatekeepers to the new capital, the bayou inhabitants were poised to profit greatly from this expansion of the territory. New neighbors quickly joined the long-standing residents along what is now Moss Street, forming a burgeoning village community.

This village was developed through strong family alliances, oftentimes resulting in multi-generational property ownership. The geography of what is now New Orleans is unique in that because of the

low elevation present within most of the city, early communities remained relatively cut off from one another because of the vast areas of swampland and seasonal flooding. As plantation tracts on the bayou were bought and sold, sometimes in rapid succession, the geography of the neighborhood we now know began to take shape.

France ceded the Louisiana territory to Spain in 1762, and further growth ensued. Commercial enterprises, as previously discussed by S. Frederick Starr, also made their mark upon the landscape in a grand way during the period of Spanish rule. When the Louisiana Purchase occurred in 1803, the urbanization of the area was well underway. Street grids were laid out essentially by 1810 with Faubourgs St. John and Pontchartrain, and the community developed. Throughout its history, the neighborhood around Bayou St. John has stood apart from the rest of the city. It has acted as a lifeline, a model, and perhaps most importantly, as the gateway to New Orleans.

A GLORIOUS VILLAGE

$\mathscr{A}$ GLORIOUS VILLAGE

Hilary Somerville Irvin

Visitors in days past traveled to Bayou St. John using various directions and modes of transportation. Native Americans pointed the way for early colonial settlers to use the naturally high Bayou Road portage, terminating at the headwaters near today's Bell Street, to travel to the current site of the French Quarter as an alternative route to the Mississippi River. In 1718 Antoine Simon Le Page du Pratz arrived for his two-year stay at the bayou, traveling from the Gulf of Mexico by way of the channels that led to Lake Pontchartrain. St. John village residents went back and forth from their city homes and places of work by carriage or horse. Pleasure-seekers during the second half of the nineteenth century flocked to Magnolia Gardens and Spanish Fort amusement areas via the city railroad lines along Esplanade Avenue.

And the Old Basin or Carondelet Canal served as the connecting waterway for oystermen, fishermen, and building materials tradesmen lugging their goods back and forth from the north shore of Lake Pontchartrain on flatboats and schooners.

This trek taken in *Gateway to New Orleans* began years ago with Mary Louise Christovich's inaugural research and vision of writing about this, the city's first European settlement. Accompanied by Robert and Jan Brantley's luminous photographs and marking the tricentennial anniversary of the founding of New Orleans, we approach the neighborhood starting with East and West

Below: The Hotel at Spanish Fort on Bayou St. John *by William Henry Buck, 1879. Courtesy of Neal Auction Company.*

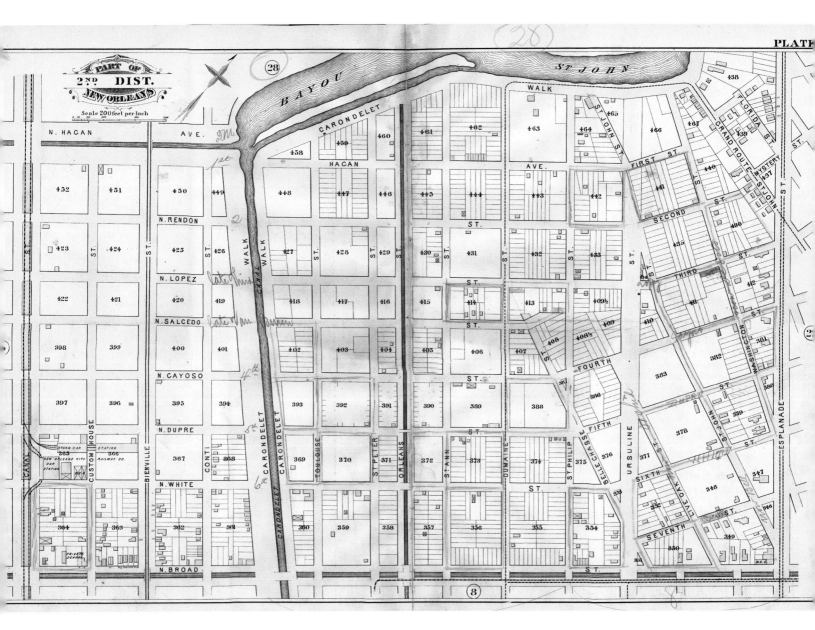

Robinson's Atlas of the City of New Orleans, Louisiana, *Plate 9: Esplanade to Canal; North Broad to Bayou St. John, 1883. Courtesy of Honorable Dale N. Atkins, Clerk of Court, Parish of Orleans.*

Moss Street, moving north from Orleans Avenue to the south side of Esplanade Avenue, and then fanning out to the streets running more-or-less parallel and perpendicular to Moss Street. Personalities, as well as architectural and developmental trends, are explored along the way, utilizing Orleans Parish's richly abundant and unique archival resources.

The boundaries of the historic Faubourg St. John set the parameters for the scope of this book to extend from the north side of Orleans to the south side of Esplanade Avenue and from the west side of North Broad to both banks of Moss Street. As a result of the early 1830s extension of Esplanade Avenue to the bayou, however, a portion of the early nineteenth-century Faubourg Pontchartrain lies on the south side of Esplanade and figures briefly in this study.

The striking theme that emerges in this exploration is this neighborhood's cohesive spirit. As with most villages universally, its inhabitants intermarried, often remaining close to home for a lifetime. Descendants of French colonial settlers Louis Blanc, early eighteenth-century émigrés Pierre Roux and Louis Nicolas Fortin, and German Redemptioner Joseph Klar stayed in the area for generations, leaving their imprint on the built environment, street names, and cultural and religious traditions. This trend applied not only to the earlier settlers but also to those who arrived during the late nineteenth-century population expansion and building boom. Because this was, and is, a close-knit community, the vicissitudes of becoming *déclassé* and ensuing decay largely skipped the Faubourg St. John.

MOSS STREET: EAST BANK

(Chemin Public/Carondelet Walk/Port Road)

700 Block: Bounded by St. Ann, Orleans, North Hagan (First)

The journey up the city side of Moss Street begins at Orleans Avenue. Unlike the architectural vistas toward Lake Pontchartrain, buildings in this block clearly postdate 1920. The area's delayed residential development lay partly in its proximity to the commercial traffic of Carondelet (Old Basin) Canal, constructed in 1794 to connect the bayou to the edge of the French Quarter. Businesses catering to the building trade lined this shallow waterway and used it for easy transport. During its heyday, the canal served as a small, busy port, carrying goods such as brick, lumber, and oysters from the north shore by way of Bayou St. John.

738 Moss Street.

As late as 1896, the entire square facing Moss Street between Orleans and St. Ann was undeveloped land and remained so in 1908, except for some cottages on and next to North Hagan Avenue. During the late 1800s, when the Salmen Brick and Lumber Company owned a sizable portion of the square, including the front Moss Street lots, the land likely served as a storage and staging area for the Slidell, Louisiana, firm's popular building materials. In 1907 George, Emile, and John Abry purchased the property for their shoring business.[1] Abry Brothers, which maintains headquarters at 3325 Orleans, subdivided the Moss Street frontage property in 1927, after which time the existing residences were constructed.[2]

The well-detailed and vibrantly painted frame bungalow at **738 Moss** was constructed circa 1929-30 for Ernest J. Miramon, who bought the corner lot in 1927. The son of French-born parents, he grew up nearby on a Metairie Road dairy. Miramon died soon after moving into his new home, but his widow and daughter remained there for many years.[3] No contract has been located to document its builder or architect, but the fanlight transom detailing in the Louisiana Colonial revival style is seen in "formula" cottages constructed by his company, Miramon Construction, in the late 1930s in Gentilly Terrace and other locations.

800 Block: Bounded by Dumaine, St. Ann, North Hagan (First)

The 1896 Sanborn Map shows two groupings of buildings on the bayou-facing portions of the 800 block. On the St. Ann side were a two-story frame mechanical shop, stables, and a shed, all belonging to the New Orleans Swamp Land Reclamation Company. As a private company, it acquired, drained, and resold land for residential and agricultural uses in the low-lying areas of New Orleans. Its president and lead investor was Charles Louque (1845-1897), a St. John the Baptist Parish native. A lawyer, New Orleans City Council member, and state senator, Louque owned and lived in the first Evariste Blanc home at 924 Moss Street between 1881 and 1891.[4] In 1893 he acquired lots 1 through 6 at Moss and St. Ann Streets from the succession of Firmin Lavasseur, a brick, lumber, and lime dealer at Carondelet Walk. Lavasseur and his heirs owned all twelve bayou-side lots in this block for over forty years, having acquired them in 1848 from the First Municipality, which had purchased them in 1834, along with many others, from Evariste Blanc.[5]

An old pottery complex was noted in 1896 at Moss toward Dumaine. These were the buildings of the New Orleans Pottery Company, not to be confused with George Ohr's New Orleans Art Pottery on Baronne

Street. Its only documented activity in its five-year life was decorating the Cotton Palace, constructed in Lafayette Square for the 1889 carnival season under the auspices of the Ladies' Unsectarian Aid Society. The "director-in-chief" of the pottery company was Mrs. William Muller, also president of the charity. In 1895 the closed factory and site, with a frontage of 132 feet on Moss and 145 feet on Dumaine, was offered at a liquidation sale and purchased by Charles Louque.[6] Although Louque's company continued after his death as the New Orleans Land Company, lots in the 800 block of Moss were sold not in the early 1900s but toward the end of the decade in 1908.

An article in the *Daily Picayune* (December 18, 1909) carried the headline, "Last square of ground in the Central Bayou St. John Section bought by National Realty Company, Certain of Early Development Demand." The article stated that the real estate company paid $18,000 for the empty land bounded by Moss, Dumaine, St. Ann, and North Hagan, "about the only remaining vacant property between Hagan and Esplanade, and the purchase was made as an investment with the idea that the closing of a portion of the Carondelet Canal will increase the value of the property." Although the canal remained open for more than another decade, the square began to develop in the 1910s, especially on the side streets of St. Ann and Dumaine, where rows of modest double cottages were constructed.

The most conspicuous house in the block, **800 Moss**, dates from 1939 to 1940.[7] Sisters Sydonia and Nina Pollatsek, daughters of Hungarian-born musician and music critic Adolph Pollatsek, commissioned this replica of the Pitot House (1440 Moss). According to architect-historian Samuel Wilson Jr., the unmarried sisters, along with their married sister Carlotta Reynolds and her two children, rented the Pitot House from Mother Cabrini before the members of the order she had founded, the Missionary Sisters of the Sacred Heart, decided to move in. According to the legend, a blind member of the family was so accustomed to the layout of the old house that a copy was desired and achieved. The sisters gave the family an original mantel from the second floor of the Pitot House for their new home, where it remains today to unite the history of the original and its copy.[8]

800 Moss Street.

900 Block: Bounded by St. Philip, Dumaine, North Hagan (First)
1000 Block: Bounded by Bell (St. John), St. Philip, North Hagan (First)[9]

Louis Antoine Blanc (1758-1825) and his descendants, notably his son Evariste, dominate the history of the bayou-facing blocks between today's Bell and Dumaine Streets from the late colonial period through much of the nineteenth century. Evariste's influence on the built environment of the east bank of the bayou also extended north to the 1300 and 1400 blocks. A native of Marseilles, France, Louis was a planter, manager of a tannery, and toll collector for the New Orleans Navigation Company. After the death in 1782 of his first wife, Louisiana-born Henriette Gauvain, Blanc married his deceased wife's sister Louise (1760-1848), with whom he fathered the following known children: Elizabeth Louise Blanc, known as Lise (1784-1861); Evariste (1785-1853); Henriette (1787-1878), widow of John Lynd; François Arsène (1792-1841); Mercedite Blanc (b. 1797), widow of Mathier Rea; and Louis Edouard (1799-1859).

Although in the 1780s Louis owned a plantation on the west bank across Bayou St. John, he first appears on the east bank in 1793, when he purchased a portion of the Langlois-Provanche tract from the Spanish notary Andres Almonester y Rojas, father of Baroness Micaëla Pontalba. The Langlois tract fronted on the bayou for eight arpents, extending from Bayou Road to the vicinity of today's Orleans Avenue.[10] Financial problems evidently plagued Blanc within a few years, inferred by a *Louisiana Courier* advertisement (March 16, 1812) for the sale of his holdings:

> The plantation belonging to Mr. Louis Blanc, situated on the Bayou St. John, fronting on one side by the said bayou and on the other the road of the said bayou [St. John or Bell], will be sold . . . by lots of half an arpent running through the whole depth of the plantation. The mansion house is built in the center of a lot fronting both the bayou and the road. This plantation, the ground of which is the highest of all the surrounding lands, is too well known to require a more minute description.

During his visit to New Orleans in the early 1830s, French naturalist Charles Alexandre Lesueur sketched scenes along Bayou St. John, including this one which depicts the demolished Louis Blanc house in the 1000 block of Moss Street at the left and 924 Moss Street at the right. Muséum d'Histoire Naturelle du Havre, Le Havre, France.

The sale did not take place, and in 1813 Louis and his wife mortgaged their property, described as the "plantation now owned and occupied by said Blanc with all building and improvements situated at Bayou St. John . . . about 7½ arpents fronting on the Bayou Road, excepting from said mortgage one arpent in front of the Bayou Road, whereon Louis Blanc now resides and which is in his recognition on the same depth."[11] In 1816 the seventy-four-year-old Louis finally sold his plantation, except for the portion with his house and gardens, measuring 98 feet front on the bayou by 563 feet in depth, to his son Evariste.[12]

Where was the home of *père* and *mère* Blanc? For years, 924 Moss Street has been likely misidentified as the "Louis Blanc House" and has been dated to circa 1798. An 1826 survey made for Evariste Blanc and an 1848 survey filed with the succession of *Veuve* Louis Blanc clearly places the elder Blanc's home in today's 1000 block of Moss Street at the corner of the Chemin Public facing the bayou and Rue St. Jean. The *fils* Blanc's house, offices, and establishment were identified on the site of today's 924 Moss Street, as outlined on an 1822 survey.

Fortunately, several available images spanning eight decades captured the Louis Blanc House before its demolition in the 1940s. Circa 1830 the French naturalist and artist Charles Alexandre Lesueur traveled to New Orleans and whimsically sketched properties along Bayou St. John, among other local sites. More charming than architecturally accurate, this small drawing shows a low, one-story, gable-ended structure in the foreground and a two-story dormered dwelling in the background. These buildings must be the Louis Blanc and Evariste Blanc houses, respectively in the 1000 and 900 blocks.

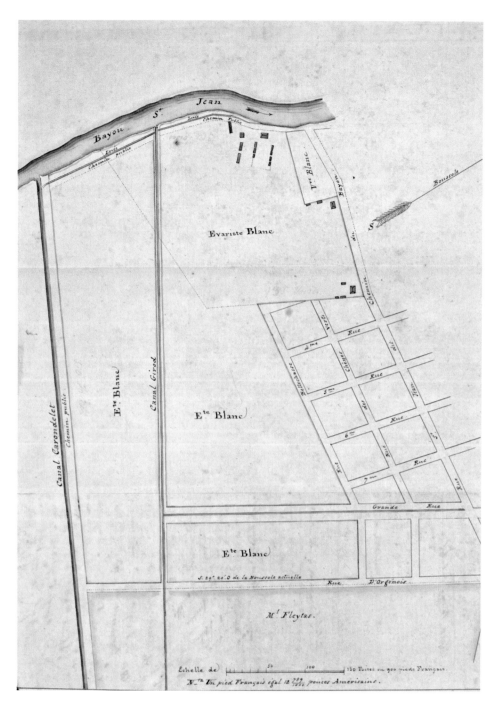

Above: Joseph Pilie's 1826 survey for Evariste Blanc outlines Blanc's homestead at 924 Moss Street and that of his mother, Veuve Blanc, at the corner of Moss and today's Bell Streets. Subdivided sections of Daniel Clark's Faubourg St. John extend east toward Dorgenois Street. Courtesy of Honorable Dale N. Atkins, Clerk of Court, Parish of Orleans.

In 1887 artist/professor/preservationist William Woodward depicted the "Old Spanish House Near Bell," with the chimney top of 924 Moss at the distant right. Woodward's painting shows a low, gable-ended building with a front gallery, sited at an angle with the bayou, a location documented by the 1848 survey and nineteenth-century Sanborn Insurance Maps. The last documented image of this old house, with 924 Moss, is in the background of a 1910 photograph of a jaunty sailor girl on the bayou. The construction date of the Louis Blanc house is not documented. Could it have been an earlier French or Spanish colonial structure that was on the land before his purchase in 1793? Or did he build it for his homestead? Sanborn Maps identify its construction material as brick-between-posts, sheathed in wood siding.

Above: Artist William Woodward's Old Spanish House on Bayou St. John near Bell Street, *1887, an oil painting of the demolished Louis Blanc House with the chimney top of 924 Moss Street in the background. Courtesy of Neal Auction Company.*

Left: Sailor girl, Constance "Tiny" Corcoran Adorno, ca. 1910. The Louis Blanc House at left and the Evariste Blanc House (924 Moss Street) at right. Courtesy of Constance Adorno Barcza.

924 Moss Street: Evariste Blanc Estate, Bounded by St. Philip, Dumaine, North Hagan (First)

Evariste Blanc (1785-1853) ranks as the leading denizen of the bayou faubourg. In addition to his first documented home at 924 Moss, he built 1342 and 1454 Moss Street and contributed importantly to the infrastructure of the burgeoning neighborhood. After his death, his wife, Marie Fanny Labatut (1791-1875), and children continued for generations to impact the area's economic, social, and religious development.

Listed in city directories as a lime merchant, Evariste owned the Blanc brickyard at the corner of Julia and St. John Streets (today's South Saratoga). This ambitious and extremely handsome son worked to reclaim the lands that his father had sold. After acquiring his father's mortgaged property in 1816, Evariste further expanded his holdings in 1821 by purchasing, from the estate of Daniel Clark, an adjoining area that his father had owned. A survey of 1822, executed when

Above: 924 Moss Street.

Below: This architectural collage by surveyor George de Armas includes the distinctively detailed façade of 924 Moss Street. The Historic New Orleans Collection, MSS 290.3.58.

Evariste Blanc (1785-1853) with youngest son, James Arthur (1833-1902), attributed to Flemish portrait artist Jacques Amans. Courtesy of Diana Lewis.

Evariste donated a strip of land to the city for the extension of the Girod Canal (Orleans Canal-New Basin), documents his holdings, which stretched from Bayou St. John to Dorgenois Street and from Rue St. Jean to the Carondelet Canal. At the same time, he pledged to build, at his own expense, a *Chemin Public* along the bayou to his own house. It was to be 1,622 feet long by 35 feet wide and suitable for vehicles in all seasons.[13]

Married in 1811, Evariste and Fanny likely built their first bayou home circa 1816, soon after acquiring the land in the 900 block from the senior Blanc. Frequently described as an example of the Louisiana plantation style, this masonry structure clearly incorporates elements of the Georgian style. While its deep galleries and slender colonnettes at

Right: Charles Zimpel's 1834 Topographical Map of New Orleans and Its Vicinity outlines the Evariste and Louis Blanc's homesteads in relation to land sold by the younger Blanc in 1834 to the First Municipality of New Orleans. The Historic New Orleans Collection, 1945.13 i-xix.

the second-floor façade are typical for eighteenth-century plantation houses, the first- and second-floor center façade entry doors, as well as the interior center-hall floor plan, reflect its early nineteenth-century construction date.

In July 1834 Evariste wrote a letter to the president and members of the city council of the First Municipality in which he detailed as follows the great advantage of his property for the city, which, he had heard, was looking for a place for a new cemetery. He offered to sell the land situated on the bayou, "where he resides, consisting of about 240 arpents superficial for 50,000 piastres": "For the public, the site has a central position and in coming one would have the choice of many routes, first that of the shore of the Carondelet Canal which the city paves with shells, and second that of the bayou and third that which would be preferable is a road which would be established along Girod Canal in the prolongment of Rue Orleans."[14]

Mayor Denis Prieur accepted Blanc's offer, and in September the sale was recorded for "a land or plantation having about 12 arpents frontage on Bayou St. John and bounded by said bayou, Carondelet Canal, the public road named Bayou Road and Dorgenois Street, the said land has a total of about 250 arpents superficial, together with all buildings, dependencies, circumstances of the said land without reservations whatsoever."[15] Concurrently with selling this tract in November 1834, Blanc acquired a site closer to the Bayou Bridge for his new home, today's

Above: 924 Moss Street. Rear elevation.

1342 Moss Street.[16] Charles Zimpel's 1834 *Map of New Orleans and Its Vicinity* outlines the Evariste and Widow Louis Blanc's homesteads in relationship with the land sold to the city.

In 1836 the First Municipality sold a major portion of the Blanc tract, including the square in which 924 Moss Street is located, to Major Henry Joseph Ranney (1808-1865).[17] A native of Middletown, Connecticut, this civil engineer came to New Orleans in 1836 to serve as chief engineer of the New Orleans and Nashville Railroad, which was to connect with the New York and Erie Railroad, until the project was abandoned in 1842. He became president of the New Orleans, Jackson and Great Northern Railroad that linked New Orleans northward to Canton, Mississippi, and played a strategic role during the Civil War, especially for the

Confederacy. As a large stockholder in the New Canal and Shell Road Company, he leased the Carondelet Canal that connected New Orleans with the lake. He invested heavily in real estate, especially in the Bayou St. John neighborhood.[18] After the death of the Widow Louis Blanc in 1848, Ranney acquired some of the lots behind the old house in the 1000 block.

Likely responding to gathering clouds of war, Ranney sold his Bayou St. John real estate holdings in October 1859. Reportedly against secession, he continued his role in the state legislature and fought for the Confederacy. Unable to return to the federally occupied city, the bachelor businessman died in 1865 in Lewisburg, Louisiana.

In 1859 Felix Labatut (1805-1889), Fanny Blanc's brother, became the new owner of 924 Moss and its grounds, which had been kept intact during the years of Ranney's ownership.[19] A resident of the French Quarter, Labatut perhaps used Evariste and Fanny's first house as a country retreat during the federal occupation. By 1864 his property had been acquired by Albert Romenzo Wise, a New Hampshire-born commercial merchant.

This square remained intact from 1876 until 1891, when Wise's daughter, Lydia Wise Schneider, sold it. The only buildings there were the circa 1816 house with its outbuildings and the small house at the corner of St. Philip Street, which had been the home of Lise Blanc.[20] As noted elsewhere, Charles Louque, president of the New Orleans Swamp Land Reclamation Company, made his home in this antebellum mansion between 1881 and 1891.

Development soon came to the Evariste Blanc estate and to the rest of the faubourg. In 1891 investors Franklin E. Rice and John E. Pierce acquired the whole square, known as the Blanc Plantation, except for the small, triangular lot at the corner of St. Philip Street. Between 1891 and 1904, when Lewis F. Levy purchased the parcel with the house, the square had been subdivided, with many houses having been constructed on the side streets.[21] Lewis Levy, manager of the sugar brokerage firm of Harry L. Laws and Company, and his physician son, Lewis Levy II, lived in the house until 1925.

Above: 924 Moss Street. First floor library.

Left: Iron latch from 924 Moss Street.

Right: 924 Moss Street. Center hall with stairway added ca. 1926-30, looking toward the rear garden.

After Levy's purchase of the grounds of the Blanc house, the bayou-fronting property in the 900 block was divided into building lots. The raised center hall cottage at **928 Moss** and the double shotgun cottages at **936** and **940 Moss** date from circa 1905. Whereas the detailing of 928 is restrained, its neighbors at 936 and 940 exhibit an exuberant display of Eastlake devices, all stock millwork items readily available at the turn of the twentieth century.

John H. Bernhard, a Dutch waterway engineer, owned and lived in 924 Moss briefly between 1925 and 1926. Bernhard had made a splash in the shipping world in 1916 when his company, the Inland Waterway Company, developed barges to travel between St. Louis and New Orleans. A vehement critic of the Dock Board's policies on public monopolistic use of the Industrial Canal, Bernhard advocated for private development of the lakefront. He was a principal with the Edgelake Land, Inc., which in 1926 offered lots for sale along Lake Pontchartrain between Downman Avenue and Little Woods.

After purchasing the Moss Street property in December 1925, Bernhard contracted with an unnamed architect in May of the following year for alterations and repairs to 924 Moss Street. A drawing of the house by Moise Goldstein points to him being the architect of record, but unfortunately it can no longer be located and his involvement therefore cannot be confirmed. In October 1926, however, Bernhard sold the bayou property to 924 Moss Street Investment Inc. Although the owner of this company is not specified, economist Walter Parker is noted in directories and newspaper articles as living at 924 Moss Street at the time. A conveyance

Top left: 928 Moss Street. Center-hall cottage built around 1905.

Top right: Eastlake-style double shotguns at 936

Left: 940 Moss Street.

of 1930 records the sale of 924 Moss, "with all furniture and fixtures," to Walter Parker. [22]

John Bernhard, Walter Parker, and Moise Goldstein figured prominently in the late 1920s as advocates for the restoration and beautification of Bayou St. John, both the waterway and its architecture. Parker served as chairman of the Bayou St. John Beautification Committee and Goldstein as the consulting architect. Plans called for "artistic" bridges at Esplanade, Dumaine, and other streets; new boat landings; and landscaped banks.

The *New Orleans States* (December 12, 1926) reported that Goldstein "would have the erection of new structures in that part of New Orleans conform in general motif to the old colonial homes." Goldstein, who had traveled to Europe in 1925, followed his principle of Colonial revival design if he acted as architect for two new dependency buildings for 924 Moss Street to replace the demolished ones, as commissioned by Bernhard and built by Parker. At some point, the exterior stair was moved inside, most likely by Goldstein. An arcaded loggia dominates the façade of the *garçonnière*, in the Spanish Colonial revival mode.

Walter Parker died in 1950, but his widow, Anita Hernandez Parker, remained in the house until 1972, when she sold it to Benjamin F. Erlanger. In 1963 Mrs. Parker had converted the buildings into the "Sanctuary," a state grant-in-aid-funded elementary school. This school closed amidst civil lawsuits regarding quality of teachers and financial woes. It had re-emerged briefly in 1964 as the Walter Parker Elementary School.[23] In 1951 a new steel stringer fixed bridge, with two twelve-foot roadways, replaced an old swing bridge crossing the bayou at Dumaine Street and was named the **Walter Parker Bridge**, in honor of the long-term bayou resident and advocate.[24]

1000 Block: Bounded by Bell (St. John), St. Philip, North Hagan (First)

When the Widow Louis Blanc died in 1848, her children inherited her property, and the lots shown on the 1848 survey were sold individually. Her daughter, Henriette Blanc Lynd, widow of Robert St. Clair Lynd, bought the corner lot with the family home. Henriette's brother Evariste bought the adjacent lots 1 and 2, the ones closest to 924 Moss.[25] The 1850 census shows Henriette's son, Robert Lynd, living with his family in the old dwelling. The small, triangular lot number 1 at the corner of the bayou and St. Philip,

which Evariste had acquired in 1848, held the home of his elder, unmarried sister, Elizabeth Louise (Lise). Both the 1850 and 1860 censuses listed Lise living there with her baby brother, Edouard.

Also at the address were Celeste Marigny and Marguerite, Leocarde, Armentine, Elizabeth, Gustave, and Oscar Blanc, all identified as mulatto. In 1850 the eleven-year-old Gustave was the subject of a lawsuit, *Leocarde, f.w.c. v. Cammack, administrator of Blanc*. In this case, Widow Louis Blanc, the owner of the young Gustave, had stated in her will that her slaves could choose their owners among her heirs. The child, valued at $400, chose Lise Blanc, who agreed to turn him over to his free mother, Leocarde, after she reimbursed Blanc for his estimated value. Leocarde paid the required sum, but the remaining Blanc heirs had Henriette interdicted and declared her not in possession of her faculties.[26] The court, however, ruled to free the child. In addition to placing the mulattos with the sire name of Blanc in the Bayou St. John home of Lise, the 1860 census noted that Henriette Lynd, age 73 years, lived in an "institution house."

Henriette lived until 1878, dying at the age of ninety-one. Her property, consisting of stocks, her French Quarter home, the Bayou St. John property identified as "Widow Blanc's Residence," and several properties in today's Central Business and Lower Garden Districts, went to her children, Robert Sinclair Lynd (1808-1890) and Rose Lynd (1811-1890), widow of Robert Chew Cammack.[27] In 1879 Robert purchased his sister's share of the Bayou St. John house, and Rose acquired her brother's portion of the downtown property.[28]

Robert likely continued to live in the old homestead. City directories and census records identify him variously as an accountant at Bayou Bridge (1861), retired farmer (1870), and gardener (1870). In 1884 he sold the property to Willis Emanuel Roux, who in turn transferred it to Edwin Millon Roux, representing Albert Peter Roux. Albert Peter Roux (money broker) and his sons, Willis (police sergeant) and Edwin (railroad worker), lived in their family's ancestral home at 1300 Moss Street (Spanish Custom House). The ties between the Roux and Blanc families were tight, not only as neighbors but also as in-laws, for Willis was married to Evariste's granddaughter. Perhaps they were trying to preserve the old homestead, as well as its neighborhood. During the 1940s, however, this doomed colonial architectural remnant was demolished.

1218 Moss Street. 1960s reinterpretation of an 1844 farmhouse by architect Raymond Boudreaux as his family home.

1200 Blocks: Desoto (Washington), Bell (Rue St. Jean du Chemin du Bayou, St. John), North Hagan (First)
Grand Route St. John, Desoto (Washington), North Rendon (Second)

In the 1720s, French colonial concessionaire François Dugué still owned his original 1708 land tract with a small frontage of 2½ arpents on the east side of the bayou, extending between today's Bell Street and Grand Route St. John. After a succession of sales throughout the eighteenth century, Jean Juzan, a relative of the Lorreins family, owners of the neighboring plantation to the north, acquired the land and soon afterward had it subdivided.[29] The 1200 block of Moss Street derives from the front of the Dugué-Juzan plantation.

The portion between Bell and Desoto is comprised of two squares designated as 465 and 466, which are joined because Ursulines Avenue

was never extended to Moss Street, as planned. Throughout the nineteenth century, this bayou-fronting area resembled a rural village, with an expanse of farmland, small-scale homes, and several neighborhood stores and a coffee house. Its inhabitants were long-term residents, most related to each other and familiar as early Bayou St. John personalities. The oldest extant building in this long block is **1218 Moss Street**. Located on a deep lot, this cottage was constructed circa 1844, soon after the Baden, Germany, native Jacob Weingarten (1822-1898) acquired the entire square 465, which ran 236 feet on Moss Street and extended back at an oblique line to front on both Bell Street and North Hagan Avenue. In 1966 New Orleans architect Raymond Boudreaux designed this modernization of the early cottage, following architectural trends of the 1950s and 1960s, as his family home. Today the house presents as a modernist interpretation of a center-hall cottage with a deep front gallery.

Interior, with portrait of owner's wife, Hilda.

Interior, entrance hall looking toward dining room.

*Interior, looking toward
the bayou.*

The only buildings on this large expanse of land throughout the nineteenth century were Weingarten's agrarian complex, which he shared with his French-born wife, Magdalena, and children. In addition to the grounds behind his house, he also owned three lots of the original Louis Blanc estate across Bell Street to use for his suburban farm, where he grew vegetables to sell at the downtown French Market.[30] After the deaths of their parents, the Weingarten heirs subdivided the property, which was sold at a public auction in 1900. The large area with the farmstead, described as "a neat cottage containing five rooms and hall, kitchen building containing three rooms, large hot house and other buildings," was bought by thirty-two-year-old Marie Weingarten, who lived there for a while with her four unmarried older sisters until she moved to the French Quarter to establish her millinery business.[31] Later owners in the early twentieth century included Bourbon Street saloon proprietor William Bernhard and Bertrand Ader, vice president of F. Laudumiey, undertakers.

The "plantation" style, two-story masonry home at **1200 Moss** resulted from a 1978 remodeling by architect Arthur Middleton for owners Eugenie and Bill Faust. The earlier home, a circa 1913 bungalow, was constructed on a corner lot of the subdivided Weingarten farm by John J. McCormick, a horseracing

and boxing enthusiast with training stables along the bayou. In 1920 this sophisticated dwelling was described as having a butlery, glass-enclosed sleeping porch, built-in features, a flower garden, and terraced lawn, as well as the expected living spaces.[32] The new owners continued remodeling when they moved the older home from a diagonal location to face the bayou, raised the ceilings 9½ feet to accommodate a second floor, and added an attic floor with dormers.[33]

The Sanborn Map of 1896 provides the first indications of buildings in Square 465, which extended from the intersection of the uncut Ursulines Avenue to Desoto. Of the three dwellings outlined, one of these remains at **1248-50 Moss** as a modified double frame shotgun. A survey in 1902 shows the footprint of this cottage and the adjacent one, later demolished (lots A and B), at the corner of Desoto. At the time of the survey, the circa 1890 double houses were part of the extensive real estate holdings in the succession of Victor Petit

Above: 1256 Moss Street.

Left: The appearance of 1200 Moss Street resulted from a 1978 remodeling of an early twentieth-century bungalow.

(1848-1892), grocer at the corner of Moss and Grand Route St. John.[34] Petit had acquired the land in 1888 from Felicité Klar Roux, whose husband, Albert Pierre Roux, owned the Spanish Custom House. Her father, Joseph Klar, a German-born gardener, maintained a homestead in the 3300 block of Esplanade. Felicité and Albert's son, Willis Roux (1859-1901), married Louise Clemence Blanc (1865-1914), daughter of James Arthur Blanc, the youngest son of Evariste, further interweaving the first families of Bayou St. John.

1200 Moss Street addresses continue in the short block between Desoto Street and Grand Route St. John. The Eastlake double cottage at **1256 Moss** postdates 1905, when the succession of Willis Roux sold the site for his widow on behalf of their minor child, Clemence.[35] The judicial advertisement for this "neat raised cottage on picturesque Bayou St. John, corner Moss and De Soto Street" described the property with a frontage on Moss Street of sixty feet and a dwelling, set back nine feet from the street, with front and side galleries, five rooms, shed, cistern, and privy. This corner cottage was the home of Louise and Willis Roux before his death in 1905. The widowed Louise moved into one of the two double cottages at **3301** and **3307 Grand Route St. John**, behind her in-laws' ancestral home at 1300 Moss. Their diminutive three-bay, side-galleried cottage stands today at **1260 Moss Street**, where it had been moved circa 1905 after being acquired by French-born grocer Jean Marie Dorginac (1870-1934). Outlined on the Robinson Atlas, this vernacular Italianate dwelling may date from the 1870s but was updated in the early 1900s with new glazing and window lintels.

The two-story frame building with a wraparound gallery at **1264-66 Moss** retains only its corner entrance to suggest its origins as a neighborhood grocery and saloon. In 1934 this structure was described in the partition of Dorignac's estate as "a one-story building occupied by a grocery and a barroom and a private market, large anteroom." A native of the Hautes-Pyrénées region of France, Dorignac came to New Orleans as a teenager and bought the store in 1902 from the estate of Victor Petit.[36] As noted above, Petit possessed extensive real estate in St. John Faubourg in

Top: 1260 Moss Street.

Center: 3307-09 Grand Route St. John.

Bottom: 3301-03 Grand Route St. John.

Left: Watercolor of a small grocery facing Grand Route St. John, 1870. Courtesy of Honorable Dale N. Atkins, Clerk of Court, Parish of Orleans.

Below: Bayou Bridge at Grand Route St. John, looking north, taken in 1867 by photographer Theodore Lilienthal. Courtesy of bpk-Bildagentur, Napoleon Museum, and Art Resource, NY.

addition to his grocery, and when he died in 1892 at the age of forty-four, his succession included the luxuries of a schooner and two race horses.[37] Petit had acquired the property in 1889 from Felicité Klar Roux, who bought it in 1882. Petit's purchase included "the contents of the grocery store established in the property herein sold, consisting in goods, shelving, liquors, bottles, glasses and in general all the moveable effects," except those of the personal use of the vendor.[38]

The parcel on Moss between Desoto and Grand Route St. John was part of the early nineteenth-century estate of Louis Nicolas Fortin (1777-ca.1819), which extended to the future site of the Luling Mansion and Jockey Club. A native of Champagne, France, Fortin came to New Orleans by way of the French fur-trading post at Vincennes, Indiana, where he had married Suzanne Bosseron (1780-1865) in 1801. With Louis Blanc, Fortin in 1809 established the Faubourg Pontchartrain, to the north of Faubourg St. John. After the death of the Widow Fortin in 1865, her remaining holdings, including this block, were partitioned and sold. Two main buildings existed at that time on Rue du Port.[39] Toward Desoto stood "a frame dwelling, bricked between posts, containing one large room occupied by a coffee house, a corner room used as a grocery, two cabinets and a large gallery on the rear . . . with awning, also

a kitchen, cellar, stables, cistern, privies;" and toward Grand Route, "a frame dwelling containing three large rooms, two cabinets, one gallery, also back building." Jean Carambat and Jean Monguillot bought the first property and Isaac Magendie, the second. An 1866 survey outlines these buildings.

Shown on the Robinson Atlas, this old building at the south corner was gone by 1896. From 1866 until his death in 1875, Isaac Magendie, a grocer listed in the 1872 city directory at Carondelet Walk, corner Grand Route, owned the corner lot as well as adjacent ones fronting on Desoto and Grand Route. Magendie operated the store there until his death in 1875.[40] Today, 1264-66 Moss may well incorporate elements of the mid-nineteenth-century corner store. Grand Route St. John seems to have served as the main street of the bayou village. Not only were there a coffee shop and grocery/barroom facing the waterway, a notarial watercolor from 1870 depicts a small, frame store facing Grand Route near North Rendon Street.

Above: Charles Alexandre Lesueur view of the Old Bridge, *looking across to the left bank from the home of his friend Albin Michel, the French consul who lived at today's Pitot House before it was moved from the 1300 block. Muséum d'Histoire Naturelle du Havre, Le Havre, France.*

Early Bayou St. John (Jean, Juan) Bridges

Trudeau's map (1798) depicts Bayou Road leaving from the lower end of the Vieux Carré toward Bayou St. John and crossing an early bridge to continue on the western side of the bayou, north toward the lake. This bridge stood between today's Bell and Desoto Streets, just north of Louis Blanc's plantation. After the opening of the Carondelet Canal in 1794, the accompanying flow of schooners and small craft necessitated a drawbridge to allow their passage to and from the canal. In 1795 the Cabildo approved the construction of a new bridge at the city's expense and, in 1796, appointed Louis Blanc to police and supervise the new bridge.[41] The next year, a watchman was hired to monitor the boats going through the drawbridge, and a hut was built for him. (Not surprisingly, this employee soon established a tavern nearby.) The bridge, erected within a year, fell apart almost as quickly. In 1806 the mayor solicited bids for the construction of its replacement.[42] When completed in 1810, its new location was two hundred yards lakeside of the old bridge, near the intersection of Grand Route St. John and the Spanish Custom House.

During his 1830 bayou sojourn, Lesueur made several sketches, one noted as having been drawn from the home of his friend Albin Michel, the French consul who lived at today's Pitot House before it was moved from the 1300 block. Romantically fanciful, Lesueur's drawings may not be precise in detail. On the other hand, an 1867 camera shot by New Orleans photographer Theodore Lilienthal accurately captured this bridge, perhaps with the Weingarten farm cottage in the foreground. This bridge was known as the Old Bridge, and in May 1866, the city authorized its repair and alteration to make it suitable for "foot passengers."[43]

1300-1400 Blocks: Esplanade Avenue, Grand Route St. John, Vignaud (Percée, North Hagan), Ponce de Leon (Florida)

The long swath of bayou-fronting land between Grand Route St. John and Esplanade Avenue abounds with properties significant to the history of the village from its founding in 1708 to the present day. Unlike in the lower blocks, no perpendicular streets from Grand Route St. John to Esplanade Avenue were cut through to the bayou, therefore leaving behind an unspoiled architectural diorama that survives today. During the early eighteenth century, the site of these blocks was acquired through concession and acquisition by early Canadian settler Antoine Rivard *dit* Lavigne, whose plantation eventually extended from today's Grand Route St. John to a point south of Desaix Boulevard. Much of Rivard's land later came into the possession of Jacques (Santiago) Lorreins, called Tarascon, who was born in Mobile to French parents.[44]

The Spanish Custom House today.

1300 Moss: Lorreins-Roux House
Bounded by Esplanade, Grand Route St.
John, Vignaud (Percée, North Hagan),
Ponce de Leon (Florida)

This, the oldest remaining house on Bayou St. John, also popularly known as the Spanish Custom House, directly connects with the earliest bayou pioneers, with original ownership by Santiago Lorreins. A steep, double-pitched roof, deep galleries, and delicate second floor turned columns, all evoking West Indian and Upper Mississippi Valley French colonial architectural prototypes, enhance the charm of this rare pristine example of the evolved Louisiana raised-basement plantation house type. When the elder Lorreins died in 1784, one of his properties, surely this one, was described as "A plantation measuring 20 arpents of land fronting on Bayou St. John, with a depth up to Santilly [Gentilly] with various fruit trees. New house 34 feet front with the same depth, with four rooms, gallery 8 feet wide on three sides." [45]

After acquiring the property in 1807, Lorreins's son sold the house with a 99' front on the bayou and 220' on Grand Route St. John to Captain Eli Beauregard. For a few years between 1809 and 1816, Louis Nicolas Fortin and Louis Blanc, together and separately, owned the house, perhaps explaining the appellation of the Spanish Custom House, for in 1807 Louis Blanc, "residing at the settlement of the bayou," was appointed toll collector for New Orleans Navigation Company, owner and builder of the Carondelet Canal, "on every vessel whatever, coming from Lake Pontchartrain into the said Bayou by the channel which the company have made." In 1809 Blanc and Fortin carved the Faubourg Pontchartrain from a portion of the former Lorreins plantation, covering from approximately today's Vignaud Street to Fortin Street, according to a plan from that year by surveyor Jacques Tanesse.

Between 1816 and 1901, this stately residence was home to Pierre Roux and his descendants.[46] The elder Pierre (1773-ca. 1834) had come to New Orleans following a route familiar to the Francophone bayou dwellers. After immigrating to Canada from his fatherland, he slowly worked his way down south to

Louisiana through the Midwestern French fur-trading settlements. Along the way, he married Marie Angelique Mallet in Detroit, Michigan, and fathered his first child, born in Indiana. The 1834 auction record of the property for the first Roux's succession noted three buildings and included a description of the house:

> A lot of ground fronting the Bayou St. John immediately opposite the bridge and forming the corner, having 220 feet front on the Bayou Road by 99 feet fronting the Bayou and the bridge on one side, and 155 feet fronting Percee Street, with all the improvements consisting of a two-story dwelling house divided into two rooms, a cabinet cellar and gallery below, and two rooms, a cabinet front and rear above.

> The first story of the house is of brick, and the second story brick between posts and weatherboarded. The whole is in good condition, having been lately repaired. The outhouses are a kitchen of two rooms, a stable and servants' room. There is also another building fronting the bayou rented as a cabaret. There is also on the lot another house at the corner of Percee Street. The whole is under lease."[47]

That this iconic house dates to ca. 1780 has been challenged by a theory that the surviving building either was rebuilt in the early 1800s, reusing the original materials, or extensively remodeled. A comparison of the description from 1784 with that from 1834, which offers the same floor plan as the earlier one, suggests that the original house remained, albeit with updates, as new owners are wont to make.[48]

Architecturally imposing, the Spanish Custom House originally had an intimate floorplan, consisting only of two adjacent rooms on each floor, with anterooms (cabinets) and open gallery at the rear, typical of early Louisiana raised plantation houses, all to capture the breezes and direct them toward the interior. As noted in the 1834 description, the dependencies consisted of a stable, kitchen, and servants' rooms. This was not a capacious home for an extended family. The principal rooms on the second floor still retain boxed mantels in the French manner, and narrow, plastered chimney breasts. In 1934 noted architect and pioneer preservationist Richard Koch photographed this property for the Historic American Buildings Survey.[49]

Top: The Spanish Custom House in 1934. Historic American Buildings Survey, Library of Congress, Prints and Photographs Division.

Bottom: 1300 Moss Street. The second-floor principal rooms in the Lorreins-Roux House, also known as the Spanish Custom House, contain such French-influenced features as this boxed mantel, photographed in 1934 by architect Richard Koch. Historic American Buildings Survey, Library of Congress, Prints and Photographs Division.

Above: This ca. 1895 cottage at 1308 Moss Street occupies the site of the "cabaret" that stood on the grounds of the Roux House in 1834.

Between 1909 and 1935, local author Helen Pitkin Schertz made her home here. In 1927 the Spanish revival rear addition was constructed as a music room for this owner, prominent in local art and theatrical circles in the 1920s and 1930s. From 1947 until 2009, Dr. and Mrs. Ignatius M. Dematteo owned the house. During their tenure, the one-story detached kitchen was constructed. The circa 1895 three-bay cottage at **1308 Moss** occupies the site of the "cabaret" noted on the grounds of the Roux house in 1834. Modifications include front porch ironwork and the center entrance's cut glass door, sidelights, and transom that fancified a straightforward example of a vernacular New Orleans Italianate building type.

1342 Moss Street: Evariste Blanc House (Our Lady of the Rosary Rectory) Bounded by Esplanade, Grand Route St. John, Vignaud (Percée, North Hagan), Ponce de Leon (Florida)

In September 1834, Blanc sold 924 Moss Street, along with his extensive Bayou St. John land holdings, to the First Municipality of New Orleans. He acquired the site of his second home a couple of months later and built his new, more elaborate residence, basically an "American plan" house that, like his first home, showed decidedly French colonial influences. Typical of raised-basement Louisiana plantation houses are the deep, shading galleries, sturdy ground-floor Tuscan columns, graceful wooden colonettes on the second level, and French doors. The center-hall plan is American in influence. Local architectural parlance identifies the well-detailed façade center entrances, with fanlight transoms and Ionic pilasters supporting the

Right: Holy Rosary Rectory (1342 Moss Street), with dome of the church in the background.

Above: The Evariste Blanc House, 1342 Moss Street, in the 1930s. Photographed by Charles L. Franck Photographers. The Charles L. Franck Studio Collection at The Historic New Orleans Collection, 1979.325.1425.

entablature cornice, as "Transitional" between Creole and Greek revival building traditions. Its most conspicuous feature is the distinctive widow's walk crowning its hipped roof. Also noteworthy is the fine original wall composed of a stucco base and columns with globe finials and hand-wrought iron pickets. Although Evariste contributed three architectural landmarks to the Bayou St. John streetscape, no architect was recorded for any of them.

Evariste lived here until his death in 1853, and his family stayed until the early twentieth century. Artist William Woodward's painting *Bayou Saint John at end of Grand Route Saint John* portrays a lush rural landscape on the bayou shore, with both 1300 and 1342 Moss in the background. An 1876 inventory accompanying the succession of Widow Evariste Blanc (Fanny Labatut) documented the furnishings of the house at that time, with a cumulative value of $1,430.35.[50] The *premier étage* included the main parlor, family rear parlor, front bedroom, back bedroom, hall-room, and hall. On the ground floor were the downstairs hall, dining room with silver and platter ware appraised for the large sum of $660, pantry, front downstairs bedroom, and billiard room. Also on the grounds were the kitchen and stable, with a barouche and cow, but no mention of horses.

At the behest of son and executor Jules Arnaud Blanc, the real estate was subdivided, per an 1876 survey by surveyor Louis H. Caire.[51] Sandwiched between the estate of J. L. Tissot to the north and that of Widow Roux or Coulter to the south, the

Blanc property edged the "public road running long the bayou" for 270 French feet and extended to front on Esplanade. Evariste Blanc acquired his land in 1834 from David Olivier, who with Louis Lecesne, had bought it from John McDonogh in 1811.[52] Earlier owners were Louis Nicolas Fortin and Lavigne, Kernion, and Lorreins.

Evariste and Fanny's daughter, Sylvanie Denegre, lived in the family home for many years before giving the dwelling and four adjacent lots on Esplanade Avenue to the Society of the Roman Catholic Church of the Diocese of New Orleans in 1905 in memory of her mother, Fanny Labatut Blanc.[53] Sylvanie made the donation "upon the express condition that there shall be created thereon and perpetually maintained

a Parish Church, for the purpose of providing the residents of the neighborhood . . . with a Parish Church and necessary accessories and dependencies, such as a parsonage, school or other purposes." She directed that its name would be the Church of Sainte Marie du Rosaire and that a "pew in the centre aisle shall be perpetually reserved and set apart for her [and] the donor's family."[54]

Reporting for the *Times-Picayune* in 1922, G. William Nott floridly recalled life in this mansion in the days before the gift to the diocese. He described the front yard, laid out in the "Italian style: a series of carefully planned terraces, and at regular intervals, graceful statues and urns."[55] At the rear of the house were grape arbors, hot beds, and, further back, an orchard. The 1908-09 Sanborn Map documents changes made after the Denegre donation. The family home had become the Priest's House. Behind a newly constructed small chapel toward Esplanade Avenue, the earlier rear dependencies remained until the larger church was built in 1924.

Below: Artist William Woodward's 1887 painting, Bayou Saint John at end of Grand Route Saint John, *portrays a lush rural landscape on the bayou shore, with both 1300 and 1342 Moss in view. The Historic New Orleans Collection, Gift of Laura Simon Nelson, 2006.0430.15.*

The picturesque cottage at 1318 Moss Street was built in the 1870s by Jules Arnaud Blanc on the southern end of the grounds of the family home, 1342 Moss.

When the Widow Blanc's estate was partitioned in 1876, her son Jules acquired the irregularly shaped lot designated B, as well as the rear lot C. By 1885 he had built a small house on lot B, still standing though perhaps in a stylistically updated form, at **1318 Moss**. A 1904 advertisement by Jules's estate described the property as a "single house, containing four rooms, two cabinets and bath."[56] Originally rectilinear in form, the cottage had a gallery on its south side. After 1909 an addition was made on this same side. Today, the picturesque cottage has screened porches on the façade and side elevation. Its tripartite gables feature applied jigsaw work in a fern pattern, repeated on the spandrels of the porch colonettes.

Just south of the campus of today's Cabrini High School stand two late nineteenth-century cottages. Formerly part of the grounds of the Michel-Pitot House, their sites were sold in 1894 by Widow Jean Louis Tissot and her son, Aristée L. Tissot. **1354 Moss** features a three-bay frame shotgun with an unusual center Classical-style entrance, described in a 1936 for-sale advertisement as an "artistic front door."[57] Old-fashioned planting adds to the charm of this rustic dwelling. The raised Craftsman-style bungalow at **1364 Moss**, originally constructed circa

1895, was advertised for sale by the estate of Judge Ernest Morel as a "charming, nearly new double cottage on picturesque Bayou St. John, in the healthiest portion of the city and on its highest ridge, opposite the Southern Park, near the City Park and Jockey Club, in close proximity to the fine properties of our esteemed citizens, Cucullu, Widow A. L. Tissot, B. Cabirac, D. Cefalu, A. Roux and E. Blanc."[58] In 1917 the owner of the double cottage, Pauline Paterno Sparicio (Mrs. Leon), engaged contractor August Frank for "reconstruction, repairs and additions" at the cottage.[59] The modifications included front and side galleries with Doric columns.

Two of the bayou neighborhood's most architecturally and historically significant properties, the Michel-Pitot House and the Fernandez-Tissot House, formerly occupied the site of the modern Cabrini High School building, circa 1964-65, designated as 1400 Moss Street. The Pitot House was relocated in 1964 from 1370 Moss to 1440 Moss, and the Fernandez-Tissot House was demolished at the same time.

1440 Moss Street: The Pitot House
Bounded by Esplanade, Grand Route
St. John, Vignaud (Percée, North Hagan),
Ponce de Leon (Florida)

Although the fight to rescue the Tissot House from demolition ended in failure, its neighbor was saved. Another fine example of a Louisiana plantation house, the Michel-Pitot House was moved from its original location at 1370 Moss and restored, beginning in 1964, under the auspices of Louisiana Landmarks Society, which is currently headquartered there. Founded in 1950 "to focus attention on Louisiana's historical buildings as living remains of Louisiana history and physical reminders of the rich heritage bequeathed us by Louisiana forebears,"[60] Landmarks has expanded its mission to include advocacy for many aspects of New Orleans's quality of life beyond the built environment. Because of its public accessibility and the high visibility of its lush setting, the Pitot House has become a beloved symbol of the Bayou St. John neighborhood.

In 1964 this colonial dwelling was acquired through negotiations with the Missionary Sisters, owners since 1904, and, with the support of then-Mayor Victor H. Schiro, was moved approximately 150 yards north to the city-owned Desmare Playground. For many years, the new site, running from Moss to Esplanade, held the wooden barn and stables of the New Orleans City and Lake Railroad and, later, the Engineering Department of the New Orleans Railway and Light Company. By 1940 the vacant lot served as a staging yard for the New Orleans Public Service Inc. An 1864 photograph by federal soldier Marshall Dunham, a New York native, depicts the demolished railway buildings next to the Bayou Bridge.

Former occupants significantly modified the old house from its original circa 1800 design. When the building was moved, the decision was made to restore/ reconstruct it to its early nineteenth-century appearance, as documented by a circa 1830 sketch made by French naturalist Charles Alexandre Lesueur during his sojourn in New Orleans. This sketch captured the broad hipped roof, deep façade, and side galleries with hefty ground-floor masonry Tuscan columns and upper-floor delicate wooden colonettes. Clearly visible is the wooden gallery railing with its distinctive x pattern, removed during the late nineteenth century and replaced with a simple vertical balustrade. The characteristic Creole double-pitched roof had been modified to a single-pitched one, pierced with two dormers. Architect-historian Samuel Wilson Jr., first president of Louisiana Landmarks Society, was instrumental in the reconstruction and restoration process. The complex moving procedure included removal and salvaging of ground-floor columns, jacking up and bracing the frame second floor, and demolishing the masonry first floor.

The house's early owners and occupants included many of the city's most influential individuals and families.[61] In 1799 merchant Bartolomé Bosque, born on the Spanish island of Majorca, briefly owned the property, which he acquired from large landowner Santiago Lorreins. Active in the shipping business, Bosque understandably would have been attracted

Charles Alexandre Lesueur's 1830 drawing of the Michel-Pitot House, formerly located at 1370 Moss, served as the guide for the restoration of this landmark to its original appearance. Muséum d'Histoire Naturelle du Havre, Le Havre, France.

Above: The Michel-Pitot House as a convent in 1964, before its move slightly north from 1370 Moss to its current location. Historic American Engineering Record, National Park Service, U.S. Department of the Interior. Prints and Photographs Division, Library of Congress.

Left: In 1864 Union soldier Marshall Dunham photographed the Magnolia Bridge (also known as the New Bridge), shortly before its collapse and reconstruction. On the right side are demolished buildings that served the New Orleans City Rail Road. Marshall Dunham Photograph Album (Mss. 3241), Louisiana and Lower Mississippi Valley Collections, LSU Libraries, Baton Rouge, Louisiana, USA.

The Pitot House, 1440 Moss, today serves as the headquarters of the Louisiana Landmarks Society.

to this site on an important waterway. He may have intended the house as his country residence, for his circa 1795 city townhouse remains today at 617 Chartres Street, attributed variously to French architect-surveyor Barthélémy Lafon and architect-builder Hilaire Boutté. Six months after his purchase, Bosque sold the unfinished house to his business associate, Joseph Reynes, who also had a home downtown, the Spanish colonial landmark at 601 Chartres. The next owner, Madame Vincent Rillieux, like her predecessors, was engaged in the import-export business. She may have finished or rebuilt the home to its present, reconstructed form with the assistance of Boutté, whose will noted $4,000 owed his estate for the building of a house for Madame Rillieux on Bayou St. John.[62]

In 1810 James Pitot (1761–1831), born in Normandy as Jacques-François Pitot, became the house's new owner and remained there for another nine years, although as a tenant during the last six. Despite the brevity of his residency, the reclaimed building bears

his name because of his role in the transition of New Orleans from a colonial town into an American one. After the Louisiana Purchase, Governor W. C. C. Claiborne chose Pitot to become mayor after the resignation of Etienne de Boré. Because he had already attained American citizenship, Pitot may be considered New Orleans's first American mayor. After holding the office for one year, Pitot continued an active public life, serving, among other roles, as president of the New Orleans Navigation Company, judge of the parish court, and a public auctioneer. Among the Pitot House Museum's collections is a portrait by Flemish artist Jacques Amans of Sophie Gabrielle Marie, Pitot's daughter, born in 1817 to his second wife.

From 1819 until its acquisition in 1904 by the Missionary Sisters, the house passed through the hands of several owners, each of whom modified it to suit individual needs and tastes. The French consul, Albin Michel, made his home there from 1819 to 1839, during which period Lesueur created

Pitot House. Parlor, second floor, overlooking the front gallery with its bayou views and breezes.

Pitot House. Rear lower loggia with exterior stairway, defining features of Louisiana Creole architecture.

Right: Pitot House. Dining room.

Below: Pitot House. South bedroom, second floor.

his drawing. In 1848 Michel's son sold the bayou plantation to Felix Ducayet, a storekeeper at the United States Custom House. During his tenure, the land served as a hog and chicken farm.[63] Ducayet's property was sold at a sheriff's sale in 1857. At that time, an advertisement provided a description of the house and outbuildings: "A two-story dwelling, shingled roof, built partly in brick and partly in wood, with front and side gallery, with three rooms (one with a fireplace) and cellar and cabinet on the first floor; a one-story brick kitchen and oven attached to the dwelling; four large rooms with fireplace and cabinet on the second floor; overseer's house, frame stables, coach-house, cow-house, pigeon and chicken house, etc., splendid garden, orchard, hot house, cistern, walls, pumps, etc."[64] Although architectural books recount the structural beauties of nineteenth-century houses, resplendent with draperies, drawings and other art, carpets, vases, and statuary, it is in these newspaper advertisements of impending sales that one finds a description, stripped to its bare bones, of the building and all that it encompasses.

In 1859 Jean Louis Tissot bought the former Michel house. A year later his son acquired the neighboring, now-demolished Fernandez-Tissot House, which the father, in turn, bought in 1870 from his son. The Tissot family used the Pitot house as rental property until selling it in 1903.

During the Cabrini period, 1904 to 1964, the nuns rented out the Pitot house residentially to tenants such as the Pollatsek family until around 1935. For approximately the next twenty-eight years, the building served as a convent. During its occupancy, the religious order made additional modifications, including removal of fireplaces and chimneys, demolition of the original external stairway on the south side, and removal of some interior walls.

Opposite: Pitot House. Parlor detail, highly ornamented boxed mantel and chimney breast in the French manner.

Fernandez-Tissot House (demolished)
Bounded by Esplanade, Grand Route St. John, Vignaud (Percée, North Hagan), Ponce de Leon (Florida)

Built circa 1800 by Andres Fernandez, an official of the Spanish colonial government, this early raised house, now lost, had side gables in the American manner. Its appearance fortunately has been documented in several archival images and in material compiled by the Historic American Buildings Survey when the building was threatened with demolition in 1964.[65]

Built on a portion of the vast holdings of Santiago Lorreins, the house was owned and enjoyed in the 1820s as a country estate by the prosperous German-born financier and real estate entrepreneur Samuel Kohn (1783-1853). Kohn, in 1806 a freshly arrived émigré, and his business partner, H. Labruyère, announced the opening of a Bayou St. John tavern named Tivoli, "in the most elegant style, where may be enjoyed the air of the country, a prospect of the bayou, and the agreeableness of a charming garden, as a pleasant walk."[66] The duo must have leased the site of Tivoli before Kohn's purchase in 1826, for as early as 1806, this piece of land, which Kohn acquired from Morel, was the scene of social gaiety, visited and described by the English adventurer, Thomas Ashe: "There is an assembly held every Sunday evening in the bayou, about two miles

Top: Built in the early 1800s by Andres Fernandez, an official of the Spanish colonial government, this now-demolished raised cottage served as the country retreat in the 1820s for German-born financier Samuel Kohn. Historic American Buildings Survey, Library of Congress, Prints and Photographs Division.

Right: Historic American Buildings Survey drawings of Tissot-Fernandez House, which stood at 1400 Moss before its demolition in 1964. Historic American Buildings Survey, Library of Congress, Prints and Photographs Division.

out of town. . . . The place of entertainment is called Tivoli. The room is spacious and circular, well-painted and adorned, and surrounded by orange trees and aromatic shrubs, which diffuse through it a delightful odor. I went to Tivoli and danced in a very brilliant assembly of ladies. The Spanish women excel in the waltz, and the French in the cotillion."[67]

In 1825 Kohn bought the Fernandez house from the creditors of Vallery Robert Avart. The following year he purchased an adjacent arpent on the lake side of the Fernandez tract from Pierre Louis Morel.[68] Kohn tried to sell his complex for several years before finally doing so in 1831, shortly before retiring to Paris. This bucolic estate was described in enthusiastic detail in the *Courrier de la Louisiane* (March 8, 1828): Situated at the

> Bayou St. John, that beautiful country seat, the residence of Mr. Samuel Kohn; measuring one-acre front by about 16 acres in depth; on which is a large two-story house, well distributed and in excellent repair, newly papered and painted. . . . In the yard adjoining, a spacious stable with coach-house, pigeon house and shed. The property is under a new fence; a vegetable garden under excellent cultivation; an orchard of about three hundred fruit trees of the choicest qualities from Europe and the States, principally in bearing; fronting the house is a parterre laid out with taste. . . . Fronting on the bayou a very convenient Bathing House, with a pump and catching tub.

In 1831 and 1832 Kohn sold the adjacent, deep parcels to Frederick Frey.[69] After a succession of owners, Felix Labatut, a church warden of the St. Louis Cathedral, sold the property in 1849 to the cathedral to establish a new cemetery.[70] Only the portion beyond the prolongation of Esplanade was dedicated to cemetery use, and that between the avenue and bayou was divided into lots and sold. The two lots upon which the house and outbuildings were located are shown on an 1854 notarial plan. Julie Fortin Ramos, daughter of early nineteenth-century bayou settler Nicolas

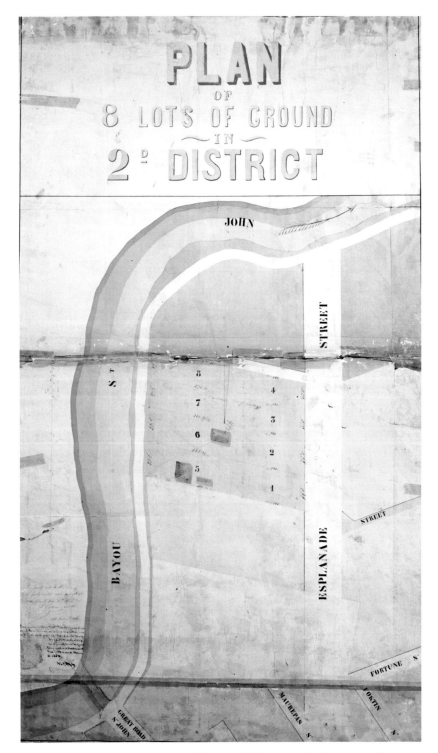

An 1854 survey outlining the buildings in the Fernandez-Tissot complex. Courtesy of Honorable Dale N. Atkins, Clerk of Court, Parish of Orleans.

Fortin, owned the house and grounds between 1851 and 1858. Jean Louis Tissot and his son, Judge Aristée Louis Tissot, made their family home here from 1866 until 1903, when the Columbia Brewing Company purchased it. In 1905 the brewery made the sale to the Missionary Sisters, sealing the fate of the house that had been an integral part of the bayou's social life for so many years.[71]

Magnolia Bridge (New Bayou Bridge, Cabrini Bridge)

Although the truss bridge today spanning the bayou in front of Cabrini School to the west bank at Harding Drive was moved there in 1908 from the Esplanade Avenue terminus, an earlier one, photographed in 1864 by Marshall Dunham, occupied this location. This bridge dramatically collapsed soon after being photographed, as reported in the *New Orleans Times* (February 6, 1865): "Bayou Bridge is in ruins. It has been broken. Long ago broken in to bridge uses, used so often, its timber snapped like a pipe stem. A wagon making an attempt to cross, drawn by six mules, the timber of the bridge refused support, and the wagon, mules, driver all fell in the swollen current of the Bayou St John. . . . Three mules arrived safe on the banks with the driver."[72]

Lilienthal's 1867 photograph of the same location shows that the bridge indeed is no longer there; however, a new one would soon be constructed. The *Times-Picayune* (June 1, 1866) reported, "We have taken notice [of] the fact that a bridge for vehicles, in lieu of the foot bridge at first contemplated, was to be built across Bayou St. John, upon the site of the old bridge opposite the Esplanade depot of the city cars." By the end of 1867, the Bayou Bridge near the Central Railroad was noted to "be right once more."[73] Located near the Canal and Esplanade rail line and leading across the bayou to the popular Magnolia Gardens park, this bridge was well traveled. The *Times-Picayune* offered the following summer's day excursion: "A very pleasant trip just now early in morning is to take the Esplanade Street cars at the Clay statue, and after reaching the Bayou Bridge, to get on board of the little streamer there awaiting, and off for the lake, where a delightful bath will fit one nicely for the lake, all this for thirty cents."

When the city decided to move the late nineteenth-century drawbridge from Esplanade to make way for a new, wider one, the chosen location was to be at the foot of Grand Route St. John, like the earlier nineteenth-century bridge. Before the erection of the drawbridge at Esplanade, there was only a narrow footbridge. The city could not gain the approval of the Canal Navigation Company for the revised location, and the bridge was relocated across from Magnolia Gardens, where it remains today.[74] Repairs were made in 1934 by the Works Progress Administration, and in 1989 it was rehabilitated for pedestrian use.

Above: Magnolia Bridge, 2017.

Left: Theodore Lilienthal's 1867 photograph of the Fernandez-Tissot House at right and the railroad buildings at the left. The collapsed Magnolia Bridge has not yet been rebuilt. The Historic New Orleans Collection, Courtesy of Fritz A. Grobien.

Boats on Bayou St. John near the Esplanade bridge. Courtesy of the Collections of the Louisiana State Museum, Accession #08482.160.

1454 Moss Street: Musgrove-Wilkinson House
Bounded by Esplanade, Grand Route
St. John, Vignaud (Percée, North Hagan),
Ponce de Leon (Florida)

This large, frame, villa-type center-hall house with gable ends also was constructed for early bayou citizen Evariste Blanc, who purchased the one-arpent, bayou-fronting site in 1847 from the succession of Etienne Reine and his wife, Celeste Cousin. The imposing raised cottage in the simple early Greek revival style was built for Blanc's daughter Elma, wife of Robert Gill Musgrove, agent in New Orleans for the London and Lancashire Fire Insurance Company.[75] Its ample grounds, classical styling, and size contrast attractively with the earlier, smaller plantation-style dwellings on the east bank of the bayou. Notable features include a deep front gallery with boxed columns and diamond-patterned railing, rusticated façade sid-

ing, and grand center entry, framed with a surround with crossetted corners and embellished with rosettes. The English-born Musgrove participated prominently in rowing activities, an integral part of social life on the bayou after the Civil War, and was an active member of the St. John Rowing Club. In Evariste Blanc's succession proceedings in 1859, his daughter exercised her preferential rights to keep the house built for her by her father. In 1876 the widowed Elma transferred the family home to her son, Emmanuel Musgrove.

In an 1882 public auction, the Musgrove estate, with over 260-feet frontage on the bayou, was adjudicated to Dominique and John Baptiste Cefalu. The Cefalu brothers, natives of Palermo, Sicily, were said to be pioneers in fruit importation in this city. In addition to their warehouse in the French Quarter on Madison

In the late 1840s, Evariste Blanc commissioned the villa at 1454 Moss Street for his daughter Elma.

Right: 1454 Moss Street. Simple but elegant detailing in the Greek revival style abounds in this home.

Below right: 1454 Moss Street. This pilastered marble mantel dramatically contrasts with boxed Creole-style mantels seen in earlier bayou cottages.

Street near the French Market, the business partners owned schooners, one of which was seized in Honduras and its captain imprisoned in 1881. The Bayou St. John site would have been useful for mooring the watercraft. Dominique acquired his brothers' interest in the property, and after his widow died in 1907, the inventory of her estate was taken in her home, the now-demolished double frame cottage at 1492 Moss. The villa and another house toward Esplanade, constructed circa 1885, were leased out.[76] The three houses and several empty lots on Moss near Esplanade, all owned by the Cefalu estate, were auctioned in 1908. Captain Luther D. Ott, a riverboat pilot, acquired the raised cottage and lived with his family in this house overlooking the bayou until his death in 1924.[77]

In 1935 Hugh Miller Wilkinson (1890-1973), a trial lawyer and former law partner of Governor Huey P. Long, bought the old Musgrove house, as well as the neighboring bungalow at 1460 Moss. Wilkinson and his family retained ownership until 2016. A sketch by artist Ellsworth Woodward shows the house before the enlargement of the dormers. In addition to raising the roof at both ends to provide more upstairs space and making building extensions at the downstairs rear, the Wilkinsons expanded the grounds by acquiring a large vacant lot extending back to the rear line of the houses facing Esplanade.

Artist and Newcomb College professor Ellsworth Woodward's Bayou St. John near City Park, *ca. 1910, also depicts the Wilkinson House. The Historic New Orleans Collection, 2008.0203.3.*

after a jewelry heist from his employee resulted in huge financial losses.[78] Colonel R. E. E. de Montluzin bought 1460 Moss at the auction "for old times' sake." Constructed in 1912 for Traverse, this was the first bungalow built by de Montluzin, who had just returned in 1911 from travels to California to study bungalow communities and would use the imported form in his Gentilly Terrace development.[79] Located at the point where the bayou takes a deep turn to the northeast, the house's façade and side elevation both face Moss Street. The *New Orleans Item* (October 29, 1933) featured a photograph of de Montluzin's bungalow, described as a "two-story brick building with weatherboards" and such "distinctive features as a flagstone paved patio reached by horseshoe steps." In 1935 Wilkinson bought 1460 Moss, as well as 1454.

1492 Moss is the last house before Esplanade Avenue on the east shore. This raised, frame, center-hall bungalow, with front and side galleries, is an extensive 1912 remodeling of the circa 1885 simple double shotgun built and lived in by fruit merchant Dominique Cefalu.[80] Although the design was updated to rival contemporary houses in the City Park neighborhood, late Victorian millwork hints at its earlier origins. A 1916 auction notice details the transformation of the modest cottage into a flamboyant house that "contains large center hall, parlor, dining room, breakfast room, four bedrooms with stationary wash stands, 2 bath rooms, large finished attic, suitable for billiard room," and a detached servant house.[81] In 1977 a zoning battle over whether restaurants could be allowed along the bayou centered on this house. Agostino Mantia, operator of an Italian restaurant in Metairie, applied for a zoning change to allow such a use in his newly purchased property. Neighbors, led by preservation stalwart Margaret Lauer, fought this application, which was denied by the City Planning Commission.[82]

The circa 1912 modified frame shotgun at **1450 Moss** occupies the southern corner of the original Musgrove estate grounds, and the circa 1912 residence at **1460 Moss** sprawls at the northern end. The sites of both buildings were part of the Musgrove estate and that of Dominique Cefalu in 1908, and were subsequently carved from the larger grounds. An auction in 1926 of properties belonging to diamond merchant Joseph Traverse offered both these properties, along with others in the "Race Track" vicinity. Most of Traverse's acquisitions were near Esplanade and Broad and included such "modern" structures as a filling station and stuccoed apartment buildings. As noted in his obituary, this French-born merchant invested in real estate as soon as he had more money than he could use for gems, intending to save for his retirement. Unfortunately, he died of a paralytic stroke as a broken man,

Above: The raised frame center hall bungalow at 1492 Moss Street resulted from an extensive remodeling, in 1912, of a ca. 1885 double shotgun.

Below: In 1912 diamond merchant Joseph Traverse commissioned construction of 1460 Moss Street, the first bungalow built by Colonel R. E. E. de Montluzin, developer of Gentilly Terrace.

MOSS STREET: WEST BANK

(Chemin de la Metairie/West Bayou St. John Road/West Lake Road/North Jefferson Davis Memorial Parkway)

A location on the left bank of even a small body of water such as the Bayou St. John seems to make a difference in both perception and reality of an area. Perhaps considered too far from town and unsettled, the west side of the bayou was not covered in the Robinson Atlas of 1883 or the Sanborn Insurance Maps of 1885 or 1896. From individual conveyance records, though, it can be determined that this area developed in a pattern much different than did the city side of the historic stream. Colonial land grants and plantations originally shared the area with eighteenth- and early nineteenth-century homesteads, but those remaining in the 1920s perished with the onslaught of planned residential enclaves. Before then, the west side seems to have appealed to a proletariat population, those whose livelihoods benefited from the area's rural environment and proximity to the water, such as vegetable growers, florists, dairymen, and boat-builders. Their homes were simple and utilitarian. On this side also was the popular public recreational area known first as Magnolia Gardens and later as Southern Park, adding to the egalitarian tenor of the area. With the post-World War I housing explosion, however, larger tracts were subdivided, and more costly houses, many bungaloid in type, were constructed. Affluent residents flocked to the neighborhood and lived in new, restrictive developments such as St. John Court, Parkview, and City Park Court.[1]

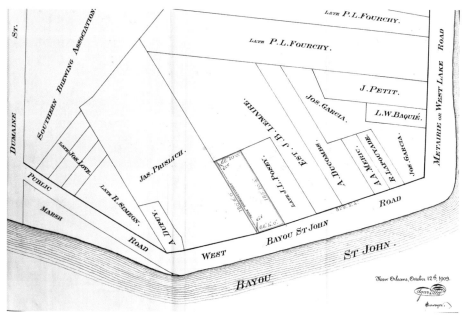

700-1000 Blocks: Bounded by Elaine, Dumaine, St. John Court, Orleans, Wilson, Harding

Only Orleans Avenue and Dumaine Street continue today from the east side of Moss Street to the west. Although shown on early surveys, St. Ann, St. Philip, and Ursulines were never established. Existing streets that do enter Moss Street date from the residential developments of the 1920s. The 1909 Sanborn shows no buildings on Moss between Orleans and Dumaine, other than a tiny "old" structure at the foot of Orleans. Two deep basins extended west from the bayou to an area designated as "swamp land." By 1940 a few buildings punctuated this stretch facing North Jefferson Davis Memorial Parkway or Moss Street, including the circa 1925 Spanish revival-style duplex at **809 North Jefferson Davis Parkway** and a Louisiana Colonial revival home at **919 Moss**. With land reclaimed, the embankment in this section is wide, and a small green space marks the corner of Moss and Orleans, contributing to a park-like atmosphere.

A 1909 survey outlines the bayou-fronting property and its owners between Dumaine Street and today's 1347 Moss. At that time, the Aztec Land Company and the

Quaker Realty Company, which commissioned the survey, were actively acquiring building sites for development in this area, as well as throughout the city. The grounds of Southern Park stretched from its waterfront entrance around to the corner of Moss and Dumaine. The 1909 Sanborn shows one structure between Dumaine and 1001 Moss Streets: a boat building on the banks. Today there are **919 Moss**, a Louisiana Colonial revival residence dating from between 1909 and 1940, and **921** and **925 Moss**, both postdating 1940.

The estate at **1001 Moss** sprawls around the bend of the bayou at the corner of uncut St. Philip Street. The north section of this modified home incorporates the circa 1890 Dutch Colonial-style home of John Frederick Dupuy (1837-1918), a mechanical engineer. Born in the Mississippi River town of Bayou Goula, Louisiana, Dupuy served in the 1890s as supervisor of the Swamp Land Reclamation, then located across the bayou, and with his sons was the proprietor of a boat yard that specialized in raising sunken ships. Until the late 1940s, the Dupuy family remained in this bucolic location, from which they sold wild cherries to make cherry bounce. A 1947 advertisement for the sale of the property included a photograph of the pre-renovated house, which had a 132-foot frontage on the bayou.[2]

Right: Another example of the Louisiana Colonial revival style, 921 Moss Street postdates 1940.

1031 Moss Street.

James Prislich, an Austrian-born French Quarter grocer, owned the large parcel just north of 1001 Moss Street in 1907. The 1910 census shows Prislich residing there, as well as Raoul Chaignaud, a vegetable farmer. The two men were married to sisters, Marie and Pauline Cabirac. Earlier nineteenth-century buildings that had stood on these extensive grounds were described in an 1869 auction notice as "a neat raised cottage, with five rooms, rear, front and side galleries, stable for eleven head of stock, feed room, two cisterns, chicken houses, privies, etc."[3] The site remained in the Chaignaud family as late as 1957, at which time it was divided. Today two modern homes—**1017** and **1021 Moss**—occupy this farmstead.

Next door, **1031 Moss** presents as a replicated plantation-style house but actually was constructed in the 1920s as a duplex, the form of which is evident in the side elevations. In the 1930s, brothers Emile and Charles Stopper sold their raised cottage at 1347 Moss and moved to this double dwelling. From 1828 until 1891, Augustine Gregoire and then his widow had owned this 66-foot-front site, which, during the early American period, figured as part of the Alpuente family holdings. Now a vacant lot, **1035 Moss Street** held a brick-between-posts dwelling as late as 1950. One of its last residents was George Drysdale Leverich, nephew of artist Alexander Drysdale, who died in 1947.[4] In a succession sale following the death in 1917 of wholesale grocer Charles Lester Hopkins from an "accidental shooting," the improvements consisted of a "raised cottage with high basement, spacious halls, parlor, dining room and four bedrooms."[5]

Developed between 1917 and 1923, **St. John Court** hosted the first private residential communities on the west side of the bayou. As early as 1918, developer Jean Lafont, who lived up the street at the two-story, circa 1900 Colonial revival-style home at **1335 Moss**, advertised several of his new, five-room "bungalows" for $17.50 a month. A "beautiful community garden or circle that is used as a playground by the children" stood at the center of the complex.[6] The residence at **1043 Moss**, more a simple cottage than a bungalow, dates from this real estate venture.

1047, 1055, 1065, and 1317 Moss Street:
François d'Hébécourt (1768-1832) and family
Bounded by St. John Court, Harding

The five houses at **1047, 1055, 1065, 1069,** and **1317 Moss Street** were constructed after 1907, when Marie Louise Alice d'Hébécourt, widow of Stephen Escoffier, and her son divided a larger tract and sold building lots.[7] Although inherited by the

vendors from their husband and father, ownership of the land reverted to Louise Alice's grandfather, François d'Hébécourt. Born in the town of Epernay, in the province of Champagne, France, d'Hébécourt came to New Orleans around 1802 and opened a school in the Vieux Carré for young men. In the 1820s, he moved the school to the Bayou St. John area, where he had bought extensive property. The city directory of 1822 lists his Bayou St. John Academy near the bridge, presumably meaning near Grand Route St. John in today's 1300 block. D'Hébécourt died in 1832, and a few years after the death of his widow, their estate was partitioned in 1847 among their three children—Adelaide, wife of Ramon de la Torre of Tampico, Mexico; François Napoleon; and Cornelia Eulalie, wife of Christoval Morel.[8] A survey accompanying this notarial act divided the land into three parcels, with lot "one," at the northern end of the tract, going to Cornelia; "two," at the southern end, to Adelaide; and middle

Above: 1047 Moss Street.

Left: 1335 Moss Street.

73

1347 Moss Street.

1347 Moss Street: Morel-Wisner House
Bounded by Harding, St. John Court

lot "three" to Napoleon. Lot three is the site of the building lots sold in 1907 by Widow Escoffier and her son. In the early 1850s, Cornelia and her husband built their villa, 1347 Moss, on their inheritance and also bought her sister Adelaide's share. In 1885, after the deaths of Cornelia and Christoval Morel, their son and heir, Ernest, sold his inherited properties at auction. At that sale, the elder Escoffier bought a sixty-foot, bayou-fronting portion that comprised part of the 1907 tract divided by his heirs.[9] The five houses on the Escoffier tract range from the raised-on-brick-piers, three-bay, circa 1905 Colonial revival cottage at **1047 Moss**, built by French-born carpenter Lucien J. Joly, to the circa 1930 two-story apartment building, **1069 Moss**.

This large, Greek revival-style raised cottage survives as the earliest documented building on the west side of the bayou. As noted above, the site figured in the holdings of schoolmaster d'Hébécourt until his daughter, Cornelia (1814-1884), inherited it. Similar to 1454 Moss Street in construction date, form, and style, the Morels' home assumes a prominent presence, with its deep façade gallery supported by boxed columns and surrounded by a wooden balustrade. Other stylistic features include the center hall entry, with pilastered surround and sidelights and pedimented dormers illuminating the one-story attic space. A stairway leading from the façade gallery to the main floor was moved in 2016 to an interior location. Although no visual images of the main house or the extensive grounds

Right: 1411 Moss Street.

of this estate have emerged during research, the 1885 auction notice for the sale of the property by Morel's son, Ernest, gives the following description: "a handsome raised family residence on six-foot pillars, having in the centre hall, front and back galleries, parlor and living room, with sliding doors and six bedrooms, pantry, cellar, well, etc."[10]

Owned from 1885 until 1897 by Paul Louis Fourchy, Christoval's reportedly unscrupulous nephew-in-law, the country house was taken over in 1904 through bankruptcy proceedings. For several years, the Eagle Poultry Farm rented the estate, and veterinarian Louis Morey Holmes acquired it in 1905 as a breeding farm for racehorses.[11] Long-lasting change, however, came to the property after its purchase in 1921 by Charles Stopper, and in 1924 by his sister-in-law, Lena Stopper. The grounds behind the main house were carved into building sites that would be consumed by Parkview Place, the residential development that replaced Southern Park in the early 1920s. To accommodate the new use, Stopper sold a strip of land to the city for the establishment of Harding Drive, which today separates 1347 Moss Street from the neighboring houses. In 1935 Elizabeth Wisner acquired this architecturally and historically significant house and saved it from its recent use as a rooming house. Wisner, director of Tulane University's newly established School of Social Work in the 1930s, and her partner, Florence Sytz, also a trained social worker associated with Tulane as a specialist in child guidance and psychology, remained at 1347 Moss for over forty years. Like their neighbor at 1437 Moss, Margaret Lauer, these two pioneering women fought for the integrity of their neighborhood, founding with others the Committee for St. John, which lobbied against the proposed demolition in 1964 of the Pitot and Tissot Houses across the bayou.

Magnolia Gardens / Southern Park

From approximately 1865 until 1922, West Moss Street between today's Harding Drive and **1413 Moss Street**, reaching back to Dumaine, served as a popular public amusement grounds. First known as **Magnolia Gardens**, it was renamed **Southern Park** in the 1880s after its acquisition by the Southern Brewery. The park had five hundred feet of frontage on the bayou and was about two thousand feet deep. A few months after the Civil War ended, the public was invited to a Fourth of July *Grand Fête Champêtre* at the Cedar Magnolia Garden, Bayou Bridge, complete with "games of all kinds, ball, day and night, balloon ascension splendid illumination, grand fireworks."[12] Accessed by public rail lines and from the east side of Moss Street by the Magnolia Bridge, the park seems to have taken the place of Tivoli, the early nineteenth-century rural pleasure gardens located just across the bayou. For over sixty years, the West Moss park was the lively scene of benevolent and fraternal society festivals, brass band concerts and dancing, baseball games, and convivial merriment in

Right: Young Men's Gymnastic Club boat house in front of Southern Park, originally built for St. John Rowing Club, 1907. The Historic New Orleans Collection, Gift of Boyd Cruise, 1958.85.345.

Y. M. G. C. ROWING CLUB, NEW ORLEANS, LA

Below: St. John Rowing Club, ca. 1873, before the second floor was added, with Magnolia Gardens in background. The Historic New Orleans Collection, 1951.41.33.

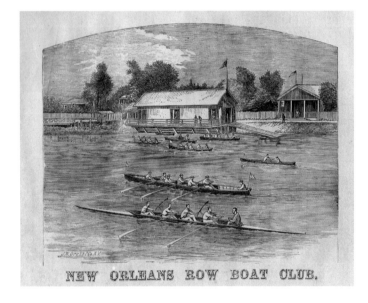

NEW ORLEANS ROW BOAT CLUB.

the beer hall. In 1911 the Louisiana branch of the German-American National Alliance held its second annual German day celebration there. Volksfests and other such German celebrations would cease with the onset of World War I.

The 1909 Sanborn Insurance Map outlines the park grounds with a dance pavilion, carriage shed, and a few small buildings scattered toward the front. On the south side of the park was the range of the New Orleans Rifle Club and nearby, next to the embankment, the two-story frame **Young Men's**

Gymnastic Rowing Club (YMGRC), an extension of the Young Men's Gymnastic Club (today's New Orleans Athletic Club). The sport of rowing had grown immensely in popularity in the 1870s and became an integral element of Bayou St. John social life. Under the headline, "A Gay Time on Bayou St. John," the *Times-Picayune* (October 28, 1872) reported that the polluted water had been cleared to its former purity and as a result, "two large, flourishing and rival row clubs with boat houses anchored on the margins of this beautiful outlet to the lake." On that day, the St. John and Pelican Clubs raced from the south side of the bend of the bayou to the island and back, with hundreds of onlookers thronging the shores and the boat houses. Founded in May 1872 by a group of "elite young men of the city," including bayou residents Jules Blanc, Henry Denegre, Robert Musgrove, and the younger Evariste Blanc, the St. John Rowing Club House was located initially in the building later occupied by the YMGRC. In 1877 the St. John Club moved from the bayou to a new place on Lake Pontchartrain, where the waters were more challenging for the oarsmen. Beginning with two boats, by 1891 the club owned thirty-five.[13]

A casualty of the Eighteenth Amendment and the onset of Prohibition in 1920, Southern Park closed, and the Anti-Tuberculosis League bought its large grounds for construction of a hospital. Neighborhood opposition, however, led the organiza-

St. John Rowing Club ribbon. The Historic New Orleans Collection, 2005.0336.7.

tion to abandon its plans and the site was divided and sold as building lots in 1921, with N. J. Clesi as the selling agent. The *Times-Picayune* (July 10, 1922) announced, "Pop only drink served at Southern Park Wake where the Benevolent Knights of America conducted the obsequies with the sounding of the funeral march over the site of the famous old outing place." Shown in the accompanying photograph was Captain Maurice Picheloup, long-time resident of the northern end of West Moss Street, drinking a bottle of pop. Plans were drawn up, and the name for the new development, **Parkview Place**, was selected from entries in a contest. To accommodate the new residential neighborhood, Charles Stopper, owner of the nearby 1347 Moss, sold a strip of land between his house and Southern Park to the city, and Harding Drive was laid out. By summer 1923, all but three of the house lots had been sold, with five houses almost completed and another fifteen getting started. **1349, 1352, 1361,** and **1405 Moss Street** were constructed in the 1920s on the grounds of Southern Park, while the Colonial revival home at **1359 Moss** dates from circa 1950.

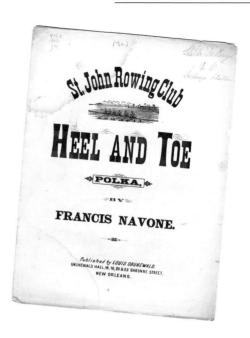

Above: "St. John Rowing Club Heel and Toe Polka," composed by Francis Navone and published in New Orleans by Louis Grunewald, 1880. Sheet music cover. Courtesy Louisiana Sheet Music Collection, Hogan Jazz Archive, Tulane University.

Below: A group of girls playing on the field at Southern Park. Photograph by John Tibule Mendes. The Historic New Orleans Collection, Gift of Waldemar S. Nelson, 2003.0182.545.

1413, 1415, 1417, and 1431 Moss Street: Johan George Merz Estate Bounded by Delgado, Carrollton (Chemin de la Metairie), Wilson

Just north of the former park are four houses dating from circa 1900, nearly two centuries after settlement of the Bayou St. John area began. The sites of **1413, 1415, 1417,** and **1431 Moss Street**, measuring 180 feet front on the bayou by 377 feet in depth, were part of the holdings of Johan George Merz from 1864 until 1883, after his death. Owner of a short-lived brewery and planing mill nearby, next to the Carondelet Canal, the German-born Merz is said to be the first in New Orleans to produce lager beer. An auction notice from 1883 describes the property as "a raised frame dwelling with two-story kitchen attached to the main building having four rooms, cabinet in the kitchen three rooms above, and three rooms below, two stables, about twenty-five orange trees, four plum trees, well, two cisterns, privies, chicken-house, garden in the front, gallery all around the house."[14] Merz acquired the rural estate from George A. Freret, a cashier with the Union Bank, listed in the 1860 census as residing on Bayou St. John. Located next to Magnolia Gardens, Merz's spacious grounds were well-situated for a brewmeister's retreat.

1415 Moss Street.

1431-33 Moss Street.

Ship carpenter and boat builder John Lewis Kennedy bought this wide stretch of water-facing land with buildings in 1883. According to the 1891 city directory, he lived on Bayou St. John near the footbridge and worked at his shipyard near Esplanade. In 1889 Kennedy sold a portion with an eighty-seven-foot frontage to his daughter, Theresa, married to Thomas J. Mullen, another shipwright. After her father's death in 1904, she inherited the remainder of his property. The Mullen family included several generations headed by Irish-born Thomas J. They built three of these houses, each in a distinctively different style, in which varying

Opposite: 1838 watercolor of a colonial raised cottage with attached treehouse overlooking the bayou. The cottage once stood on the Merz Estate, approximately at the site of 1431 Moss, and may have been the habitation of Etienne Roquigny and his wife, Maria Isabel DesRuisseaux. Courtesy of Honorable Dale N. Atkins, Clerk of Court, Parish of Orleans.

groupings of the extended family apparently resided. The circa 1898 front- and side-galleried two-story frame house at **1415 Moss**, probably the first of the three, blends the vernacular Carpenter's Gothic and Stick styles and certainly exhibits the family's ship-building skills. Before the construction of this attractive residence, the Kennedy and Mullen clan lived in the older home at **1433 Moss**. After its demolition, they moved to its replacement at **1431**, a circa 1910 raised Classical revival-style, villa-type duplex with a prominent gallery and center portico bay. Also constructed around the turn of the twentieth century was the simple cottage at **1413 Moss**, which has a front and side gallery. The deep façade gable and side porch terminate in scallop trim, pointing to a carpenter's touch.

In 1909, after the death of the matriarch, Theresa, her widower sold, for the benefit of the estate, a forty-seven-foot bayou-fronting strip of ground on the north side of 1415 Moss to Robert Paul de Lapouyade. A survey accompanying this

1417 Moss Street.

transaction shows the lot sandwiched between the properties of father Thomas and son James.[15] Born in Covington, Louisiana, de Lapouyade, a noted scene painter, was under contract with the French Opera House from 1911 to 1915. With the demise of legitimate theater and the advent of the burgeoning motion picture industry, he became involved with the Diamond Film Company and its doomed efforts to make New Orleans the American movie capital.[16] The sculptural—almost eccentric—stucco bungalow at **1417 Moss** was built circa 1910 as the artist's home and also housed at the rear a barn-like, fifty-foot-tall studio. As noted thirty years later by writer Harnett T. Kane, "The studio was thrown up in what was then an unsettled area along the bayou selected for large open space, the attractive scenery, distance from industry that might interfere with sunlight facilities, etc." [17] This important relic from the early heyday of filmmaking in the city remains in the same family today.

1437, 1451, 1455, and 1459 Moss Street:
Gustave Laroque Turgeau Estate
Bounded by Delgado, Carrollton
(Chemin de la Metairie), Wilson

Until the early 1900s, yet another now-demolished two-story, brick-between-posts, Louisiana raised house faced the bayou next to the Mullen complex. It was located on a portion of the Girardy-DesRuisseaux-Roquigny plantation. The last residents of this colonial house were Donaldsonville, Louisiana, native Gustave Laroque Turgeau (1823-1907) and his wife. Turgeau had acquired his bayou property in two transactions—the first in 1850, with a frontage of seventy-five feet, from the widow Guillaume Herries; and the second in 1886, with a frontage of 145 feet, from the succession of N. M. Benachi.[18] After the deaths of the Turgeaus, their heirs sold the property to Arthur Duvic, French Quarter ship chandler and member of the Progressive Union, which advocated for federal supervision of reconstruction and maintenance of the mouth of Bayou St. John. Duvic divided the tract into five lots, the site of today's **1437, 1451, 1455,** and **1459 Moss Street**. He reserved one

1437 Moss Street.

of the lots for himself and there, around 1910, built his new bungaloid home, 1459 Moss.

One of the "modern" homes built on the subdivided Turgeau tract was 1437 Moss, an imposing, two-story residence in the Louisiana Colonial revival style, marked by a broad front gallery with Ionic columns in the Colossal order, a center entry on the primary (second) floor, and exterior galleries. For many years beginning in 1953, this was the home of staunch preservationist Margaret Lauer, whose leadership and financial backing saved many of the city's landmarks, such as the Factors and Julia Row, and lesser structures, including 1450 Moss and 3320 Bell. In 1916, in addition to the residence, 1437 Moss housed the Nola Film Company, producer of photoplays made locally such as "The Folly of Revenge," which opened with "intimate views of an artist's studio, showing a sculptor at work on the statue of a nude woman, for which a beautiful model

is posing." Could this have been filmed next door in the de Lapouyade studio? An advertisement in 1919 offered for sale "practically new materials" salvaged from the Diamond Film Company's building, under demolition at the time at 1437 Moss.[19] This circa 1913 residence briefly was home around that time to dentist Armand Mary and his wife, and in 1920 to Yugoslavian lawyer George Sladovich and his two children. The subject of several lawsuits and ethics violation investigations, Sladovich lost his property, which was sold at auction, along with "antiques and modern furniture." A more detailed description of the estate accompanied a 1925 auction notice: "Handsome raised stucco bungalow, overlooking beautiful Bayou St. John. The handsome residence is of semi-colonial architecture on grounds measuring 50' by 300', contains four bedrooms, two baths, living room, dining room, reception hall, kitchen has hardwood floors. Italian marble mantels."[20]

1451 Moss Street.

Above left: 1451 Moss Street, dining room, looking toward living room.

Above right: 1451 Moss Street, living room looking into the dining room.

Left: 1455 Moss Street.

Below: 1455 Moss Street, entrance hall looking toward dining room and kitchen.

No building contract has been located for this early use of the Louisiana Colonial revival style, most examples of which date from the late 1920s and 1930s. In 1911 Duvic sold the lot to Excelsior Homestead Association. Excelsior, which advertised its many services including "buying you a lot and building you a house," likely constructed this one.[21] Such organizations played a major role in the circa 1900 residential development of the Bayou St. John neighborhood, as well as other booming areas of city.

Constructed around 1918, the raised stucco bungalow at 1451 Moss was home in the 1920s to French Quarter restaurateur Anthony Tortorich. In 1921 it was advertised as a "swell home" with a large front porch, rear gallery and other living amenities on the first floor, bedrooms and nursery on the second floor, basement with servant quarters, and a three-car garage, also with residential spaces. For the Italian-born Tortorich, whose first employment in America was as a fruit peddler in the Poydras Market neighborhood, owning a grand house on spacious grounds must have been gratifying.[22]

For many years the home of banker and real estate developer Hippolyte Dabezies, the raised, one-story bungalow at 1455 Moss was distinguished by the application of cobblestones to the lower façade and south side wall. A photograph accompanying an advertisement in the *Times-Picayune* (July 6, 1919) for this "country water side home with great City Park at your door" shows the completed house with two full stories and an attic. A comparison of

the appearance today with the 1919 photograph reveals that the entrance portico remains as illustrated but that other elements vary, notably its height and porch and dormer designs. The fourth house built on the subdivided Turgeau land was Duvic's sprawling bungalow at 1459 Moss, today the home of noted jewelry designer Mignon Faget. Like its two neighboring structures, this horizontally oriented residence has a prominent red tile roof, punctuated by numerous dormers. Other distinguishing features are the projecting eaves with rafters and purlins projecting further. Duvic and his wife remained in their home until their deaths. His 1934 obituary noted that he was the first in the south to "conduct a gas-engine boat business."[23]

Opposite: 1459 Moss Street.

Opposite, below: 1463 Moss Street.

1463 and 1467 Moss Street: Picheloup Tract Bounded by Delgado, Carrollton (Chemin de la Metairie), Wilson

In 1922 local newspapers announced sale of the "Picheloup Tract, one of the last residential parkway sites available."[24] Captain Maurice Picheloup sold the land, extending from the corner of West Moss Street and North Carrollton Avenue back to Dumaine, for $100,000 to New Orleans Realty Investment Company, which divided it into a hundred large building lots known as City Park Court.[25] Restrictions applied to this subdivision "to insure only the better class of homes," with all businesses excluded. A longtime resident of the area, Picheloup operated a dairy on the extensive property. His cottage home and barn on Moss Street near the corner of North Carrollton were illustrated in a drawing that accompanied an 1897 newspaper article.[26] Picheloup's father, Louis, was a wood and coal dealer who employed at least eleven laborers, all French-born like him. The 1860 census lists Louis on St. Philip Street, in the Fifth Ward, which would have been part of the tract.

Three buildings were built circa 1923 on the Moss Street portion of the Picheloup tract. Both **1463** and **1467 Moss Street** are well-designed, sprawling, and expensive versions of the raised bungaloid form. In 1930 the owner of 1463 Moss was wholesale vegetable dealer Joseph Bossetta, who became director of the newly renovated Farmer's Market in the Vieux Carré in 1937.[27] Its neighbor at 1467 Moss was advertised for sale in 1926 for the large sum of $30,000, which included expansive grounds with twenty fruit trees, one hundred rose plants, and a four-car garage. This was the home of Ferdinand J. Alciatore, proprietor of La Louisiane Restaurant and Hotel, at the time of his death from apoplexy at forty-seven. Omar H. Cheer, owner of Solari's Grocery, took over Alciatore's home, restaurant, and hotel.[28] **1056 North Carrollton**, corner of Moss Street, is a large, stucco apartment building comprised of four units, each with about seven rooms and a bath. Scheduled in 1928 for demolition to make way for a fifteen- to twenty-story apartment hotel, this complex perhaps was spared by the Wall Street Crash of 1929.

Below: This 1897 newspaper illustration shows the bucolic "neat" cottage and barn of Maurice Picheloup, where his wife died as result of an affirmed suicide. The dairyman, however, questioned this verdict. "The Scene of the Shooting," Times Picayune, March 20, 1897.

THE SCENE OF THE SHOOTING.
The Cross Marks the Window of the Death Chamber.

BELL STREET

2630 Bell (St. John) Street
Bounded by Orchid (Live Oak),
Crete (Seventh), North Broad

Sited dramatically at an angle on abundantly planted grounds, this late Victorian Italianate-style frame raised villa commands attention from several directions, especially from the vista across Esplanade Avenue through verdant Capdevielle Place. This architecturally impressive property is steeped in rich history, figuring prominently during the late Spanish colonial and early American periods, and later as the home of such diverse personalities as mercantile giant Daniel H. Holmes (1816-1898) and abstract artist Robert Gordy (1933-1986). Its plan consists of a main block placed diagonally across the lot with two wings, with the façade located in the northern one and the rear elevation at the south. Its sophisticated but restrained detailing includes an entry gallery supported with columns fitted with spandrels with rondel cut-outs, repeated in the bracketed architrave. A series of small rectangular windows pierce the deep frieze, a feature that continues across a portion of the main building block. The recessed entry casing has pilasters and an elliptical arched head, leading to the door framed with pilasters and sidelights.

Stylistic analysis indicates a construction date from the late 1870s, when its owner was French Quarter grocer Pierre Noel Canton (1834-1880). This French-born merchant acquired the property, which included nine lots, at an auction in 1878 from

This Italianate-style raised villa at 2630 Bell Street sits on the site of the complex shown in the 1837 plan on the opposite page.

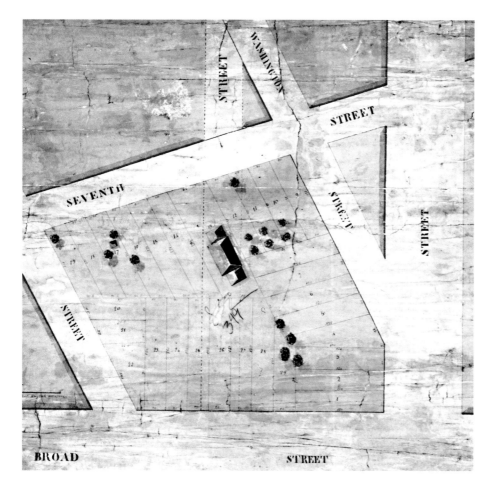

The habitation of Spanish colonial intendant Nicolás Vidal may be outlined in this 1837 notarial watercolor plan advertising the sale of 27 lots in Faubourg St. John. Courtesy of Honorable Dale N. Atkins, Clerk of Court, Parish of Orleans.

drawing is a main block with side wings, the temptation to conjecture that the existing house may date back to this late colonial house is great, but there is no evidence to confirm this from external analysis.

Daniel Clark, merchant, land speculator, and vice-consul for the United States during the late 1790s, purchased Vidal's tract in 1804, along with some property from Louis Blanc. Out of these holdings, he developed the early Faubourg St. John. After Clark's death in 1813, his executor, Richard Relf, sold the subject property, including "maison et terrain," to Dame Jeanne Desalles (1767-1833), wife of Pierre Dulcise Barron. In 1840 the widowed Barron conveyed the same to Louise Prevost Bertus (1819-1843), wife of Mortimer. When she died, her husband was named as executor of the indebted estate and natural tutor of her three minor children, and, as such, inherited her nine lots of ground with buildings in Faubourg St. John, as well as property in Tremé and on Metairie Road in Faubourg Jackson.[5] Subsequent mid-nineteenth-century owners of the nine lots included François Bouvier, 1846-1854, who had a nearby dairy on Esplanade between North Broad and North White Streets, and Mary Clara Fontenelle, wife of Richard Stockton, 1854-1862. Clara Stockton acquired the lots for $4,250, funds that she received from her older husband through their marriage contract.[6] The conveyance act notes improvements but no buildings on the lots. If the act is correct, the colonial buildings were demolished by the 1850s, if not earlier. Clara ran a boarding house in the French Quarter in the 1870s, after her husband's death, and maybe the Stockton Hotel in 1850s Bay St. Louis, Mississippi. Perhaps she was planning on such a venture in the Faubourg St. John or, more likely, was investing for her and her children's future.

Joseph Girard, who had bought it in 1862.[1] Noted in the 1880 census as retired, Canton died in that year at the age of forty-six years, leaving a wife and two minor children. An inventory taken for his succession listed the house's contents room-by-room—parlor, hall, octagon, first bedroom, closet, second bedroom, dining room, kitchen, and servant's room.[2] His widow, Marie Anne Tropc, in 1882 married blacksmith Pierre Larroux and retained ownership until 1892, when D. H. Holmes became the new owner. In 1905, several years after their father's death, Holmes's heirs sold his former home to coffee dealer Daniel Hubert Hoffman (1865-1925), president of Southern Coffee Mills. During Hoffman's years of ownership, the lots at the rear of the house facing Crete Street were sold as building sites.

The roster of notable owners before Canton's acquisition and the likely construction of the cottage begins with late Spanish colonial intendant Nicolás Vidal (1740-1806), whose habitation may be outlined on a notarial watercolor plan from 1837 for a "plan for 27 lots in Faubourg St. John."[3] The house is shown on the projected route of the Esplanade Avenue extension, which was not done as indicated here.[4] Since the building depicted on this

2805 Bell (St. John) Street
Bounded by Desoto (Washington),
North Dupre (Fifth), North White (Sixth)

Located on a prominent, lushly planted corner lot, this five-bay cottage appears to have served originally as a single-family, center-hall home but actually was built as a double cottage. The neighboring cottage at 2815 Bell, which has almost identical Italianate-style detailing, fenestration pattern, and façade configuration, has always been a one-family home. After concert singer Nelville Mercier bought the lots in 1901, she and her husband, "capitalist" Henry Bier, commissioned both houses. The couple both were native Parisians, and he was in Cannes when he died at fifty-eight years in 1903. His remains, however, were returned to New Orleans, and his funeral was held at his newly constructed home. Known locally as a vocal soloist, giving concerts in Grunewald Hall in the 1870s, Nelville was a relative—perhaps sister—of Dominique Mercier, the free man of color who established a flourishing men's clothing business in the French Quarter in the 1860s and went on to amass a real estate empire in the French Quarter, most of which his descendants retain today. The Biers also speculated successfully in real estate, especially in the emerging residential development adjacent to City Park.[7]

2734 Bell (St. John) Street
Bounded by Orchid (Live Oak),
North White (Sixth), Crete (Seventh)

One-family cottages on spacious lots with space for a pretty garden, and maybe even a vehicle, lured families with moderate means to the Bayou St. John neighborhood in the early twentieth century. This well-maintained and architecturally intact circa 1905 Italianate-style cottage with a side hall leading to a gallery fit the bill for several families, including those of bartender Henry Quatrevaux with his wife, stepchildren, and their families around 1910 and, later, Austrian Karl Kramel, a clerk with the United States Railroad Mail Services, and his wife, a stenographer. Real estate agents made such homes available to working families by offering low monthly payments. A real estate advertisement in the *Times-Picayune* (April 14, 1912) described the property as a "neat retired cottage, iron fence, six rooms, bath, gas and shed with servant's room."

Above: 3017 Bell Street.

3017 Bell (St. John) Street
Bounded by Desoto (Washington),
North Lopez (Third), North Gayoso (Fourth)

After Henry Bier's death, his namesake son from a previous relationship challenged his succession, claiming to be his only child. As a result of this successful lawsuit, Bier properties in the subject square, including 2815 Bell, 2833 Bell, and 1202 North Dupre, were auctioned in 1908.[8] The one at 2805 Bell, however, was sold privately to real estate agent Robert Upshur, who also served as secretary and treasurer of the Mercier Reality and Investment Company. Upshur and his family lived in and owned 2805 Bell through the 1920s. Theodore Soniat du Fossat, scion of an old Creole family, was listed in the 1920 census as owner of 2807 Bell, another half of the cottage.

Opposite: 2805 Bell Street.

Presenting today as a sophisticated architectural assemblage, 3017 Bell Street dates from before 1896, when it appears as a diminutive, one-story cottage on the Sanborn Insurance Map, the sole building on this side of the square facing Bell Street. By 1908 its footprint had expanded to that of a longer cottage with a front gallery, and by 1940 it had been raised to create two stories. For over forty years, from approximately 1910 through the 1950s, this was home and probably workplace to the Italian-born gardener Eduarde Gai and his wife, Cecile, and, after the father's death in 1927, to his heirs. Located on a double lot, the property historically included a stable and several outbuildings. The current appearance resulted from a major renovation project in 2016, which added a gallery and dormers to the post-1940 side addition. Historically, this site's ownership—like most of those on the city side back to North Dorgenois—traces back to Louis Blanc in the early eighteenth century and later to Daniel Clark.

BROAD STREET, NORTH

1015 North Broad Street.

1015 Broad Street, North
Bounded by Bellechasse, Ursulines,
St. Philip, North White (Sixth)

A lonely and deteriorating historical survivor on the west side of North Broad Street, this picturesque cottage dates from 1906, in which year clothing merchant Leonard Meyer contracted with carpenter/builder Alfred Mazzei for "erection of a house and dependencies" for $5,835.[9] The twin turrets with copper pavilion roofs dominate the design of this unusual residence, also elaborated with Eastlake-style devices. Meyer had acquired the site, which included two lots with an approximate frontage of sixty feet on North Broad Street, in fall 1905 and demolished earlier buildings to make room for his new home.

From 1859 until 1894, gardener Joseph Torregano and his daughter, Helena, wife of butcher Romain Lagleyze, owned the property. The 1896 Sanborn Insurance Map outlined multiple small structures on the wide, deep lot, including a blacksmith shop, a one-story frame dwelling, and a target practice. A *Times-Picayune* for-sale advertisement (June 5, 1895) for this address described a frame cottage and other improvements on a lot belonging to a rifle club, a popular sport in the late nineteenth-century Bayou St. John neighborhood. In 1913 French Quarter fruit merchant John Moncado acquired the property from Meyer. This native of Palermo, Italy, lived there until his death in 1930. His daughter denied allegations of suicide, telling police that her father mistook poison tablets for rheumatism medicine (*New Orleans Item*, May 7, 1930). In 1931 Moncado's bankrupt estate sold at auction the "large single cottage with large grounds and room for five cars" (*Times-Picayune*, June 18, 1931).

DESOTO STREET

2934 Desoto (Washington) Street
Bounded by Bell (St. John), North Gayoso (Fourth), North Dupre (Fifth)

Buying empty lots from various owners, Joseph Paul Florio wove together spacious grounds, extending from Desoto Street west to the middle of the block and north to front on North Gayoso. His new home, built circa 1895 on Desoto Street—larger, more decorative and picturesque than the earlier one at 1239 North Dupre—displays an inviting front porch, supported by turned columns and surrounded by a spindled balustrade, a motif repeated at the gallery frieze and long stairway. A bay of windows on one side of the center hall creates an asymmetry not seen in traditional center-hall cottages. A curved walkway radiates from the central stairway, both framing the building and guiding the eye to the abundant landscape. Florio died in this idyllic place after residing there for fourteen years. The house was offered for sale at a public auction as a "modern raised cottage," with magnificent grounds, measuring 120 by 160 feet with a garage entrance on North Gayoso (*Times-Picayune*, February 9, 1913). The floor plan consisted of a large hall, double parlors, two dining rooms, three bedrooms, servant quarters, and a finished basement.

Buying the property soon after 1913, Charles Mauthe created magical gardens, celebrated locally and internationally, and still visible today to charm the onlooker. A master painter and interior decorator by profession, Mauthe remained there with his family until his death in 1942. An author writing under the pen name of Lady Banksia published an article in the *Times-Picayune* (January 20, 1935) under the headline, "Fashionable Europe Knows Rare Plants Originated in Gardens of New Orleanian." An accompanying photograph shows the Desoto Street grounds, with its water garden and greenhouse "filled with marvelous plants." Although his horticultural specialty was as a caladium hybridizer, Mauthe perfected new forms of plants, with new colors of flowers and leaves. His caladium specimens, it was reported, were displayed in Parisian shop windows.

2934 Desoto Street.

Left: 3020 Desoto Street.

3020 Desoto (Washington) Street
Bounded by Bell (St. John), North Lopez (Third), North Gayoso (Fourth)

This cottage presents restrained, almost feminine elegance, expressed by lacy millwork spandrels located between turned porch columns and delicate, rounded sidelights and transoms surrounding the façade entry. Constructed circa 1894 for Soline Louise Bertus, newly widowed by her French-born husband, Adolph Faure, a cotton office clerk, the comfortable home has a center hall, parlor, dining room, breakfast room, and three bedrooms.[10] She lived there for just four years with her son, George Paul Faure, also a cotton broker, before her death in 1897. Subsequent owners included police captain Francis Warren Calongne, 1896-1906; Louis Gagnet, 1906-1921, secretary with Gaiennie Limited, a plumbing company; and Daniel Buckley, born in the "Free State of Ireland." A wholesale vegetable and produce dealer in the French Market area at 1209 North Peters Street, Buckley died at the age of fifty-five in February 1937. New Orleans newspapers reported his "mysterious" death after his partially decomposed body was found in the New Basin Canal near the Carrollton Avenue Bridge. His British widow retained ownership of their home until 1944.

3123 Desoto (Washington) Street
Bounded by Grand Route St. John, Esplanade, North Rendon (Second), North Lopez (Third)

This five-bay center hall house stands on the western (North Lopez) half of lot O, the former site of the circa 1840 raised cottage at 3129 Desoto. Subdivided by then-owner John Joseph Bermingham in 1894, the property was transferred circa 1903 to bartender Charles Seruntine, whose family's strong ties to the Bayou St. John neighborhood dated from the 1870s. Listed in the 1905 city directory at this address, he is the first recorded occupant of this simple cottage with refined Eastlake style detailing. Not shown on the 1896 Sanborn Map, the house dates from circa 1903. Between 1905 and 1910, bar pilot John T. Small made his home here until the death of his wife, when it was sold for the benefit of a minor child. Subsequent owners included clerk August Laux, 1911-1916, and Louis William Robert, 1916-1926. Described in a *Times-Picayune* real estate advertisement (April 20, 1924) as a comfortable house with four large independent bedrooms, living room, dining room, large central hall, beautiful flower gardens, and fruit trees, the dwelling inexplicably did not seem to attract long-term residents.

Right: 3123 Desoto Street.

3129 Desoto (Washington) Street
Bounded by Grand Route St. John,
Esplanade, North Rendon (Second),
North Lopez (Third)

"Weak in body but sound in mind," the dying book dealer Fidele Kellar dictated his last will from his bed in Charity Hospital in May 1875: "I own . . . sixteen lots of ground in the Faubourg St. John in the city of New Orleans having on this property a dwelling house, etc., and I own a book store on St. Charles near Common Street and sundry debts due to me."[11] His home was this circa 1840 raised cottage, simply detailed with front gallery and dormers. The four-bay façade configuration retains two original French door openings; the two double-hung windows replace similar doors. The Swiss native went on to state that although he bought the above-stated assets during his marriage to Louisa Casserly, he acquired two book stores and a private library before his marriage—worth more than the house—and these were not part of the community assets. He bequeathed all

his possessions to his five children—John, Willie, Thomas, May Antoinette, and Chickahominy. Since just two were of majority age, their mother was to act as natural tutrix.

According to his 1844 naturalization paper, Kellar arrived in New Orleans more than five years earlier at the age of eighteen years. He lived and worked in the French Quarter before acquiring the bayou property in 1862.[12] The city directory of 1867 included a listing for "Fidel Keller, medical, law and antiquarian books, 97 Royal." In addition to the 127-foot frontage on Desoto Street, his holdings included an adjoining parcel with a frontage of 105 feet on North Rendon. Originally part of Daniel Clark's vast estate, Kellar's purchase featured among the many properties contested by Clark's daughter, Myra Clark Gaines, who in 1872 executed a quit claim for this Desoto Street property.[13] From 1832 until 1847, Elizabeth Louise Blanc (1784-1861), the eldest child of Louis and Louise Blanc, owned a

Below: 3129 Desoto Street.

93

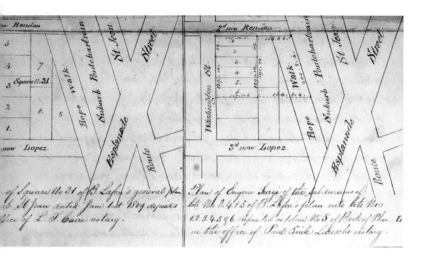

3139 Desoto (Washington) Street
Bounded by Grand Route St. John, Esplanade, North Rendon (Second), North Lopez (Third)

A compelling history envelops this eye-catching cottage, perhaps representing three stages of development. From 1870 until 1907, it was home to Jean Valentin Cathalougne and his wife, Marie Louise Vitter. A partner in the Faubourg Tremé grocery firm of Jean Jeanneaud and Company, Cathalougne in 1870 acquired two lots of ground, numbers one and two, at the corner of Washington and North Rendon Streets from attorney Victor St. Romes. City directories from the 1870s confirm that this was his residence, outlined in the Robinson Atlas, which, though published in 1883, was surveyed in the 1870s. Natives of France, the couple participated in the Francophile community—he served as a director of La Société de Demoiselles de la Nouvelle-Orléans. After her husband's death in 1887, the widow remained at the address for the rest of her life, which ended in 1907. The inventory of her succession, with the younger Evariste Blanc as one of the appraisers, was taken at her home, which consisted of two parlors, a dining room, two bedrooms, and a shed in the yard.[15] Her real estate holdings included a Creole cottage at 814 Barracks Street, which her husband bought in 1860, and two late nineteenth-century houses at 2329 Ursulines and 2861 Ponce de Leon. A survey attached to her succession shows the footprint of 3139

larger lot at the corner of today's Desoto and North Rendon Streets, the location of both 3129 and 3139 Desoto. The earliest documentation of buildings here dates from 1847: a *maison* with two rooms, four cabinets, front and rear galleries, and a building in the yard serving as a *boulangerie*.[14]

In the late 1880s, John Joseph Bermingham, identified in city directories only as a manufacturer's agent, bought numerous lots in this square, including this site, where he lived in the 1890s. He subdivided the property in 1894 to create a separate building lot on the North Lopez side and lot P on North Rendon Street. Beginning in 1907, the old cottage was home to Walter Parker, who in 1926 bought another Blanc property, 924 Moss Street. His widow retained ownership until 1975. In 1926 it was described as including "large and screened rear porch, large grounds, flowers, trees, patio fountain and playground for children."

Above: This drawing, executed in 1809 by surveyor Barthélémy Lafon, shows the rope walk located between Suburbs Pontchartrain and St. John in the 3100 blocks of Grand Route St. John and Desoto Street. Courtesy of Honorable Dale N. Atkins, Clerk of Court, Parish of Orleans.

Right: 3139 Desoto Street.

3212 Desoto Street.

3212 Desoto (Washington) Street Bounded by Ursulines, North Hagan (First), North Rendon (Second)

This comfortable, single-family residence, built circa 1910, combines elements of the Queen Anne and Colonial revival styles, as did many homes of its era in New Orleans's fashionable University Section near Audubon Park. Constructed for Joseph Lallande, freight agent for the Southern Pacific Railway, this two-story dwelling was built on an empty lot, one of many in the Ursulines Avenue vicinity handled by the Home Realty Company. Between 1907 and 1912, this real estate venture acquired future building lots and sold them to individual owners, either as vacant lots or with a residence constructed to suit the purchaser. All buyers had to commit themselves to build single residences only—no doubles or stores—costing more than $3,200. A survey in 1907 outlined the available sites in the neighborhood, offered by the Fellman Company.[16]

The square bounded by Desoto, Ursulines, North Hagan, and North Rendon remained vacant in 1896, with the exception of a few small buildings at the corners of Desoto and Ursulines at North Rendon. In 1907 the Home Realty Company acquired twenty-four lots in this square from George Donnerhaser Eicke, who had inherited the property from his mother, widow of George Eicke. Both the German-born stepfather and his adopted son were shingle dealers, located at the Carondelet Canal. When the lot at the corner of Desoto and North Rendon was sold, the vending company acknowledged its responsibility to remove the old buildings, including stable and shed.[17]

Desoto at that time, as well as the adjacent structure on North Rendon Street. Their daughter, the widow of Alexandre Bisconteau, inherited the estate.

The original Cathalougne home likely was a simple rural cottage of the 1870s type, without the prominent façade gable and highly decorative gallery detailing. These features, as well as the developed attic level, could date from the late 1800s, while the widow was still living there, or they could have been added after 1908, while Hippolyte E. Capdau owned the property. Stylistically, however, these modifications are characteristic of the 1890s rather than the early 1900s. A druggist by profession and a member of the White League by avocation, Capdau was noted in his obituary as a participant in the "historic battle of Canal Street against the Carpetbaggers" (*Times-Picayune*, April 25, 1929). When Capdau refinanced his property in 1914, he may have made additional modifications, including the façade windows in the Tudor style. His daughter Louise remained at this address until 1945.

3217, 3219, and 3233 Desoto Street.

3217, 3219, and 3233 Desoto (Washington) Street, Bounded by Grand Route St. John, Moss (Port), North Rendon (Second)

The oldest house in this streetscape is the cottage in the background at **3233 Desoto Street**, built circa 1891 by Marie Agnes Seruntine, widow of carpenter William Langhetée. Before her husband's death in 1890, the family lived on Desoto Street on a parcel closer to the bayou, purchased in 1874 from Charles Beaulieu. Beaulieu had acquired it from the 1873 estate sale of cotton broker Emile Torregrossa, owner of vast holdings in the Bayou St. John area and elsewhere in the city. The 1910 census lists the sixty-four-year-old widow as head of household, living with a daughter and sons, Joseph and Emile, both of whom, like their father, engaged in the wood-working trade. In 1911 she subdivided the large grounds into three lots, retaining the one upon which her house was located, and sold the future site of **3217 Desoto** to Vincent Picolo for $2,500.[18] A wholesale oyster dealer in the French Quarter at 1215 North Peters, Picolo apparently constructed the house before 1915, when the city directory gave 3217 Desoto Street as his address. In 1924 Mary Agnes Langhetée sold 3221 Desoto to Myrtle Baker, wife of Jules d'Hémécourt, daughter-in-law of the city engineer and surveyor with the same name who created numerous drawings accompanying conveyance acts for properties in the bayou neighborhood and throughout the city. When the junior d'Hémécourt, the last surviving son of the city surveyor, died in 1925, his obituaries noted that he had served for twenty-five years as a passenger conductor on the Texas and Pacific Railroad.

The three houses that stand on the parcel acquired in 1891 by the Widow Langhetée well illustrate the evolution of residential design from circa 1891 to 1917, using a watered-down classical vocabulary. The three-bay cottage at 3233 Desoto, dating from 1891, has a hipped roof, characteristic of late Victorian Italianate cottages in New Orleans, and a façade gallery supported by simple Tuscan columns, with altered fenestration. At **3219 Desoto**, the raised stucco-and-frame bungalow also nods to the Classical revival and Louisiana Colonial revival styles. The more ambitious design of 3217 Desoto represents the City Beautiful movement, eclectically combining classical detailing with Queen Anne-style massing and a Chippendale-patterned gallery railing.

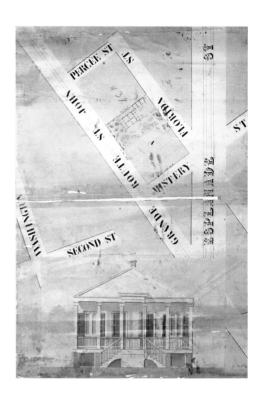

In 1873 the estate of deceased cotton broker Emile Torregrossa sold many properties in the Bayou St. John neighborhood, including this unusual raised cottage, which, before its demolition, sat amidst a free-form, English-style landscape on the site of today's 3213 Desoto Street. Courtesy of Honorable Dale N. Atkins, Clerk of Court, Parish of Orleans.

After the Civil War, Emile Torregrossa, a descendant of Spaniards who came to New Orleans in the late colonial period, amassed significant holdings in the Faubourgs St. John and Pontchartrain. At the time of his death in 1872, he owned most of the properties located on Grand Route St. John, as well as many on Desoto Street in the area bounded by Esplanade, Mystery, Desoto, and the bayou. The auction announcement in the *New Orleans Republic* (March 15, 1873) specified thirteen parcels in the neighborhood, many with "handsome cottages," a few of which, such as the altered 3100 Grand Route St. John, remain today. Three plan book watercolor renderings date from this sale—one of a circa 1840 raised cottage that stood, before its demolition, at the site of today's 3213 Grand Route Street; a second of a double Creole cottage in the 3100 block of Grand Route St. John; and the third of "The Folly," a pleasure grounds that faced the bayou on the lake side of Esplanade Avenue. Spread over six lots, this complex included a pavilion with a circular gallery; arbor; pigeon and chicken houses; fishing ponds with bridges, crossings, and sidewalks; and thickly planted orchards. Torregrossa's widow, Angelina Durapau, remained in the family home on Grand Route St. John near Esplanade for many years, then moved with her daughter, Mrs. Charles Dittmann, to the extant cottage at 3224 Grand Route St. John. The *Times-Picayune* (September 5, 1922) pictured five generations of Torregrossa women in front of this simple circa 1870 house, headed by Angelina, who credited her longevity partly to the mealtime consumption of claret until the onset of Prohibition in 1920.

An 1847 watercolor depicts an early Bayou St. John rural complex, now demolished. It consisted of a Creole cottage with an unusual configuration of galleries and cabinets on both the front and rear, an écurie (barn), and a kitchen, facing today's Desoto and North Rendon Streets, backed by Esplanade Avenue and Grand Route St. John. Courtesy of Honorable Dale N. Atkins, Clerk of Court, Parish of Orleans.

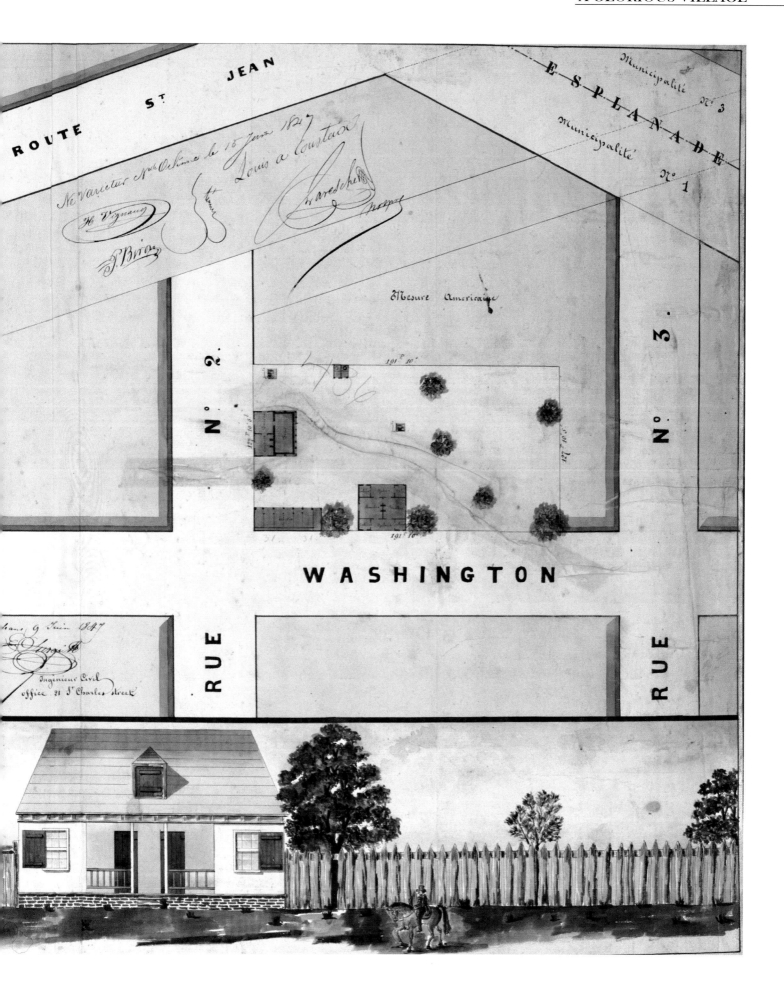

3238 Desoto (Washington) Street
Bounded by Ursulines, North Hagan (First),
North Rendon (Second)

Properties offered for sale between 1907 and 1912 by the Home Realty Company included lot H, upon which this commodious residence sits. Although the seller required that no doubles be constructed on the building sites, this Colonial-revival-style-influenced duplex of significant size and cost, constructed circa 1912, evidently was permitted, perhaps because of family ties connecting residents of both sections. One half was home to George E. Briere and his family, and the other to his son, Dr. Joseph Briere, with his wife and two sons. In 1920 the elder Briere sold his ownership to Joseph, with the provision that he be allowed to stay in the house as long as the doctor retained the property. Seven years later, Dr. Briere sold the family house to Marie Josephine Michel, wife of Pierre L. Sarrat, for $10,750. The Sarrat family, which in 1940 included five daughters and a granddaughter, stayed there for many decades.

Left: 3238 Desoto Street.

Below: This 1907 survey shows empty lots along Ursulines Avenue, offered for sale between 1907 and 1912. They were handled by the Home Realty Company and offered by the Fellman Company. Courtesy of Honorable Dale N. Atkins, Clerk of Court, Parish of Orleans.

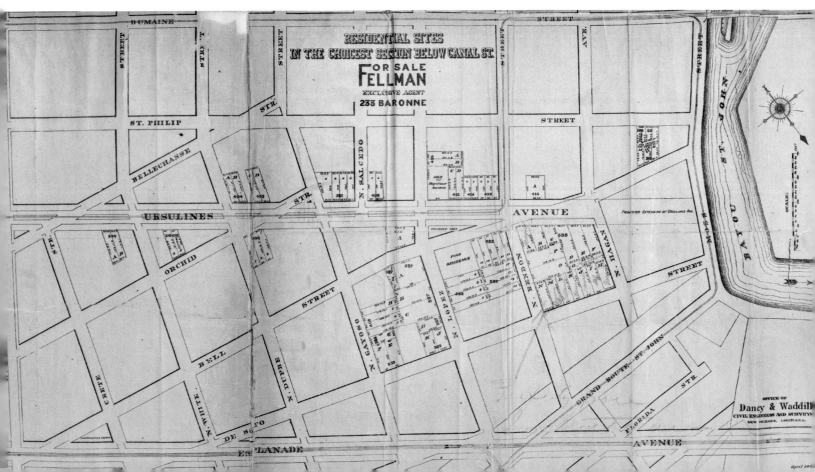

1141 North Dupre Street.

DUPRE STREET, NORTH

1128 Dupre (Fifth) Street, North
Bounded by Bell (St. John), Orchid
(Live Oak), North White (Sixth)

Typical in design for its Faubourg St. John neighborhood, this four-bay shotgun cottage with subtle Italianate detailing always served as a single-family residence. Constructed circa 1900 with a raised, eight-foot basement level, it readily accommodated a large household. Across the street from more expensive homes, this cottage also evidences pride of ownership. An advertisement in the *Times-Picayune* (June 9, 1910) called it a "swell Second District gem, "a raised cottage with double parlors, dining room, four bedrooms, bath, clothes closet, big lot." In the early 1900s, collector William G. Gautier resided here with his wife and three children.

1141 Dupre (Fifth) Street, North
Bounded by Bell (St. John), Ursulines,
Orchid (Live Oak), North Gayoso (Fourth)

The oldest house on its block, this wide cottage dates from circa 1895, shortly after Henry Joseph Fremeaux (1862-1922) acquired the corner lot for $583.33 from the New Orleans Real Estate and Collecting Company. In 1896 this was the only structure in the five-sided parcel bounded also by Bell and North Gayoso, Orchid, and Ursulines Streets. A projecting three-bay, gabled section jauntily angled toward the corner joins another three-bay, deeply gabled portion set back to allow a side entry in the front bay, an unusual arrangement that provides two façade entries. Highly decorative and idiosyncratic detailing includes overhangs that have multiple brackets with cut-out work, and, in the set-back segment, surrounds with pilasters topped by tripartite cornices. A non-original concrete porch and steps with brick posts replaced the original wooden elements. After his wife, Ida Jung, died in 1901 in Covington, Louisiana, where the couple owned property, Fremeaux remarried. He held the New Orleans house until 1920, when Mrs. Leonice Bonnecaze purchased it. She retained ownership until 1936.

1239 Dupre (Fifth) Street, North Corner Desoto (Washington), Bounded by Bell (St. John), North Gayoso (Fourth)

During the late 1800s and early 1900s, many recently arrived European immigrants of sufficient means chose the Faubourg St. John neighborhood over the expanding uptown areas. Joseph Paul Florio, a prominent stevedore, built this handsome raised cottage circa 1891. Although Florio listed his nationality as Austrian, today's Italian port city of Trieste was his birthplace. Florio commissioned his new home shortly after marrying his business partner's widow, Annunciata Buja, a native of the western Italian coastal town of Livonia. Florio came to New Orleans while working

as captain of the bark *Mississippi* and decided to give up sailor life and settle down there. While en route, the *Mississippi* wrecked off the coast of Florida, and he and some of his crew were rescued and transported to New Orleans. In 1908, a year before his death at the age of fifty-nine, he joined the military staff of Louisiana governor Jared Young Sanders and became known as Major Florio.

The couple's first home, which they shared with her children by her first marriage, sits on a generous corner lot near Esplanade Avenue. A gallery extends across three-quarters of the façade, with a projecting bay in the remaining portion. Eastlake ornamentation enlivens the façade and side bays. The family remained at this location only until around 1895, when Florio gathered various adjacent parcels and built a larger home next door at 2934 Desoto.

From around 1910 until his death in 1931, Paul Eugene Sahuque made his home here. Immigrating in 1869 from Tarbes, France, Sahuque established a grocery in 1889 at 719 Royal Street, a property that his descendants still control. Residing with the grocer on North Dupre Street were his wife, his sister-in-law, and his German-born gardener. His obituary in the *Times-Picayune* (January 1, 1931) noted that the deceased was "one of the oldest and best-known members of the French speaking colony of the city."

Above: 1239 North Dupre Street.

Left: Outsider art? Maybe, but also Bayou St. John residents joining the city's love fest for the New Orleans Saints, who symbolically lifted the city up after Hurricane Katrina with their February 7, 2010 victory in Super Bowl XLIV.

2936 Esplanade Avenue.

ESPLANADE AVENUE

2936 Esplanade Avenue
Bounded by Desoto, North Gayoso (Fourth),
North Dupre (Fifth)

When Charles J. Bier bought vacant land at 2936 Esplanade Ave in 1882, he wasted no time before building, for the house appears on his property on the 1883 Sanborn Map. By 1900 it was home to Oliver O. Provosty, who, the following year, was named an associate justice of the Supreme Court of Louisiana (he became chief justice in 1922). Provosty sold the house between 1910 and 1912 to Jules Andrieu, whose widow had it auctioned in 1924. By the 1970s, the house was the local headquarters of the International Society of Krishna Consciousness.

The house is described in *The Esplanade Ridge*, volume 5 of the *New Orleans Architecture* series, as having "an American center hall plan on top of a raised basement" and a "wide, gabled front with deep overhang." A railing of sawn balusters encircles the gallery and central staircase. A 1907 photograph in the *Times-Picayune* shows additional details, including a side gable that terminates with Swiss chalet-style stick work and a central square tower with a roof hipped in all directions. Ads for the 1924 auction list an entrance hall, dining room, living room, library, three bedrooms, bath, breakfast room, rear porch, paved basement, finished attic with one bedroom, and asbestos slate roof. Jigsaw cresting on the gable rake boards is an especially fanciful characteristic.

3018 Esplanade Avenue.

3018 Esplanade Avenue
Bounded by Desoto (Washington),
North Lopez (Third), North Gayoso (Fourth)

A good example of an Eclectic-style design from the pre-World War I building boom, this duplex, converted for single residency, may incorporate an earlier building, shown on the site as early as 1885. The existing appearance displays elements typical of the period between 1910 and 1917, such as Queen Anne-style asymmetrical massing, Tudoresque window detailing and faux framing, and columns in the Neoclassical mode, all executed in mixed building materials. Although research has failed to yield conclusive documentation, the shields embossed on the brick piers, as well as the nod to Neoclassicism, point to creation by the firm of Toledano and Wogan.[19]

Between 1899 and 1920, Ralph L. Schmidt, Royal Street antiques merchant, owned the property. The 1900 census shows the twenty-three-year-old Schmidt living at this address with his stepfather, Raoul Tanneret, also an antiquities dealer, and his mother and step-siblings. After Tanneret died in 1910, his "beautiful objects d'art" were auctioned from his home. Schmidt retained ownership of the house until 1920 but lived elsewhere in the neighborhood, in a bungalow at 1221 North Gayoso. He may have renovated or torn down the older, circa 1910-13 home and built a revenue-producing duplex. The attorney and banker John Legier briefly owned the property between 1920 and 1922 but did not live there. Legier, a resident of Gentilly Terrace as a young married man and later, for many years, of the Emlah Court, designed in 1913 by Moise Goldstein, must have been interested in au courant design. In 1927 he commissioned Goldstein for his new home in Pass Christian, Mississippi. Legier therefore could have built 3018 Esplanade circa 1920, but the presence of Toledano and Wogan's trademark shield ornamentation strongly suggests otherwise. From 1922 to 1935, this was the home of Edgar Battistella, French Quarter seafood merchant and proprietor of a stall in the French Market. The *New Orleans Item* (October 31, 1934) reported that Battistella died after mistaking ant poison for cough medicine.

3100 Block Esplanade Avenue (Fortier Park)
Bounded by Grand Route St. John, Mystery

Nestled in the triangular parcel formed by the convergence of Grand Route St. John and Mystery Streets with Esplanade Avenue, a little vernacular Gothic-style frame schoolhouse hosted generations of Bayou St. John children from 1891 until a modern new school replaced it at 2733 Esplanade in 1925. Its construction signified the population boom that took place in the neighborhood in the late 1800s, and, with just eight classrooms and a capacity of 337 pupils, it became overcrowded in the 1920s. Likely designed by architect William Freret as a "cottage school," it was raised on brick piers, the primary floor reached by exterior stairways that later came to worry parents, and a partition that divided the front gallery for separate use by girls and boys. After demolition of the building, the newly landscaped space was dedicated in 1926 as a public park, named in honor of Alcée Fortier, romance languages scholar and longtime resident of the neighborhood. For generations, it has remained a favorite oasis.

3102 Esplanade Avenue
Bounded by Grand Route St. John, Desoto (Washington), North Rendon (Second), North Lopez (Third)

This late nineteenth-century version of a raised center-hall cottage dates from circa 1890, after Victor J. Botto, shipping merchant and consul to Nicaragua, had pieced together parcels of land to form a large lot at the corner of Esplanade Avenue and North Lopez Street. Late Italianate stylistic features include a post-supported gallery with columns linked by arched spandrels in the upper sections, shiplap siding, and segmentally arched window heads. The two-over-two configuration of façade windows likely dates from circa 1906, when the house was moved approximately twenty feet east to the existing corner location (the 1896 Sanborn Insurance Map had outlined it in the middle of the lot). As part of the holdings of the heiress Myra Clark Gaines, the square, with the exception of its Grand Route St. John side, remained undeveloped until her

death in 1885. After 1886, building lots in this square, as well as in many other areas of Faubourg St. John, were sold to individual owners.

Botto lived in the cottage, listed in 1902 as 3106 Esplanade, until 1905, when he sold it to Pierre Montagnet and moved to Covington, Louisiana. In separate acts in 1906 and 1907, Montagnet sold the corner portion of the subdivided property to Emile Vergnes, a sixty-five-year-old whiskey broker. A survey accompanying the 1907 conveyance shows the dimensions of this lot and the adjoining sliver of land.[20] Either Vergnes or Montagnet moved the house to the corner, as shown on the 1908-9 Sanborn Map. Also shown on that map is a dwelling on the western part of the lot, outlined "according to plans," at 1308 Esplanade. An advertisement in the *New Orleans States-Item* (March 22, 1908) described 1302 Esplanade as a "handsome and modern single residence, $10,000, comprising parlor, octagon reception, dining and five bedrooms, six-foot hall, large gallery." If Vergnes planned to sell his updated house, he apparently failed to attract a buyer, for he resided there until his death in 1912. His daughter, Cecile, remained in the home until 1917, when George J. Deynoodt, superintendent of the nearby St. Louis Cemetery No. 3, acquired it.[21] The Deynoodt family retained ownership of this villa until 2010.

Right: 3102 Esplanade Avenue.

Joseph Klar Properties
3330, 3336, and 3342 Esplanade Avenue
3243 Ponce de Leon (Florida) Street
Bounded by Moss (Port), Ponce de Leon
(Florida), Vignaud (Percée, North Hagan)

Walking or driving along Esplanade Avenue between Moss and Ponce de Leon Streets, passersby might feel as if they have stepped back in time to a mid-nineteenth-century country village. **3330, 3336,** and **3342 Esplanade**, as well as **3243 Ponce de Leon** located directly behind these frame cottages, differ from their neighbors in the simplicity of their detailing and apparent earlier dates of construction. All four properties belonged to the German-born gardener Joseph Klar, who in 1834 had acquired seven lots (84 through 90) bounded by Mystery, Florida, and Maurepas Streets from the heirs of Faubourg Pontchartrain developer Louis Nicolas Fortin.[22]

Born around 1806 in Baden, Klar arrived in New Orleans as a Redemptioner in 1818 with his father,

Steffan. His mother and sister had died en route, and his father died a few years later. According to his obituary in the *Times-Picayune* (August 16, 1887), the young man found work in the "vegetable garden of old Mr. Blanc, on Bayou St. John, near where the bayou bridge now stands." He saved enough money to buy the land in front of the Jockey Club, on which he built "tenement" houses. Klar and his New-Orleans-born wife had nine children, including Felicité Klar Roux, wife of Albert Pierre Roux, owner of the Spanish Custom House. Klar's grandson, Willis Roux, married Louise Clemence Blanc, daughter of James Arthur Blanc, the youngest son of Evariste, whose property adjoined Klar's. Daughter Marie Josephine's husband, George Oscar Reinecke, was a cotton factor and Bayou St. John resident. According to city directories, sons Henry and Zenon lived on Esplanade near their father and worked respectively as a carpenter and a grocer.

The extension of Esplanade Avenue toward the bayou necessitated the reconfiguration of lots owned by the elder Klar, a process that consumed much of

3330 Esplanade Avenue.

Above: 3336 Esplanade Avenue.

Below: 3342 Esplanade Avenue.

the land he had purchased in 1834 and resulted in houses being moved to face Esplanade. After Klar died in 1887, his succession described four cottages on lots A, B, C, and D that comprised his estate. A circa 1935 apartment building at **3340 Esplanade** replaced the cottage on lot B that the octogenarian had willed to his daughter Henriette in 1884 "as a remuneration for her attention paid to him." The other three properties, the cottages that remain today at 3336 Esplanade, 3342 Esplanade, and 3243 Ponce de Leon, were sold at auction.

In 1873 Klar had sold the one-and-a-half story side-gabled Creole cottage at **3330 Esplanade** to John Hager, a foreman with the New Orleans and Carrollton Railroad at Bayou Bridge, and therefore Klar's succession omitted it.[23] Typical of the 1840s in type and style, this four-bay house has a post-supported façade gallery and rear cabinets.

According to the auction notice (September 17, 1887), all the properties shared a common denominator: ornamental gardens. On lot D stood a "very elegant one-story frame slated cottage retired from the street, with nice gallery in front, containing six rooms in all, kitchen shed, cistern, privies, large yard, garden in front, etc." The Classical style, three-bay, galleried home at today's **3336 Esplanade** has sophisticated circa 1870 detailing, including a rusticated façade and an entry framed with pilasters. Alice Trist, wife of notary public Nicholas Trist, paid $1,200 for this property. On lot A, the "elegant cottage" with front gallery at **3342 Esplanade** also was retired from the street. It contained three rooms and had grounds with a kitchen cistern, privies, and "a small ornamental garden in front."

Behind the Esplanade cottage, at the end of a cul-de-sac created by short Vignaud Street (North Hagan or Percée), stands **3243 Ponce de Leon**, a wide cottage with a post-supported gallery that dates from the late 1830s or early 1840s. Before its restoration in the late 1900s, a façade addition obscured the original configuration. In the 1887

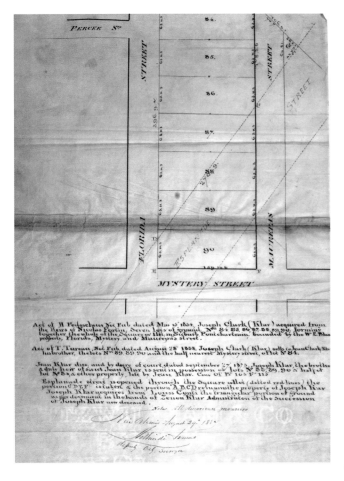

Above: 1887 survey showing the impact on the Klar properties by the extension of Esplanade Avenue to the bayou. Courtesy of Honorable Dale N. Atkins, Clerk of Court, Parish of Orleans.

Above, right: Cottages and dependencies offered for sale in 1887 by the estate of the German-born gardener, Joseph Klar. Courtesy of Honorable Dale N. Atkins, Clerk of Court, Parish of Orleans.

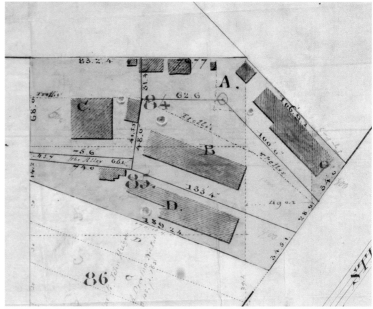

sale, son Henry Klar bought this property, noted as a "one-story and attic frame cottage retired from front street and containing front and rear gallery, two large rooms, two cabinets, kitchen, cistern, privies, chicken house, etc., nice ornamental flower garden in front of property containing several orange and other fruit trees."

In 1864 the inventory for the succession of the Widow Nicolas Fortin, the vendor of Klar's land in 1834, was taken at this house, "sitting at the corner of Florida and Perceé [sic]," where she lived with Joseph Klar's son-in-law, Oscar Reinecke.[24] Although she did not own the house, her belongings were listed as bedding, armoire, rocking chair, etc. in the front room facing the yard, table in back gallery, French silver, goblets, etc., clothes and a milk cow and calf in the stable. Her only heir, daughter Julie Fortin, wife of Clement Ramos, inherited her estate, including considerable real estate in the Faubourgs St. John and Pontchartrain. The 1860 census shows the eighty-five-year-old Widow Fortin living with the Reinecke family. No blood relationship has been determined; perhaps the connection was as longtime neighbors in the old village.

Left: 3243 Ponce de Leon.

Opposite: 3356 Esplanade Avenue.

3356 Esplanade Avenue
Bounded by Moss (Port), Ponce de Leon
(Florida), Vignaud (Percée, North Hagan)

Constructed in 1895, this three-bay cottage combines late Italianate detailing (segmentally arched openings) with subtle, Eastlake-style ornamentation (bull's-eyes in the surrounds, scalloped verge boards in the façade gable) to form an attractive late nineteenth-century component of its streetscape. Located on the rear portion of the Evariste Blanc estate (known today as the Holy Rosary Rectory), the site was one of nine building lots facing Esplanade Avenue that were subdivided in 1876 at the request of Jules Arnaud Blanc, executor of the estate of his mother, Fanny Labatut Blanc. In 1892 the vacant lot was transferred to the widow's daughter, Sylvanie Denegre, who in 1905 donated four adjacent lots on Esplanade Avenue, as well as the Moss Street family house, to the Archdiocese of New Orleans. She sold the subject lot in October 1894 to Robert E. Saucier, a sheriff and crier for the Civil District Court, who, soon after, contracted with builder John Lotz for construction of a "one-story frame slate residence," according to the plans by architect Alfred E. Theard.[25] For many decades, beginning in the late 1910s, this was home to Alice and Edward Guenard, listed in the 1920 census as a "drummer" with a tobacco company. Next-door at 3354 Esplanade resided his brother, Hamilton Guenard, a tobacco manufacturer.

3368 Esplanade Avenue, Our Lady of the Holy Rosary.

3368 Esplanade Avenue
(Church of the Holy Rosary)
Bounded by Moss (Port), Ponce de Leon
(Florida), Vignaud (Percée, North Hagan)

On November 22, 1925, Archbishop John William Shaw consecrated the newly completed Church of the Holy Rosary, fulfilling the wish of Sylvanie Denegre to endow a church in memory of her mother, Fanny Labatut Blanc. For this purpose, in 1905 the daughter of Evariste and Fanny donated the family home at 1354 Moss Street and four adjacent lots facing Esplanade Avenue "upon the express condition that there shall be created thereon and perpetually maintained a Parish Church, for the purpose of providing the residents of the neighborhood . . . with a Parish Church and necessary accessories and dependencies, such as a parsonage, school or other purposes." In the two decades between the bequest and completion of the new church, a smaller chapel was located behind the old family home, which then was used as the "priests' house."

New Orleans architect Rathbone DeBuys (1874-1960) chose the Roman basilica style for the new church. Details include buff limestone and textured brick exterior walls, dominated by a façade portico with six massive, thirty-foot-high columns with Corinthian capitals. A forty-foot-diameter dome crowns the building, providing a thirty-foot-high beacon from many vantage points in the

neighborhood. On the interior, intersecting Roman arches spring from piers and point up to the dome. The sanctuary is made of marble, with a Carrera marble altar, trimmed in marble mosaics. Two side altars have similar detailing.

The church forms part of the Holy Rosary/Cabrini campus, today including the rectory (Evariste Blanc house) and the 1964-65 Cabrini High School. The Sacred Heart Orphan Asylum at 3400 Esplanade, constructed in 1905 according to the plans of architect Robert Palestina, also figures in this religious complex. Located directly behind the now demolished Tissot house and Pitot house before its relocation, the pre-existing orphanage fueled the Cabrini Sisters' insistence on having the new school at its current location. Mother Frances Xavier Cabrini (1850-1917) founded the orphanage to house children without parents, many of whom perished to yellow fever, with the financial backing of Captain Salvatore Pizzati. The orphanage ceased its mandated use in the late 1950s and was converted to the Cabrini High School for Girls.

Above: Sanctuary of Our Lady of the Holy Rosary.

Below: 3400 Esplanade Avenue, constructed in 1905 as the Sacred Heart Orphan Asylum, is shown on a 1907 postcard. The Historic New Orleans Collection, 1981.350.48.

GAYOSO STREET, NORTH

823-25 Gayoso (Fourth) Street, North
Bounded by Dumaine, St. Ann,
Salcedo (Van Buren)

Built circa 1904 as an investment property, this exuberant Eastlake-style double cottage retains its original detailing, unlike those at 817 and 819 North Gayoso, the other two in this row of three. Millwork companies such as Chicago-based E. L. Roberts & Company provided stock elements such as those seen here—brackets, spindle band frieze, turned columns, pierce-work window cornices; the terra cotta rooster comb finial, for example, recurs next door at 819. Builders, therefore, could individualize their buildings as wished, giving personality through decoration rather than color, which, in New Orleans, remained traditional throughout the late nineteenth and first half of the twentieth centuries.

Vacant land in 1896, the square bounded by North Gayoso, Salcedo, St. Ann, and Dumaine Streets was fully developed by 1909, with rows of double cottages that filled the need for inexpensive, working-class housing. German-born Katie Schweitzer, who ran a boardinghouse downtown at 520 Chartres, acquired the subject lots from Cecile Avegno Rousset and her sister, Catherine Avegno West, daughters of French Quarter denizen Philip Avegno. Avegno and several business associates had bought land in this square in 1848 from the First Municipality. Interestingly, the 1870 census shows Cecile Rousset living on Gayoso with her husband, a milkman; two children; and two servants.

1302 Gayoso (Fourth) Street, North
Bounded by Esplanade, Desoto (Washington),
North Dupre (Fifth)

This asymmetrical, late Queen Anne-style cottage sits on a portion of land carved in 1902 from the grounds of the Gothic villa at 2936 Esplanade Avenue, after Edward Carriere acquired the land from his father-in-law, Supreme Court of Louisiana chief justice Oliver Provosty.[26] Located at the corner of Desoto Street, the house features an inviting front porch extending on the north side from an open bay with a pavilion roof and, at the south end, an enclosed half-octagon culminating in a turret. The suggestion of rustication between the openings in this bay con-

823-25 North Gayoso Street.

1302 North Gayoso Street.

tinues the Medieval motif. Decoration is restrained, limited to garland appliques in the demi-lune above these windows, a nod to the Adamesque revival style. A spindled frieze located between supporting columns unifies the façade elements.

A prosperous stave exporter, Carriere moved uptown to Jefferson Avenue with his wife, Olive, after a few years. He ran afoul of the law in 1915 and declared bankruptcy after being indicted by a federal grand jury, accused of issuing false bills of lading and the selling thereon of bills of exchange, a fraud that created an international banking crisis. In the 1920s this was the home of attorney Charles Rivet, whose mother, Maria Anna Deynoodt, was a member of the family that owned 3102 Esplanade.

GRAND ROUTE ST. JOHN

3216 Grand Route St. John.

3216 Grand Route St. John
Bounded by Desoto (Washington), Moss (Port), North Rendon (Second)

The detailing of this Italianate-style cottage, with its exaggerated parapeted cornice, faux rusticated façade, and pilastered entry, points to a construction date between 1865 and 1875. Its two lots were vacant in 1878 when Alexandre Seruntine, a cotton broker, acquired them. His purchase also included two lots on North Rendon Street where buildings already stood, and Seruntine could have moved one of them to the current site. After his death in 1920, his daughter, Clara, and son-in-law, French Quarter jeweler Louis Zaeringer, inherited the property. Together with all the other houses facing this street, this residence is located in Faubourg Pontchartrain, whereas those on the river side, fronting Desoto Street, fall within Faubourg St. John.[27]

The boundaries of the historic Faubourg St. John set the parameters for the scope of *Gateway to New Orleans* to extend from the north side of Orleans to the south side of Esplanade Avenue and from the west

side of North Broad to both banks of Moss Street. As a result of the extension of Esplanade Avenue to the bayou in the early 1830s, however, a portion of the early nineteenth-century Faubourg Pontchartrain lies on the south side of Esplanade and figures in this study. This four-block-wide suburb, carved from the former Lorreins plantation by then-owners Louis Blanc and Louis Nicolas Fortin, stretched from approximately today's Vignaud Street to Fortin Street, as shown on an 1809 plan by Jacques Tanesse.[28]

The expansion of Esplanade Avenue isolated the 3100-3300 blocks of Grand Route St. John, the diminutive square edged by Esplanade, Grand Route St. John, and a triangular portion of property bounded by Ponce de Leon, Esplanade, and Mystery Streets, from the remainder of the Faubourg Pontchartrain. With squares running together toward Moss Street, the faubourg's boundary lines are so indeterminate that even nineteenth-century conveyance records are unclear as to which suburb a property belonged to. The resulting bizarre configuration of the impacted blocks meant that one block could be located in two suburbs, and several squares run together with no clear division lines. For example, square 436, bounded by five streets—Esplanade Avenue, Desoto, North Lopez, North Rendon, and Grand Route St. John—incorporates both faubourgs. Historical surveys depict Faubourgs Pontchartrain and St. John separated in this block by a rope walk, an elongated space where workers laid out twine and twisted it into rope.[29] As geographer Richard Campanella pointed out, this light-industry activity was common in port cities, and linear, interstitial spaces sufficed as locations.

Below: Copy made by Claude Jules Allou d'Hémécourt of a plan, originally delineated in 1809 by Jacques Tanesse, depicting the subdivision of a number of blocks into lots within the Bourg Pontchartrain, extending from Grand Route St. John to Fortin Street and from Bayou St. John to Bayou Sauvage. The Historic New Orleans Collection, 1966.34.16.

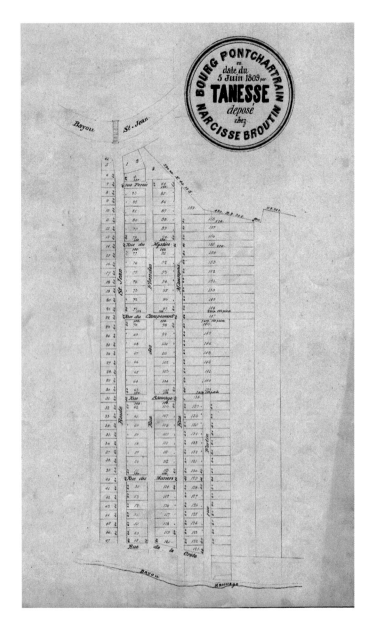

3300 Grand Route St. John
Corner Moss (Port) Street

This oxidized Birdsill Holly cast iron fire hydrant, which bears the date September 24, 1868, may be the oldest of such firefighting apparatuses remaining in the city. Named after its inventor and manufactured by his namesake company in Lockport, New York, this technologically advanced equipment served to protect the Bayou St. John village in the days when there were only volunteer fire company units scattered throughout the city's neighborhoods. The Valiant Fire Company Number 3, established in 1846 with bayou resident Albert Roux as one of its founding members, served the bayou neighborhood among others—perhaps the reasoning for the placement of the hydrant adjacent to the Lorreins-Roux House at 1300 Moss Street. At this location, the hydrant helped to pump water directly from the bayou with much-needed extra pressure.

HAGAN AVENUE, NORTH

700 Block Hagan (First) Avenue, North
Bounded by St. Ann, Orleans, Moss (Port)

This intact row of six double shotgun houses on the bayou side of North Hagan Avenue between Orleans and St. Ann Streets charmingly displays the great variety of design and millwork options available to builders and real estate speculators at the turn of the twentieth century. Round-headed windows here and straight ones there, truncated roofs and gabled ones, all prevent monotony. These cottages today contribute richly to the streetscape, especially with the softening of the landscape created by the small trees. Constructed between 1896 and 1908 as rental properties for less affluent families, these houses illustrate the delayed residential development in the neighborhood near the Carondelet (Old Basin) Canal, which remained commercial and industrial through the early 1900s. The opening in 1906 of the nearby American Can Company surely created a demand for low-rent housing.

700 block (odd) North Hagan Avenue.

LOPEZ STREET, NORTH

925-27 and 931 Lopez (Third) Street, North
Bounded by St. Philip, Dumaine,
North Rendon (Second)

In the late 1800s, the large swath of undeveloped squares in the Faubourg St. John bounded by the south side of Ursulines Avenue, Orleans Avenue, North Broad Street, and North Hagan Street emerged as a neighborhood of predominantly lower-income families, explained by its proximity to the still-operative Carondelet (Old Basin) Canal and the canal's semi-industrial usage. Originally part of the Evariste Blanc holdings, acquired in 1848 from the First Municipality of New Orleans, this area largely includes double shotgun cottages, some elaborated with Eastlake ornamentation and others with simpler late Italianate characteristics. In the early twentieth century, Edwardian features also appeared in the housing stock. Commercial buildings such as corner stores comingle with the residential buildings. The aggregate lends a completely different tenor than that found nearer Esplanade Avenue and Moss Street in the more prosperous areas.

The two Eastlake-style cottages at 925-27 and 931 North Lopez date from circa 1906, when the Crescent City Building and Homestead Association constructed them.[30] Around the turn of the twentieth century, financial organizations such as this played an important role in the residential development of the Faubourg St. John, as well as of other parts of the expanding city, both by acquiring vacant building sites for resale and by building homes on the sites. One of the occupants of 931 North Lopez was, for example, Eliza Coates, widow of barber Onofrio Disimone, who lived there with some of her children from 1907 until her death in 1930.

Following Page: 925-27 and 931 North Lopez Street.

1219 Lopez (Third) Street, North
Bounded by Desoto (Washington), Bell (St.
John), North Rendon (Second)

Above and below: 1219 North Lopez Street.

The *Illustrated Sunday Magazine* section of the *Times-Picayune* (December 27, 1908) pictured the residence of Mrs. M. L. Sieward at 1219 Lopez Street as one of two featured "Beautiful New Orleans Homes." One of the most unusual homes in the bayou neighborhood, this raised cottage combines elements of the Mission style (parapeted dormers) with features decidedly influenced by the Art Nouveau movement (glass entrance door, sidelights, and transom etched with delicate organic forms). A rusticated stone basement or foundation level adds to the design's solidity and gravity. According to architect/writer Robert Cangelosi, New Orleans native Robert Spencer Soulé drew the plans for this early twentieth-century residence. Educated at Cornell University, Soulé, along with fellow architects Jordan Mackenzie and Francis J. MacDonnell, experimented

117

with a variety of styles in an attempt to break away from Beaux-Arts traditions. Soulé's remaining work, mostly located in the University section of the city, represents such varied modes as the Craftsman, Southern Colonial revival, Mission, and Tudor revival styles.

Mary Louisa Sieward, freshly widowed in 1906, immediately acquired the building sites to build her new home, where she remained until her death in 1937. Her late husband, Adolph Sieward, had served as president of the New Orleans Gas and Light Company and had established one of the first rice mills in the city. At his death, he left an estate of over $500,000 to his second wife but neglected to mention his children and grandchildren from an earlier marriage. This omission resulted in several lawsuits, based on legal precedent that in Louisiana a parent or grandparent cannot disinherit a child. In 1917 Adolph's deceased son's daughter, living in Baltimore, Maryland, received her $62,000 share of the estate, as did another son living in New Orleans.[31] Relationships between the stepmother and the Sieward children, however, appear to have been friendly enough that she served as administrator of her stepson's estate in 1925.

1325 Lopez (Third) Street, North
Bounded by Grand Route St. John, Esplanade, Desoto (Washington), North Rendon (Second)

Built circa 1890, this center-hall cottage with attached two-story ell served for decades as home for J. Henry Lafaye and his large family of eleven children until his death in 1911 and his wife's in 1928. President of the Board of Trade and city council member during the administration of Mayor Walter C. Flower (1896-1900), Lafaye acquired the deep building site in 1889 from John Joseph Bermingham, who owned a number of lots in the subject square. Featuring a tripartite façade gable, a front porch with a side bay, and fine Eastlake detailing such as spindle bands and a raised sunburst motif in the side gables, this cottage was featured in the *Illustrated Sunday Magazine* section of the *Times-Picayune* (June 13, 1909). The gallery railing appears at that time to have been constructed of wrought iron, and multiple prominent, double-stack brick chimneys rose from the roof.

1325 North Lopez Street.

ORCHID STREET

2765 and 2775 Orchid (Live Oak) Street Bounded by Bell (St. John), North White (Sixth), Crete (Seventh)

John Nicolas Karcher, a native of Alsace Lorraine, and his family owned the property at the corner of Orchid and North White Streets from 1883 until 1930. Karcher, a truck farmer, built both the simple but vividly hued three-bay cottage at **2775 Orchid** and the more demure Eastlake cottage at **2765 Orchid Street** circa 1906. The 1896 Sanborn Map outlined the earlier buildings that had comprised Karcher's homestead before he constructed the existing buildings. At that time, only a small frame dwelling with façade and side galleries or porches and a stable stood on the large, L-shaped lot that fronted on both Orchid and North White Streets. According to the 1880 census, his farm at that time was located on Gentilly Road. Widowed in 1877, Karcher married his wife's younger sister in 1880 and, a few years later, moved to the Faubourg St. John neighborhood. The 1900 census finds him with his wife and nine children, ranging in age from two to nineteen, at 2753 Orchid, the address of the earlier, smaller cottage. Such a large, growing family required a larger home. His extended family lived on the property, with sons Alphonse and Oscar running a grocery in a now-demolished structure at the corner of North White. This family should not be confused with the closely related Karcher clan headed by Bernard. This branch operated the John Karcher Marble and Granite Company, located at 3425 Esplanade Avenue.

Above right: 2775 Orchid Street.

Right: 2765 Orchid Street.

RENDON STREET, NORTH

**800 Rendon (Second) Street, North
Bounded by Dumaine, St. Ann,
North Lopez (Third)**

The great influx of working-class families to the Bayou St. John neighborhood in the late nineteenth and early twentieth centuries created a concomitant need for public educational facilities nearby. Therefore, in 1904 the Orleans Parish School Board commissioned construction of McDonogh No. 31 at the corner of North Rendon and St. Ann Streets. The architectural firm of Andry and Bendernagel drew the plans for the Spanish Renaissance-style brick school, which the *Times-Picayune* called "one of the most modern school buildings in the city, situated in the thriving and fast-growing part of New Orleans" (November 15, 1908). This school supplemented the 1891 frame Gothic revival-style school in the 3100 block of Esplanade and taught boys and girls from kindergarten through the fifth grade. Operated for a while as the Morris F. X. Jeff Elementary School but shuttered for a number of years, this large structure now is under private ownership and is the subject of a proposed multi-family residential redevelopment.

Above right: McDonogh No. 31 School, photographed by George François Mugnier, [ca. 1908]. Louisiana Division/City Archives, New Orleans Public Library.

Right: 800 North Rendon Street, entry influenced by by Spanish Renaissance style.

1320 Rendon (Second) Street, North
Bounded by Grand Route St. John, Esplanade, Desoto (Washington), North Lopez (Third)

The cohesiveness of the Bayou St. John village, from its establishment through the twentieth century, defines its essence and appeal. Descendants of French settlers such as the Blanc, Fortin, and Soniat du Fossat families still lived in the area in the early twentieth century and later, retaining old homesteads and building new ones in au courant styles. Newer arrivals to the community remained there for decades, with other family members living nearby. This Eastlake cottage numbers among four built in this square by produce broker J. Henry Lafaye and his namesake son, the first cottage being the elder Lafaye's home at 1325 North Lopez, circa 1890. The junior Lafaye lived at another cottage at 1326 North Rendon before moving next door to his parents to a circa 1907 raised bungalow at 3101 Desoto Street. The residence at 1320 provided rental income for the Lafayes. It was inhabited in 1910 by cotton broker Scott Reinecke, related to George Oscar Reinecke, who married the daughter of an early Esplanade Avenue resident, the German-born gardener Joseph Klar (see 3300, 3336, 3342, and 3243 Esplanade). The Klars also intermarried with the Roux family of the Spanish Custom House and the Blancs. In the 1980s this small cottage was modified with a camelback addition.

SALCEDO STREET, NORTH

716, 722, and 724 Salcedo Street, North
Bounded by St. Ann, Orleans, North Gayoso (Fourth)

Rows of simple double shotgun cottages with detached outbuildings provided vitally needed low-cost housing in the areas near Orleans Street and the Old Basin Canal. Styled in the vernacular Italianate mode, this circa 1910 row's gabled roofs and overhangs supported with brackets lend a decided rhythm to the streetscape.

Above left: 1320 North Rendon Street.

Left: 716, 722, and 724 North Salcedo Street.

ST. ANN STREET

2824, 2820, 2816, and 2812 St. Ann Street
Bounded by Orleans, North Dupre (Fifth), North White (Sixth)

This circa 1907 row of four houses displays an idiosyncratic combination of details that defies facile stylistic classification. The windows' heads are rounded, not arched as in the Italianate style; the sash has diagonal mullions in a lattice pattern à la the Tudor revival mode; the shed dormers reflect the English Arts and Crafts movement; and finally, the brackets seem to have been thrown in as a nod to this city's late nineteenth-century vernacular shotgun architecture. Similar double cottages dot the Bayou St. John neighborhood, as well as the adjacent area across Orleans Avenue, and frequently are admiringly commented upon as an endearing component of the streetscape. With the exception of number 2820, where the dormered roof was modified, these doubles retain their original detailing, sans the wooden stoops.

Francis and Paul Maestri, scions of furniture store entrepreneur C. N. Maestri and the father and uncle, respectively, of New Orleans mayor Robert Maestri (1936-46), commissioned the construction of these cottages and others in the early 1900s, advertising them "as the cheapest cottages for rent in the city for the money" (*Times-Picayune*, January 16, 1909). Similar cottages lined the 600 and 700 blocks of North Hagan Avenue, as well as nearby Dumaine and North Alexander Streets, all adding to the Maestri real estate empire. Built in rows, they display variations on a theme—some with truncated roof, others with dormered ones, rounded fenestration, and square-headed ones—that avoids monotony.

With their furniture store located on the fringe of the French Quarter at Iberville and North Rampart Streets, the Maestri family also was closely associated with the Bayou St. John area. Before fire demolished their circa 1903 furniture manufacturing plant in 1905, it faced Moss Street between St. Ann and Dumaine. And the Maestri Market stood on the west side of North Broad Street at the corner of Orleans. A strong connection existed between the Maestri family and builder John Minot (1871-1914), whose lumber yard was located in the 2800 block of St. Philip. Minot, who also worked in the Maestri store before returning to his contracting business, may have helped to design the "Maestri cottages."

Above left: 2821 St. Ann Street quoins

Above right: 3009 St. Ann Street quoins

Right: 2824, 2820, 2816, and 2812 St. Ann Street.

ST. PHILIP STREET

2739, 2743, 2747, and 2753 St. Philip Street Bounded by Bellechasse, Ursulines, North White (Sixth), North Broad

Built toward the end of the Great Depression and the beginning of World War II, this sturdy row of four gable-fronted double shotgun houses illustrates an evolved form of low-cost housing in the fringe areas of Bayou St. John. Constructed in 1939 by builder William C. Osborne for owner John B. Gries, the cottages each cost $4,063.[32] The site at the corner of North White served in the earlier 1900s as a lumber yard with an associated warehouse, likely as part of the building empire of John Minot, whose lumber yard was shown across the street on the 1908-9 Sanborn Insurance Map. After Minot's death in 1914, his widow sold their new, spacious home at 3042 Ursulines Avenue and moved across the street from this row to the raised Craftsman-style house at 2738 St. Philip Street.

Above: 2739, 2743, 2747, and 2753 St. Philip Street.

Right: This 1902 survey shows the footprint of the small cottages built by the widow of Victor Petit in the 1890s at the corner of St. Philip and North Dupre Streets, as well as the vacant sites of the row of 1906 cottages, 2815, 2821, and 2823 St. Philip Street. Courtesy of Honorable Dale N. Atkins, Clerk of Court, Parish of Orleans.

2815, 2821, 2823, 2827, and 2829 St. Philip Street and 1002 North Dupre (Fifth) Street Bounded by Bellechasse, North Dupre (Fifth), North White (Sixth)

The 1892 succession of Victor Petit inventories his estate, including ten vacant lots in the small trapezoidal square bounded by St. Philip, North White, North Dupre, and Bellechasse Streets, part of the extensive Faubourg St. John holdings of heiress Myra Clark Gaines until 1875.[33] Proprietor of a "long established grocery, barroom and private market" at the corner of Moss Street and Grand Route St. John, Petit avidly speculated in real estate. After he died at a young age, his widow inherited his estate, which was partitioned and sold at public auction in 1902 after legal challenges by their children. Between 1892 and 1902, Mrs. Petit had built the three austerely detailed two-bay cottages on lots one and two, today's 1002 North Dupre and 2827 and 2829 St. Philip, the footprints of which are outlined in a 1902 survey.[34]

Charles Lepley acquired lots three, four, and five from the 1902 auction, and in 1906 he commissioned active contractor and bayou resident John Minot to build the three cottages at 2815, 2821, and 2823 St. Philip.[35] With gable fronts and apron canopy roofs supported by turned columns, this row with the adjacent single dwellings presents an assemblage of a great variety of building types and styles aimed for working class residents.

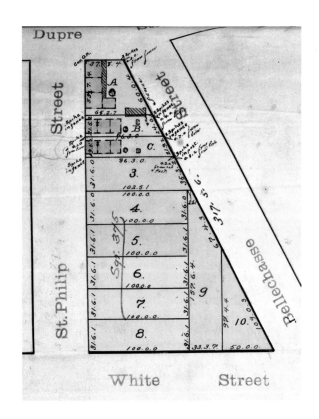

3039 St. Philip Street
Bounded by Ursulines, North Lopez (Third), North Salcedo (Van Buren)

This double cottage dates from 1906, after Peter B. Pederson acquired the property. Identified in the 1910 census as a Norwegian-born retired merchant, Pederson lived at that time at 3114 Esplanade with his son Hagnus, who dealt in real estate. After acquiring the lot at the corner of North Salcedo, which was not cut through from St. Philip Street to Esplanade Avenue until after 1896, the Pedersons built the subject rental property, as well as a single cottage at 1015 North Salcedo. They lived in the Salcedo house for a few years, offering it for sale in 1908 along with a "hot house, pretty garden and chicken or stable yard" (*Times-Picayune*, November 29, 1908). The existing

Above: 3039 St. Philip Street.

Opposite: 2815, 2821, and 2823 St. Philip Street.

house at 1015 North Salcedo, however, postdates this 1908 house. In the same year, Pederson sold 3039 St. Philip, subject to two existing leases, to Thomas Spicuzza, ferry boat captain and president of Spicuzza Brothers Transportation Company. A bayou neighborhood resident at 1201 North Dupre, Spicuzza probably used this house, also, as an income source.

Simply but elegantly detailed in a neo-classical style, the cottage as presenting today resulted from a 2012 remodeling. At that time, two full-length double-hung windows replaced original, round-headed ones; square columns were added after removal of non-original metal ones; and dentils were added to the fascia. The rear and side porches also date from this renovation, as do new openings in these areas. The remodeling retained original elements frequently classified as "Edwardian," such as its shed dormer with etched glazing and patterned transoms over the façade doors.

URSULINES AVENUE

2731 Ursulines Avenue.

2731 Ursulines Avenue
Bounded by Orchid (Live Oak),
North White (Sixth), Crete (Seventh)

A wide front porch terminating in a bay with a gazebo roof at one end and a hipped pyramid at the other, adorned with spindle bands and crowned with red tile shingles, contributes to a joyful architectural expression, suitable for a vacation cottage. Also noteworthy is the rich interplay of suggested textures, especially evident in the side bay.

Although there was a building on the site as early as the 1883 Robinson Atlas, the existing configuration does not appear until the 1908-9 Sanborn Insurance Map. In 1902 the property was sold to Anna Graw, wife of Henry M. Turpin, by the estate of John R. Bahan, who had owned it since 1891. She then resold her purchase in 1903 to Frederick William Armbruster, who within a few months transferred the same to Gracia Montes, widow of Charles E. Eggleston. The existing design dates, therefore, from circa 1902-3 when the earlier residence was likely demolished or perhaps enlarged.

Armbruster reacquired the house in 1910 as the universal legatee of Grace Armbruster, who, the *New Orleans Item* suggested (March 24, 1910), used this pseudonym rather than her real name. Twenty-eight years old, she allegedly committed suicide in 1909 as she was about to be charged with running a "disorderly house," downtown on Howard Avenue near Camp Street. Her death certificate named her as Grace Mentes Eggleston. Armbruster lost his inheritance soon after as a result of lawsuits brought by his debtors, including the supplier of the casket for the deceased. At the 1910 auction, Miss Julia Moreira, who evidently leased the property already, purchased it. When she sold it in 1920 to Clifford Lewis Purnell, the notarial conveyance act noted that the purchaser was aware that the "property is occupied by a Mrs. A. Perry, who claims possession under a pretended lease."[36] Purnell, a department manager for Woodward Wight and Company, owned the house until his death in 1952.

126

2834 Ursulines Avenue
Bounded by Bellechasse, North Dupre (Fifth), North White (Sixth)

For several decades beginning in 1904, New Orleans's preeminent seed man, Joseph Steckler, lived in this rambling, circa 1894 Victorian center-hall cottage, which he purchased in 1904 from original owner George Meyer, an officer with the Teutonic Insurance Company.[37] Situated on spacious grounds incorporating eleven lots with original frontages on Ursulines, North Dupre, and Bellechasse Streets, according to a 1913 newspaper article, the complex included "one of the finest poultry yards in the south" (*New Orleans Item*, February 19, 1913). A photograph of the back yard accompanied the piece with the caption, "Home of J. Steckler's Chicks."

Growing and importing the "choicest varieties" of plants for sale in his downtown seed store at 512 Gravier Street, Steckler had nurseries located throughout the city but hatcheries only in the country. Born in New Iberia, Louisiana, he came to New Orleans as a young man to apprentice with his uncle, horticulturist Richard Frotscher. From 1899 to 1904, the Pitot House, before its relocation to its current site, served as headquarters for his gardening enterprise. Steckler last owned this colonial landmark before its transference to the Missionary Sisters of the Sacred Heart. When it was offered for sale in 1921, the *Times-Picayune* (April 17, 1921) described the attractive Ursulines Avenue offering as "in one of the finest neighborhoods in this city planted in tropical palms and a parked neutral ground." The floor plan included a reception hall, parlor, library, dining room, breakfast room, and five bedrooms, and a stable and garage also sat on the grounds.

2834 Ursulines Avenue.

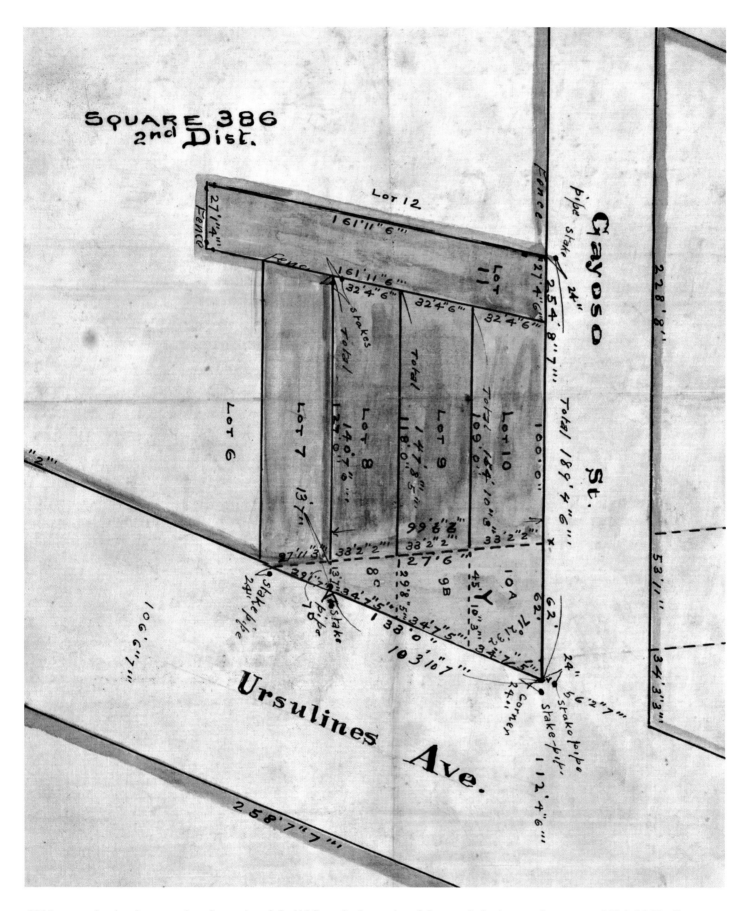

1905 survey showing the annexation of a portion of Orchid Street for the creation of front yards for the row of cottages at 2924-36 Ursulines Avenue. Courtesy of Honorable Dale N. Atkins, Clerk of Court, Parish of Orleans.

2924-36 Ursulines Avenue
Bounded by St. Philip, North Gayoso (Fourth),
North Dupre (Fifth)

2924-36 Ursulines Avenue.

This eye-appealing row of four double shotgun cottages employs all the embellishments of the Eastlake-style lexicon. Set back from the street, their angled placement provides an attractive and coherent streetscape. Downtown Sixth-Ward boss and Irish immigrant John Brewster built these revenue-producing houses circa 1905 after having acquired the empty lots from Charles E. Breckenridge in 1903 and the triangular portion of ground from the City of New Orleans in 1905.[38] Formed from the continuation of Orchid Street, this parcel created the front yards of the subject cottages. Serving in the elected position of state tax collector for the Second District,

Brewster was well positioned to acquire building sites in the up-and-coming Ursulines Avenue residential neighborhood. When he died in 1908, his obituary in the *Times-Picayune* (March 5, 1908) discussed at length this colorful politician, known as Captain Brewster, who "had a wonderful control over the Italians who lived crowded like sheep in the front portions of the ward and would gather them at the polls on election day." The history of the site, like many others, reaches back to Myra Clark Gaines, who sold it, together with much more property in the area, to Virgil Whitney of Binghamton, New York. After his death, his New Orleans property passed to his daughter, Mrs. Rodney A. Ford, also a resident of New York State, who soon sold the building lots to local speculators.[39]

129

Left: 3042 Ursulines Avenue.

C. N. Maestri Furniture Store, 731 Dauphine Street. His connection with this politically influential family may explain his many contracts for city-financed projects. Before he moved into his new home, Minot and his family lived in an Eastlake-style shotgun double at 2740 St. Philip Street.

After Minot's death, his wife, Mary Cigale, moved back to the old St. Philip Street neighborhood to 2738 St. Philip, the site in 1908-9 of the John Minot lumber yard. On April 22, 1915, the *Times-Picayune* announced an auction of the contents of Minot's large yard at North Hagan Avenue and Toulouse Street, next to the Carondelet Canal. Offered for sale were "building materials and tools including moulding of all kinds and sizes, top and bottom rails, ballisters and brackets, doors of all kinds and many other articles used in the building lines"—in other words, all the bits and pieces that make up the streetscapes.

3036 and 3042 Ursulines Avenue
Bounded by St. Philip, North Lopez (Third), North Salcedo

Contractor John Minot built the impressive Eclectic-style residence at **3042 Ursulines** as his home circa 1908-9, but he was able to enjoy it just for a few years before his death in 1914 at forty-three years. He constructed its neighbor at **3036 Ursulines** at the same time. These large, two-story buildings differ markedly from earlier residences in other areas of the Faubourg St. John, more nearly resembling those built in many cities during the pre-World War I years, overlooking parkways and verdant avenues. Loosely reflecting the influence of the City Beautiful movement, such houses above all radiate comfort and prosperity.

Minot, a leading contractor for public buildings such as schools, fire stations, and, at the time of his death, the Second City Criminal Court and Third District Police Building, also acted as builder and occasionally designer for the smaller residences that were springing up in the bayou neighborhood in the early 1900s. At one point, he worked in the

Right: 3036 Ursulines Avenue.

3100 Ursulines Avenue
Bounded by St. Philip, North Rendon
(Second), North Lopez (Third)

3100 Ursulines Avenue.

The survey in 1907 outlining the available sites in the neighborhood offered by the Fellman Company noted that the large lot at the corner of Ursulines and North Lopez had been sold for a "magnificent residence." This referred to the large home constructed that year for cotton broker Harry Russell Gould. A wraparound porch on the façade, terminating on the western end with a turret and pedimented bays on the front and side elevations, creates an asymmetry typical of the Queen Anne style,

while the detailing of the gallery points to the Classical revival mode. Gould built his home on three generous lots and acquired five nearby ones facing Ursulines Avenue, probably to ensure their proper development. In 1908 he became president of the Commissioners of Ursulines Avenue, an advocacy body created to protect the integrity of the residential neighborhood. Several years earlier, this group planted palm trees in the boulevard's neutral ground. Gould and his wife, Annie Everett, remained in their home until his death in 1942.

131

3200 Ursulines Avenue.

3200 Ursulines Avenue
Bounded by St. Philip, North Hagan (First), North Rendon (Second)

With touches of Tudor, Louisiana Colonial, and Neoclassical revival motifs, this sprawling cottage typifies the early twentieth-century Eclectic style. Algiers, Louisiana, native Mark A. Morse and his wife, Carmelite, built their new bayou home on the shaded boulevard in 1906, after his retirement at age sixty-seven from his supervisory position with the Southern Pacific Steamship Terminal. One of their daughters, Alice Terrell, later acquired the next-door residence at 3206 Ursulines. Morse purchased the empty corner property in separate transactions in 1903 and 1906.[40] For many years, this square and many others in the vicinity near Moss Street were owned by Frenchman Louis André Billaud, who with his kinsman Joseph Billaud bought the land in 1848 from the First Municipality.[41] In 1877 Billaud dispersed some of his holdings, transferring the subject two lots at the corner of Ursulines and North Rendon and three adjacent lots on North Rendon to Mary Leontine Saucier, wife of A. A. Grandpré. Mark and Carmelite remained in their home for over twenty years, until their respective deaths in 1927 and 1936.

WHITE STREET, NORTH

1206 White (Sixth) Street, North
Bounded by Esplanade, Bell (St. John), Crete (Seventh)

That beautiful residence property, comprising the entire square of ground bounded by Esplanade, St. John, White and Dupre Street, measuring about 330 feet front on Esplanade, 332 feet front on St. John, 110 feet front on White and 263 feet on Dupre Street. The dwelling is built on an elevated brick basement, containing hall, six rooms, bath, wash room and kitchen, 3 large cisterns and well in the yard. The main floor contains central hall, seven beautiful apartments, 2 closets and galleries. The attic is finished and contains 4 rooms, all finely finished and well lighted, stable, poultry house, etc. The ground is planted with a choice variety of fruit and ornamental trees, and affording ample room for stock, etc. As a gentlemen's complete residence, this property is unsurpassed.

The *Times-Picayune* (April 9, 1879) so described the former Dufour residence in a notice of the upcoming auction of the choice property by absentee owner Josephine Schreiber, wife of Jean François Beugnot. A prominent lawyer as well as an architectural connoisseur, Cyprien Dufour built this Italianate-style villa facing Esplanade between North White and Crete Streets in 1870, soon after selling his monumental mansion at today's 1707 Esplanade and a few years after the death in 1867 of his wife, Louise Donnet. Dying at the age of fifty-one in 1871, shortly after his new, more restrained cottage was completed, Dufour left four orphaned sons, two of whom were minors. Soon after, coffee merchant Pierre Pousine acquired the home for $18,600 and in 1878 transferred ownership to Mrs. Beugnot.[42]

Between 1884 and 1904, retired merchant Henry Beebe and his heirs owned this impressive complex, first as originally sited on an entire square and later carving building lots out of the ample grounds. In 1906 Louise Sarrazin Plassan, wife of cotton merchant Adolph Plassan, acquired the parcel at the corner of North White and Bell Streets, including the relocated Dufour house.[43] This extended family—consisting of numerous children and in-laws—lived there for years. In the 1920s they rented the property out as four apartments of four rooms each.

Although definitive documentation is lacking, Henry Howard likely designed Dufour's 1870 home. This noted architect was Dufour's choice for his earlier home as well as a commercial building. Also, Robert S. Brantley, author of *Henry Howard, Louisiana's Architect*, points to stylistic similarities found at 1206 North White and in Howard's other designs. At Nottoway Plantation,

Left: 1206 North White Street.

Below: 1206 North White Street, cornstalk and sunflower cast iron fence detail.

Brantley noted, Howard used a jigsaw cut on the brackets on either side of the columns, and here he did away with decoration and used a plain bracket, but with the same proportions as Nottoway's. The double-height columns, with their soaring attenuation, also harken back to Nottoway. Toward the end of his career, Howard became more conservative in his architectural creations, eliminating elaborate decorative elements on both the exteriors and interiors of his houses. As Brantley observed, in the early twentieth-century relocation from its original site, the raised cottage's basement level and façade gallery were shortened, which significantly impacted its original proportions. The front staircase and the gallery's original ironwork also have been removed.[44] Its cornstalk and sunflower iron fence, cast by Wood, Miltenberger & Company Ornamental Iron Works, Inc., the southern branch of the Philadelphia firm of Wood & Perot, figures as the most noted feature of this Orleans Parish landmark, designated as such in 1986. This is one of three such fences remaining in New Orleans, one at 915 Royal Street and the third at 1448 Fourth Street.

PHOTO INDEX

R. Stephanie Bruno

A glorious village, indeed, set along the banks of Bayou St. John, the waterway where our earliest settlements appeared, even before the official founding of the city. I think that this fact may have been the impetus behind Mary Lou Christovich's dedication to seeing to it that this book be published—ever the historian, she wanted the story to be told.

Over the last three hundred years, Faubourg St. John has managed to maintain its architectural integrity and urban scale despite pressures to the contrary. Its building inventory includes every type of dwelling, from French Colonial plantation-style homes to double shotguns to bungalows to converted corner stores and gas stations.

Meanwhile, residents have woven a thriving and diverse community, one that celebrates "Voodoo on the Bayou" or throws a "Bayou Boogaloo" for the public to enjoy.

You have read about the grand families of Faubourg St. John, about its rowing clubs and native pleasure gardens, about Bayou Road and the old Indian portage, about the commerce that once took place here. Now is your chance to explore the backstreets. Along the way, you'll encounter more than 100 nineteenth- and twentieth-century buildings and meet the storekeepers, bank presidents, plasterers and brewery workers who built the Faubourg St. John neighborhood we know today.

2608-10 Bell Street Joseph Lambert Bercier built this center-hall Eastlake-style house between 1891 and 1895, when he purchased the odd-shaped lot from Caroline Villio ($1,350). He bequeathed the property to his daughter, Louise, who lived there with her husband, Eugene F. Villarrubia, until their deaths. Its Eastlake charm is augmented by a gallery that wraps around elements of the façade, turned gallery columns, open frieze spindles, cut-work panels, and swan-neck spandrels which extend beneath the frieze. Unusual features include a "Queen Anne" attic window in the dormer, having small, stained-glass squares around the perimeter; and an exceptionally tall iron fence, probably added later.

2721 Bell Street Built between 1908 and 1917, this Craftsman-style home was constructed during the period that prominent businessman Joseph Emile Jarreau lived there with his wife, Amelie. The Jarreaus occupied the residence until 1925, when they put it up for auction and it was bought by Edward Davis McCutchon, the advertising manager for the D. H. Holmes department store. Ads for the house in the 1920s describe it as a modern "bungalow" and tout its two floors of living space, basement, and sleeping porch, among other amenities. Two steeply pitched gables in the center of the house—one at the roofline and one above the front porch—are the most prominent features.

3001-03 Bell Street This twentieth-century shotgun double appears on the Sanborn Fire Insurance Map of 1908 (but not 1896). Eclectic, it mixes elements of both Craftsman and Neoclassical revival styles. The gallery's boxed columns taper under their Doric capitals. Multi-component entries (doors with transoms and sidelights) suggest a Craftsman influence, but the steeply pitched roof and front-facing gable inset with a pair of vertical attic windows surrounded by gable-shingles suggest the Neoclassical. Narrow weatherboards were common on façades during the Arts and Crafts era and belong in both periods. As a corner property, the house fills its lot and completes the streetscape.

3135 Bell Street This stucco raised-basement house does not appear on the 1908 Sanborn Map, but records show John Lachin living here from 1924 to 1949. With brothers Angelo and Victor, he operated Lachin & Co., "Sculptors and Designers Architectural and Ornamental Work in Plaster Cement and Wood," which still exists today. Mediterranean styling, handsome landscaping, and a complimentary placement of house to property, along with a green tile roof, red terracotta tile steps, and a small terrace at the landing add to the home's allure. The asymmetrical façade is punctuated by a balustrade that stretches between and around a pair of Tuscan-style columns topped with Corinthian capitals.

2901 Desoto Street In 1896 Antoine Baumgartin owned this side-gabled corner cottage, which was shown as early as the 1883 Robinson Atlas. He acquired the property in 1867 from Joseph Beaulieu and partitioned it. Between 1896 and 1908, the ell that runs parallel to the rear property line may have been added. The 1908 Sanborn Map indicates the house was a double cottage, likely having two doors and two windows. The house has since been converted to a single-family residence, and the façade reconfigured to include an off-center, recessed front door and two windows. The façade is fronted by a small garden. The house occupies an exceptionally wide lot.

3200 Desoto Street The raised-basement Arts and Crafts house at Desoto and North Rendon was built on ground auctioned on December 18, 1900. Improvements included a single-story, frame house with a slate roof, three rooms, two kitchens, a cistern, and stables. By 1912 Charles S. Dittman Jr., a coffee broker, lived there with his bride, Emma Hincks. They remained until 1920, when, after their fourth child was born, they sold the house for $11,000. Its most compelling architectural aspects are its gables—one facing Desoto and a second facing North Rendon—with perpendicular rooflines. Supported by Tuscan columns, both gable-ended roofs cover porches.

3201 Desoto Street In January 1930, Dr. Ignatius Tedesco contracted with builder Charles Louviere to construct this Mediterranean revival raised-basement house for a fee of $7,945, replacing a previous house shown on the 1908 Sanborn. Striking features include a red tile roof, two clusters of Solomonic columns, and a multi-paned entry door with sidelights, topped with a fan transom that is reiterated above the pair of windows to the left. Rather than rest upon the porch floor, the columns extend below the porch to plinths atop pilasters. Typical of this house type citywide, stairs appear to the side of the entryway. A slight bow in the porch's forward edge creates a graceful curve.

2800 Dumaine Street The streetscape of the 2800 block of Dumaine Street expresses at a glance the tightly woven fabric of the Faubourg St. John neighborhood. A row of single-story double shotgun houses, some converted to singles but all flush with the sidewalk, share elements that include stoops, hip-and-gable rooflines, and brackets in the eaves. Although a pair of the houses have segmentally arched Italianate windows, all maintain a rhythmic repetition of door-window-window-door. The consistency of scale on the block, balanced by the variety of details, makes this block a perfect snapshot of prevailing conditions in this late nineteenth-/early twentieth-century neighborhood.

2822-24 Dumaine Street Henry Freie acquired lots at 2822-24 and 2834-36 Dumaine from John Ernest Cassard for $200 in 1893 and sold them to Jules Meunier for $425 five years later. In 1899 Freie bought the improved lots back from Meunier for $1,400 and sold them in 1922 for $10,500. A double shotgun now converted to a single-family residence, the house exhibits Italianate features, including segmentally arched windows and door transoms that are emblematic of this style, as are drop-lap siding, quoins, and fanciful, milled brackets. In recent years, owners have added a screened-in porch to the North White Street side on an adjacent key lot that they also own (2818 Dumaine).

2826-28 Dumaine Street When Henry Freie bought this house in 1899, he also purchased its twin, 2834-36 Dumaine. Freie, born in Germany, immigrated to the United States in 1875 and became president of the Crescent City Manufacturing Company in 1902. This house, like others on its block, was built in the Italianate style as a shotgun double around 1899. Among many fine late nineteenth-century features, the distinctive fleur-de-lis verge board—installed on the overhang of the hip-and-gable roof and outlining the gable—sets it apart. Although the houses have changed hands many times since Freie sold them as a pair in 1922, they are held by a single owner today.

2830-32 Dumaine Street In 1893 Emile L. J. Bernadas bought two lots at the corner of Dumaine and North Dupre Streets before building this double shotgun and the corner store to its right in 1894. Built as a double, presumably as an investment property, the house appears to have been converted to a single-family residence. The combination hip-and-gable roof creates an overhang to shelter visitors from the elements. Decorative millwork brackets support the overhang. Half-glass front doors are embellished with raised millwork panels, and simple box cornices top six-over-six windows. Drop-lap siding, a common architectural element of the day, covers the façade of the house.

2834 Dumaine Street In 1893 Emile L. J. Bernadas bought this lot and the one next door, and built a double shotgun (2830-32) and a corner store/house (the latter in 1894-95) on them. Situated at the corner of Dumaine and North Dupre Streets, it has a diagonal entrance, created by truncating the right-angled corner where the front and side walls meet. Typically, the entrance would be at ground level (to facilitate attracting customers and replenishing store produce) rather than raised. The building's original appearance, probably the image of the double next door, has been altered with replacement windows and shutters, and delicate millwork brackets under the roof overhang instead of hefty ones.

1897: 1034-36 Crete Street Built in 1897 by Louisa Trosclair, widow of Henry C. Marionneaux, this double shotgun house in the Italianate style has segmentally arched windows and door transoms framed by screen-panel shutters. Elaborately patterned double millwork brackets, together with door and window cornices, accentuate the styling, while drop-lap siding, a gable vent, and quoins on the corner boards enhance this corner four-bay double. A pair of French doors in the rear of the 1036 side suggests a side entrance, though no steps exist.

ca. 1895: 3115 Desoto Street This side-hall single house in the Italianate style appeared on the 1895-96 Sanborn Map as a narrow, one-story structure featuring galleries across the front and at the rear. It sat on an 80-foot-wide lot, hugging the property line closest to North Rendon Street. When a legal judgment cost Ruth Snaer the property in 1909, the lot was just 37 feet wide, indicating subdivision of the original parcel. At some point, the leaded glass front door with matching arched transom was moved to the center of the façade. The house retains original drop-lap siding, quoins, cornices, and Tuscan columns. A garden and iron fence complete the composition.

2900 Dumaine Street This block offers a splendid opportunity to view and consider a row of five late nineteenth-century Eastlake double shotguns, their similarities and differences. All have the same scale and proportions, imparting an important lyrical harmony to the streetscape, even if some turned columns have been replaced with iron and some houses lack their fanciful open friezes. The millwork, including fine turned columns, could well have been ordered from catalogs of the period. The balanced rhythm and similarities extend to the front stoops, which mirror each other in style and placement. This view demonstrates how these houses have changed and adapted over time—and just how much they have remained essentially the same.

pre-1895: 3019 Dumaine Street This two-bay shotgun single was built prior to 1896, according to the Sanborn Map. Frederick Scholly, a shoe fitter, lived there with his wife, Elizabeth, a dressmaker, and their children. The Italianate house exhibits defining characteristics of its style: segmentally arched, six-over-six windows; drop-lap siding; quoins on the corner boards; and a double-arched, half-glass door. Milled roof brackets, overhang, and unadorned boxed cornices above the front window add detail, with coved shingles in the gable continuing the Italianate theme. Board and batten shutters, painted blue, replace the original louvered ones. On the left, a drive leads through an added lot to a side porch and entry.

1895-96: 3245 Desoto Street Built between 1895 and 1896 by Esterene "Irene" Justi, wife of Emile Albin Maignan, this side-hall, bracketed house must have been intended as a rental property, for Justi never lived there and sold it in 1906. A handsome house with front porch, intricate milled brackets, and a hip-and-gable roofline, its entry door is Queen Anne style with small panes of stained glass encircling a large central pane. Two short windows exhibit a four-over-four configuration, and operable louvered shutters cover openings. Turned balusters and newel posts comprise the front porch, drop-lap siding covers the façade, and quoins appear on the corner boards.

ca. 1895: 3029 Dumaine Street This circa 1895 single shotgun with a hipped roof occupies a lot that is double the width of the typical thirty-foot-wide residential lot in this area. An attached second dwelling (3023-35) has a low-pitched, gable-fronted roof, unlike the steep pitch of the front building. A gravel driveway separates the two houses on the single lot. Judging by the hipped roof and floor-to-ceiling openings on the front, the house appears to have been built in the late nineteenth century as a two-bay, bracketed structure. Its brackets strongly resemble a design readily available from local millworkers or illustrated in late nineteenth-century catalogs.

3037 Dumaine Street This double shotgun occupies the corner of Dumaine and North Salcedo. Like many other houses in the area, its façade stands on the front property line, necessitating side-orientated stoops. The home's notable features include drop-lap siding, quoins in the edge boards, cast iron soffit vents, and fanciful milled brackets. Decorative coved shingles fill the gable of the hip-and-gable roof. Two attic windows, each consisting of a single pane of green stained glass, add to the appeal. Windows and doors retain the frames of original louvered shutters, the windows now fitted with screens.

2837 Dumaine Street This residence originated in the 1890s, after Hecla Marie Dalferes (wife of William M. Hicks) sold the property to Albert Charlet (1889) for just $200. Albert, Numa, and Leo Paul Charlet were brothers, born in Assumption Parish. Albert subsequently sold the property to his younger brother Numa in 1900 for $1,400. Numa, a grocer, lived here, while Leo worked across the street at 2836 Dumaine. The 1908 Sanborn Map shows this as a "store" with a wraparound shed roof overhang. The building may include a front addition to the pre-1896 cottage. The property's ornamental plantings enhance its current diagonal entrance at grade.

3041 Dumaine Street This double shotgun house with altered gable stands out among its peers, largely because of its segmented, late Italianate keystone windows and door surrounds. Arresting elements on the house, which likely was one of a number of similar ones built in the neighborhood in the early 1900s by Francis and Paul Maestri, include the oversized attic window, which also repeats the fanciful keystone on top. Whereas the façade fenestration lacks shutters, the modern interpretation of the four-bay double-shotgun is maintained. Board and batten shutters along the North Salcedo edge of the property add dimension to the side elevation, as well as privacy when closed.

3138 Dumaine Street Shotgun doubles in this Faubourg St. John village adapt to commercial endeavors, perhaps with more ease and absorption than in any other New Orleans neighborhood. Corner-orientated stores/houses abound, exhibiting widely ranging styles and degrees of sophistication. This one, situated at the corner of Dumaine and North Rendon, retains one of its original vitrines (display windows) on the Dumaine façade and clerestory windows—which admit light while conserving wall space for merchandise—on both façades near the corner. The building's gable faces Dumaine and is embellished with coved shingles. A terracotta roof finial adds an extra flourish to the composition, as does the modest amount of ornamental plantings.

3343-45 Dumaine Street Ernest Zeigler, a machinist and foreman at Novelty Machine Works on Julia Street, built this shotgun double between 1896 and 1908. Born in Germany, Zeigler immigrated to the United States in 1896 and became a naturalized citizen in time for the 1910 census. A textbook example of an Eastlake double, the house features the requisite "gingerbread"—an open frieze between turned columns, with turned spindles and pierce-work panels, and turned balusters in the porch railing. The hip-and-gable roofline features three gables, the largest inset with decorative shingles and Palladian stained-glass windows. Cornices top Italianate openings. Drop-lap siding and corner boards filled with columns of quoins, incised with rosettes, complete the composition.

2700 Esplanade Avenue This gracious cottage replaced the grand two-story center-hall Cyprien Dufour house, built in 1870, that belonged to Henry and Amelia Beebe, then to other Beebe relatives. In about 1905, Louise Sarrazin Plassan moved the Dufour house to 1206 North White Street and divided the Esplanade parcel into lots. This house, built circa 1906, features a front-facing gable that extends over the front porch and is embellished with half-timbering and an elaborate attic window that echoes the window to the left of the porch. The entry, like those of many early twentieth-century homes, is wider than other openings on the front porch and is further emphasized by pilasters on either side.

2826 Esplanade Avenue The L-shaped side-hall house was built before 1883, when it appeared (though smaller) in the Robinson Atlas. It fit snugly into one corner of the triangle bounded by Esplanade, North Dupre, and Desoto. By 1896 it had been enlarged, and the 1908 Sanborn Map shows the dramatic addition made by the two wings of the house and porch. Today it looks much as it did in 1908, when Alice Guerin owned it. With turned columns, open frieze with turned spindles and pierce-work panels, and verge board embellishing both the façade and the gable rake of the addition, it is every bit a fanciful Eastlake home.

2914 Esplanade Avenue This circa 1890 house appears to have a center hall, with the addition of a bay wing. Elaborate cornice detailing suggests the spirit of a Queen Anne style. From the sunburst patterns in the gabled bay roof, further embellished with giant spandrels, to its pediment scrollwork over all windows, harmony graces this structure and enhances its symmetry. Two one-over-one, full-length windows repeat cornice designs, while their perfect spacing balances the half-glass front door, which is protected by a wrought iron security door. Drop-lap siding, a prominent architectural feature, marks definition. A low, rare iron fence, once common throughout the district, encloses a prolific garden.

2918 Esplanade Avenue Built between 1883 and 1896, this neoclassical-style side-hall house was occupied from 1903 to 1905 by Gaston Edgar Musson, nephew of Impressionist painter Edgar Degas, and Estelle Angelina Musson, the lovely sister-in-law whom Edgar painted when he visited New Orleans, 1872-73. In 1908 James Robin, later a vice-president of the Whitney Bank, bought the property. The house is retired from the sidewalk behind a classic wrought iron fence and a front garden. It features a forward-facing gable inset with a demi-lune attic window; two full-length, six-over-six windows; and a transom with delicate tracery atop the door. A side bay, present in 1896 and 1908, remains, but side galleries do not.

3322-24 Esplanade Avenue The house currently at this address was likely built by John Hager, who purchased lots from Joseph Klar in 1873. Although the city directory lists a resident here in 1875 (when it was 739 Esplanade) and the Robinson Atlas shows a structure in 1883, the existing house was built after 1908. In the 1940s it was occupied by Fortunata Ida Culotta, the fourth wife and widow of Leon Winfield "Lee" Christmas (1863-1924), a notorious soldier of fortune. The handsome two-story double features both Craftsman elements (exposed rafter tails, deep roof overhangs) and neoclassical elements (composite columns with Scamozzi capitals, wraparound galleries, Queen Anne-style attic window). Windowpanes exhibit a one-over-one configuration.

3118-20 Grand Route St. John This pre-1883 Creole cottage with a side-gable roofline occupies an oddly shaped lot at the corner of North Rendon Street, a half block from Esplanade opposite Fortier Park. Four large openings punctuate the façade—two full-length, six-over-six windows and two doors with transoms. Wings in the rear have rooflines parallel to one another but perpendicular to the ridge of the cottage. The steep pitch of the roof affords room for living quarters upstairs. Each of two stoops leads from the banquette to one side of the double residence. Cypress trees along the North Rendon Street side lend a rural feel.

3208-10 Grand Route St. John The versatility of shotgun doubles is reflected in their fenestration, brackets, and cast iron soffit vents. Originally this pre-1896 house would have had period doors and windows, most likely in the location where they exist today. Cement steps rest, as did the original wooden ones, on the banquette because the house edges the property line. Currently the site is wide enough for off-street parking, a screened porch, and the enjoyment of a neighbor's side yard. Sensitivity to the planting of two sidewalk trees indicates an awareness of the Bayou St. John neighborhood's unification by front and side gardens.

3209 Grand Route St. John This fanciful Eastlake home was built between 1896 and 1900 for J. Alfred Reinecke, a cotton classer, and his family. By 1906 Frederick Vincent Allain lived there with his family. He raised the house high off the ground and added a basement level (about 1914). After the Allains moved to Chicago, William Feuillan, a buyer for Williams Richardson Co., owned the house for several decades. Turned columns, an open frieze (with pierce-work panels and turned spindles), fan-shaped spandrels, scrollwork in both front-facing gables, cresting atop the window and door cornices, drop-lap siding, and quoins in the corner boards combine in an irresistible portrait of late nineteenth-century style and taste.

Development in the Late Nineteenth Century

Dumaine Street

pre-1895: 3058 Dumaine Street The bracketed single shotgun at this address is retired from the sidewalk, allowing for a front porch and yard. Although the house has experienced many alterations—including a storm door and front storm window, replacement of the front door, carport on the side, paved front yard—it is a handsome house that first appears on the 1895-96 Sanborn Map. The façade features a floor-to-ceiling window and a front door and transom of equal height. Noteworthy features include the hipped roof, elaborately milled brackets, drop-lap siding, and quoins in the corner boards. The narrow house widens in the rear to increase living space, a condition not present in 1896.

Dupre Street

ca. 1899: 935 Dupre Street, North This single shotgun house with a hipped roof sits far back on its lot, appearing from the street to occupy the side lot of the house at 929 North Dupre. Although the lots were combined on the 1908 Sanborn Map, today the two houses occupy separate lots, both under the same ownership. Whereas the neighboring two-story house at 929 belongs to the early twentieth century, features of this single shotgun, such as the hipped roof, suggest it was built very soon after the turn of the twentieth century or even in the late nineteenth century. Sanborn Fire Insurance Maps indicate a construction date between 1896 and 1908.

Gayoso Street

1883-96: 917 Gayoso Street, North This side-hall/side-gallery house was built between 1883 and 1896. When offered for sale in 1928, it was described as a "retired single cottage, containing 6 rooms, bath . . . driveway and garage, large side porch." A dormer punctuates the hipped roof. Picket-shaped panes in its windows, an early twentieth-century pattern, suggest the dormer was added post-construction. Tuscan columns support the roof over the front porch, where two walk-through windows, a half-glass front door, and drop-lap siding contribute to the composition. An iron fence and gate provide a transition from the sidewalk to the small front garden.

Orleans Avenue

ca. 1899: 3027 Orleans Avenue This shotgun single occupies a wide but shallow lot between North Gayoso and North Salcedo Streets. Its façade sits at the property line, precluding a front porch or garden; rather, a side oriented stoop rests on the sidewalk. This house is one of the few in the area that appears to be largely in its original condition. The inset gable of its hip-and-gable roofline contains a small attic window. Additional late nineteenth-/early twentieth-century features include millwork brackets, drop-lap siding, a cornice above the window and door, and quoins, incised on the corner boards with a floral pattern, an uncommon and appealing decorative feature.

1895-1900: 3238-40 Dumaine Street This double residence was built between 1895 and 1900, likely as a typical Eastlake shotgun double. It was altered, probably in 1928 for the family of Pierre A. Lesseps, a collector for Louis Mondshine Furniture Company, to create commercial space where Catherine Ruello Lesseps operated a notions store. Daughter Lucille Lesseps Loga sold the property in 1980, ending the family's ownership. Before the North Hagan Avenue half was altered, the front porch likely extended the width of the house. Eastlake-style millwork—turned columns, open frieze with turned spindles, and pierce-work—remains, as do Italianate-style windows exhibiting segmentally arched tops, cornices with cresting, drop-lap siding, and a shingled gable with elliptical Queen Anne window.

1014 Gayoso Street, North An exuberant garden enhances the appearance of this cheerful Eastlake house. Once a double shotgun, it has been converted into a single-family residence. Its list of Eastlake embellishments is extensive: turned columns, open frieze, turned spindles, cut-work panels, fanciful spandrels, and filigree crowns atop window and door cornices. Full-length windows complement the half-glass doors and accentuate the vertical aspects of the façade. Raised beds between the sidewalk and the street hold pretty plantings and popular Queen palms.

3301-03 Grand Route St. John Located at the corner of Vignaud Street, this double shotgun house exhibits an array of late nineteenth-century features. French V-channel tiles outline roof ridges. The roof is visibly pierced by the original brick chimney. Cast iron soffit vents and drop-lap siding add definition to the façade, where modeled cornices cap windows and doors. Original six-over-six wood window sashes remain. Colorful flowers fill a small garden between the two front stoops, and palms grow in a second garden between the sidewalk and the street. Although the house may not look large from the sidewalk, it extends far back and features several additions that add square footage of living space.

3307-09 Grand Route St. John It is tempting to deem this bracket-style double shotgun a duplicate of its neighbor on the right, but closer observation reveals differences. The greatest changes are in the configuration of the windows and transoms on the façade. Whereas the ones on the corner house are flat on the top, their counterparts here curve gently into a segmental arch, a defining element of Italianate-style houses. Drop-lap siding, six-over-six windows, and cast iron foundation vents are present, as are verge board trim on the roof overhang and operable louvered shutters. Although covered by screen doors embellished with wrought iron decorations, the front doors appear to be in the double arch pattern.

1215 Hagan Avenue, North Built about 1925, this raised bungalow was in 1928 the home of Ulysses Daussat, treasurer for Blaise Parking. It features a Craftsman-style double gable. Other signature Craftsman elements include exposed rafter tails (though covered by a board), exaggerated gable rake boards, faux timbering in the foremost gable, and clustered half-columns resting atop masonry pillars supporting the roof over the porch. Knee brackets appear in the eaves of both gables. This house is one of just a few having a central stair leading to the porch, rather than on the side. Moreover, the height of the basement level appears lower from the front because of the terracing of the lot.

1221 Hagan Avenue, North This one-story bungalow is deceiving in that the roof appears to be flat, as is the case in many Prairie-style homes. In fact, the house has a very low-pitched roof extending over the front porch and a true side gable over the main body of the dwelling. Another peculiarity of many cottages of this arrangement is that they appear small when viewed from the front but increase in size toward the rear, as is the case here. A small bay on the left side of the house centers on the peak of the side gable, and a rear wing provides space for more rooms.

1235 Hagan Avenue, North Situated on a terraced lot, this side-gabled Craftsman cottage was built prior to 1923. Early residents were attorney Arthur Mosby "Jeff" Curtis and his wife, Julia Marie Flanagan, whose relatives lived at 1241 North Hagan. The placement of the chimney on the right and the fact that the footprint is the same on the 1940 Sanborn Map as it is today suggest that the condition is original. The roof is pitched steeply enough to afford living space upstairs, where a wide, low-slung shed dormer admits light. Exposed rafter tails and a flared brick column (supporting one edge of the roof) are additional Craftsman features.

1249 Hagan Avenue, North Built between 1908 and 1915, this camelback double house exemplifies the Neoclassical revival style. One of its earliest owners, banker Ernest Caro, shared one side with his wife, Louise Brandner, their two daughters, and Louise's mother, while leasing out the other half. A hip-and-gable roofline showcases an elaborately detailed attic vent, surrounded by shingles and scrollwork. The eave of the hip offers a space for the application of modillions, and garlands of millwork flowers embellish the frieze. Transoms atop the one-over-one window sash are fitted with opaque stained glass arranged in a webbed pattern. Fluted columns topped with Scamozzi capitals complete the composition.

1100 Lopez Street, North This exuberant two-story Arts and Crafts house was constructed between 1908 and 1919. Retired from the sidewalk, it blends a variety of styles that enjoyed popularity in the early twentieth century. The front porch appears to be squarely Craftsman, with its low-pitched, gabled roof and squared brick columns. Two more gables on the second floor are steeply pitched. Exposed rafter tails on the complex roofline and the variety of windowpane patterns animate the façade. The house likely was constructed for Frederick Albert LeMieux of New York, who worked with his brother Jasper as timber estimators. After Jasper and another brother died in 1930, Frederick dissolved the business in 1935.

1204 Lopez Street, North Almost immediately after this grand two-story house was constructed in about 1909, ads began appearing in the paper advertising it for sale or lease. By 1914 the family of Edward S. Butler, a businessman involved with various cotton-buying ventures, was in residence. The Butler family remained in the house until about 1920, when Paul Zibilich, a prominent oyster supplier, bought it for $13,000. The influence of the City Beautiful movement is unmistakable, with its paired columns, elaborate millwork, deep eaves, ornamental banded frieze (concealed by the monochromatic paint job), and especially the diamond-shaped windowpanes. The red tile roof and proportions of the dormers add an eclectic Craftsman element.

1205 Lopez Street, North This handsome, early twentieth-century house, now divided into apartments, occupies an immense lot, 158' wide by 125' deep, at the corner of North Lopez and Bell Streets. The spacious setting suits this sprawling, two-story home with porte-cochere. Several features distinguish it from other grand dwellings on its block. First, because the red tile roofline is hipped rather than gabled, it affords a sidewalk view of the tiles. Second, the pronounced second-story bay with three windows and gable in the center of the house draws the eye to the elaborate first-floor entrance. Third, clusters of two Tuscan columns and one squared, battered column flanking the steps present an unusual contrast.

1303-05 Mystery Street Constructed before 1895, this double shotgun occupies a corner lot at the intersection of Mystery Street and Grand Route St. John, directly across from the popular Alcée Fortier Park, which hosts the annual Bastille Day celebration. Though it exhibits a number of decorative embellishments, the house has undergone many alterations. It exhibits shortened replacement windows and modern doors that lack transoms. A wrought iron railing borders the porch and continues down the center entry stair. The space afforded by setting the house back slightly from the sidewalk is dedicated to a small garden containing a variety of plants.

1307-09 Mystery Street This house and its neighbor at 1303-05 Mystery may have been twins originally, but whereas the house next door has been altered, this one has not. It retains full-height windows and doors, with segmentally arched tops and banded cornices above them. The harmony of exterior siding, with drop-lap on the façade, echoes the construction of late nineteenth-century shotgun doubles abundant with brackets and soffit vents. The hipped roof is similar to the one on the neighboring house, but this one retains its original centered chimneys. The full-width front porch, with center stair and iron rail, mirrors that of its neighbor.

3121 Orleans Avenue This pretty shotgun single has Eastlake detailing and, unlike many other houses in the neighborhood, is retired from the sidewalk far enough to accommodate a front porch. Another difference is the roofline—a simple gable in lieu of the hip-and-gable configuration. True to the Eastlake style, the roof is supported at the edge of the porch by turned wood columns and an open frieze plus spandrels (square spindles in the frieze and the multi-paned front door may be replacements). Wood columns terminate a couple of feet above the porch, resting atop later masonry piers. Drop-lap siding, quoins in the corner boards, and a six-over-six window are compatible with the era.

145

1896-1905: 1019 Rendon Street, North This bracketed side-hall house was built between 1896 and 1905, likely by William Langhetée, a carpenter on his "own account" who married Marie Bordes in 1899. They remained here at least until 1957, when William died. The Italianate style is exhibited by the house's tall, arched-top windows and door transom. Trim embellished with fanciful scrollwork, cornices topped with lacy crowns, rosettes, and fluting in the vertical trim add allure. Strategically placed paint colors accentuate the many details of the elaborate millwork, still evident despite façade alterations. No matter how small a cottage may be, such millwork jewels as this decorative Eastlake window lintel with cutwork cresting will pop up to delight.

ca. 1900: 2801 St. Ann Street This building is the quintessential New Orleans corner store/house, situated with its main entrance at an angle to the corner of St. Ann and North White Streets. Built after 1896, it functioned as a grocery as early as 1905. The Ponzo family, led by Antonino and Rosa Ponzo and their son, Francesco, operated a store and "saloon" there and lived on site, from 1910 until at least 1949. The structure, recently renovated, has a hip-and-gable-style roof with a demi-lune and rectangular attic window. A metal awning supported by posts has been restored. The impression from the street is positive, thanks in part to the cheerful turquoise color with crisp white trim.

2711 Ursulines Avenue A bounty of noteworthy architectural features distinguish this side-hall Italianate house, including a one-room-deep camelback with a gallery. The façade displays a pair of segmentally arched, full-length, four-over-six windows to the left of the half-glass front door with its rounded-top transom. Cornices crown the windows and door, and columns of quoins fill corner boards. Additional features include the hip-and-gable roofline, a three-part decorative gable element including a small window, and patterned shingles in the gable. Fleur de lis verge board applied to the roof eave and gable rakes and operable louvered shutters over the front windows add charm. A garden, iron fence with pedestrian and vehicular gates and decorative cap vent cover on the roof complete the composition.

1895-1908: 824 White Street, North The two-bay shotgun single at this address was constructed between 1895 and 1908, according to the Sanborn Maps for those dates. The entrance to the house has been moved to the left side, and the front door and steps removed. Louvered shutters cover the door and half-length window opening on the façade. Simple but attractive millwork brackets appear under the eave created by the hip-and-gable roofline, and the gable is filled with shingles. A gate crafted from a six-panel door leads into the side yard. The relocation of the entrance to the side made way for a colorful garden in front.

3311 St. Ann Street This late nineteenth-century two-bay, single shotgun has classic proportions and details, accentuated by the creative use and placement of colorful paint. Façade drop-lap siding and single-side board framing also indicate a late nineteenth-century building date. Roof-gable shingles are identified as scallop style in builders' catalogs. A batten-shuttered walk-through window balances a shuttered half-glass front door, embellished with decorative wooden panels and a transom. Three proportioned boxed columns in white support the hipped-roof over the front porch, fronted by a wide entry stair. Fenestration cornices are detailed with turquoise-shaded verge board, as is the set of quoins.

2803 Ursulines Avenue This single two-bay shotgun house features original Eastlake/Stick-style millwork. Rather than a traditional open frieze with turned spindles and pierce-work panels, the builder selected a pattern using oversized spandrels and intersecting wood members. The presentation dominates the porch and effectively highlights the undecorated window and door trim. Although the house appears small from the sidewalk, it doubles in width toward the rear. Three turned columns are integral to the grille support and hip-and-gable roofline. Drop-lap siding and quoins in the corner boards suggest a nineteenth-century origin, while the cement stairs are in the stock Queen Anne style. A chain-link fence encloses the side garden.

1117-19 White Street, North The Italianate bracketed shotgun double at this address resembles houses on either side of it, but subtle differences are noticeable. This house has full-length windows that are topped—as are the doors—with cornices. Segmental arches of the window tops and transoms identify the house as being in the Italianate style. There is neither an attic vent nor a window in the gable, nor shutters on the façade. Nonetheless, set back from the sidewalk and painted a brilliant white, the house fits in nicely with its companions.

1123 White Street, North Set back from the sidewalk some twenty feet, this bracketed double shotgun is separated from passersby by a small yard. Half-glass front doors and full-length windows are topped with cornices and covered by operable louvered shutters. Segmentally arched doors and windows indicate Italianate style. The deep overhang created by the hip-and-gable roof requires large brackets for support, a need that five graceful brackets fulfill quite well. The gable window—in a Palladian style of a larger window flanked by two smaller ones—is another feature that sets this house apart from similar ones on the block.

3127 Orleans Avenue Six of the ten houses on Orleans between North Rendon and North Lopez Streets—an unusually large number—are single shotgun houses. The bracket-style single shotgun at this address was renovated in 2017, with excellent results. Although the entrance was moved to the side, drop-lap siding, original windows, and appropriate brackets were utilized. Decorative shingles in the front-facing gable were repaired, and the gable is inset with a stained-glass window. A one-story side addition—recessed at least two rooms' distance from the sidewalk—has an appropriate hipped roof. The paint palette—yellow with white trim, khaki window sashes and gable shingles, and dark blue soffit—is key to the house's appeal.

3137 Orleans Avenue This bracket-style house with a hip-and-gable roof was built as a double shotgun, as evidenced by four openings on the façade, but has since been converted to a single-family residence. Cornices above the openings, louvered shutters, and milled brackets impart elegance to the home's façade, even without the drop-lap siding and shingled gable that are common for houses of this era in the neighborhood. When the house was converted to a single, the front door on the right and its stoop were removed, making room for shrubbery. The remaining half-glass door on the left, visible through the iron security gate, is embellished with millwork panels.

3237-39 Orleans Avenue French V-channel tiles outline the ridges of this bracket-style double shotgun house's steeply pitched hipped roof, one of a handful in the neighborhood that retains its asbestos shingles. The café au lait body color contrasts with crisp white trim and black doors and mailbox. Although the window openings maintain their original size, multi-paned inserts that resemble casement windows replace the double-hung sash. The dark color of the doors calls attention to them, but neither would have been original to this house, as they are indicative of the Craftsman era. It is likely that the original doors were either four-panel or half-glass.

1219 Rendon Street, North This grand, Eclectic-style home was built between 1908 and 1914, when its residents were Andrew Chalona, a first-generation Italian-American fruit vendor in the French Market, and his wife. After Andrew died in 1914, the house was leased to A. J. Higgins before its purchase by George Mule of the Union Brewery and then by Dr. Theodore August Jung. A large, two-story residence with a porch that wraps across the front and around the right side, the house is further distinguished by arches that support the hipped roof over the porch and rest atop pairs of short columns with Scamozzi capitals, and the foundation of cast concrete "stones."

1227 Rendon Street, North August Benjamin Letellier, president of the Phillips Paper Company, commissioned a sprawling home at this address circa 1911, the predecessor of this early twentieth-century house. The Letellier family lived there until at least 1941, when August died. Distinctive features are the red tile roof, its gable-fronted dormer inset with a horizontal band of windows, and the stout Tuscan columns with Scamozzi capitals. Brackets extend from the frieze below the eaves. The front porch stretches across the full width of the house. This is a true raised basement house, as evidenced by windows visible on the sides of the lower level. Like its neighboring house, it occupies an oversized lot and is far retired from the sidewalk.

716 Salcedo Street, North This double shotgun, having a hip-and-gable roof, resembles many late double shotguns on the same block and others nearby. Elements of the house have been altered. A comparison with its neighbor at 718-20 implies that it originally had two doors and two windows, rather than one door and three replacement windows. It also had a full complement of eave brackets (five instead of four). Cornices above the openings are present but lack the delicate bird's-eye trim presented on its neighbor. The house retains its drop-lap siding and coved shingles in the gable, plus an attractive half-glass front door (likely original).

925-27 Salcedo Street, North Sited perfectly on its property with a small, recessed front garden, this double house dominates its two-bay neighbors. On the porch, the Victorian wood turnings and individual woodwork repeat designs of grilles that were purchased by size and depth. Bayou St. John houses abound in turned columns, sometimes joined by simple, cast-iron railings, as exemplified here. The fenestrations, two doors and two windows, retain excellent cornices and surrounds from ceiling to floor. Today colloquially known collectively as gingerbread, fretwork spandrels, running trim, and turned columns were illustrated and offered for sale in millwork catalogs in a variety of patterns, sizes, and prices.

2820 St. Ann Street The earliest verifiable resident of this house—constructed between 1896 and 1901—was Charles Hecknagel in 1901. This shotgun double was built in an Eclectic style, but later alterations to its roofline make it appear different from the three neighboring homes it originally mirrored. Its main façade rests on the property line, fronted by a small garden between the two sets of steps that lead to the entrances. Several of its neighbors have milled brackets, as this house does, and all possess the characteristic rounded door transoms and rounded arch windows with diamond-patterned top sashes. Drop-lap siding and quoins in the corner boards complete the composition.

2901-03 St. Ann Street This shotgun double makes a striking corner, with paint colors accentuating architectural features. Body and trim are painted olive; foundation, Bahama and batten shutters, and side-orientated stoops are cornflower blue; and the whole is enhanced by tomato red, applied to window sash, soffit vents, scrollwork, and finials of the millwork brackets. Even the quoins on the corner boards are painted the olive of the body color, forming a monochromatic backdrop. Additional late nineteenth-century/early twentieth-century elements include two-over-two windows, drop-lap siding, and half-glass doors. The front gable roof retains coved shingles and a wooden attic vent.

2909 St. Ann Street Built as a double shotgun to house two families, this cottage, now a single-family residence, edges the front property line. Its façade, one of the finest examples, presents a true late nineteenth-century structure. Two sets of cast concrete steps mark the entrances, while five roof brackets and four cast iron soffit vents serve as decorative and functional elements. Operable louvered shutters protect six-over-six windows and two doors. The turquoise and spring green color scheme expresses twenty-first-century flair. With the fortuitous purchase of the adjoining lot at 2913, the owner gained space for off-street parking, a side garden, and a covered porch.

3325-27 St. Ann Street Genetically related (if not originally identical) to the three doubles on the left, this double shotgun also shares features with the single shotgun to the right. The house has a hip-and-gable roofline, with five small, milled brackets under the overhang. Its façade, like those of its neighbors, sits on the property line, limiting room to stoops only. Alternating bands of sawtooth and coved shingles in the gable form an elaborate pattern. Recent renovations, as evidenced by the fresh paint, retained original features such as drop-lap siding and four-over-four windows, preserving the house's late nineteenth-/early twentieth-century appeal.

3223-25 St. Philip Street This hipped-roof double shotgun was built between the publication of the 1883 Robinson Atlas and of the 1896 Sanborn Map. The house retains many original six-over-six windows, as well as narrow, multi-pane transoms over the two entryways. Recent renovations, however, have introduced modern doors fronted by metal security doors, inoperable shutters, and contemporary siding. With its façade located flush with the sidewalk, the home adheres to the tradition of paired stoops rather than a front porch. Decorative wrought iron rails accent the side-orientated stoops, which adds character.

1001 Broad Street, North Crescent City Steak House has been in operation at this address since 1934, having been founded by John Vojkovich, a Croatian immigrant. The building at this address may predate the arrival of the steakhouse, for the 1908 Sanborn Map shows a one-story store having a wrap-around awning at North Broad and St. Philip Streets. By 1940 the Sanborn shows a two-story building having the same footprint, perhaps indicating that the original single-story building was raised. A balcony at the second level, lined with a cast iron railing, now wraps from the façade around the right side.

3019-21 Desoto Street This house occupies the center portion of a much larger lot that was the home of John R. Barkdull, a cotton broker, from 1882 until his death in 1924. Shortly thereafter, the lot was subdivided and the original raised cottage was demolished and later replaced with the present structure. In the appearance of a duplex with double porches, the house is balanced

with fluted boxed columns and enhanced by decorative millwork. Set back from the property line and fronted by a split-cypress fence, the location of the house within the lot allows for a somewhat expansive front garden.

3100 Desoto Street Many elements of this house repeat the features of the Bayou St. John typical four-bay, drop-lap-sided double. Its position at the corner of North Lopez allows for two attic dormers, with the addition of a truncated gable. Most likely raised between 1908 and 1940, this home retains much of its original appearance. Decorative brackets, turned columns, and quoins, in alternating paint colors, add to its charm, as does a Little Free Library box at its property line. Its attractive façade is enhanced by shrubbery, flowerbeds, and a commanding front stairwell.

3063 Dumaine Street Sanborn Maps from 1896 and 1908 show a single-level store at this location, possibly the grocery operated there by Joseph Abadie in the early 1900s. In 1927 the first mention of a two-story building appears in a newspaper advertising the sale of the property, described as a grocery with two rooms on the ground floor and six rooms upstairs. The building's most distinctive feature is the rustication of the exterior walls, made with cast concrete blocks. A small balcony on the North Lopez side, a diagonal entry with a pole supporting the corner of the second floor, and a bank of windows along Dumaine Street are additional notable features.

3200 Dumaine Street The building at this address began as a one-story corner store/house where the Brugier family (Adolphe, then George) operated a food store and sometimes a bar in 1904 until the 1950s. At some point, the roof was raised

one-half story to allow for an interior loft space, perhaps because of business storage needs. The 1900-era shingled gable with attic window remains in its original position. Although the building is residential today, its commercial past is evidenced in the entry set at an angle to the sidewalk, the wrap-around awning, and the clerestory windows.

1101 Broad Street, North This twentieth-century, two-story structure stands on a triangular lot bounded by North Broad, Bellechasse, and Ursulines. A building occupied the triangle as far back as 1896, when the Sanborn Map showed a single-story dwelling. By 1908 a shop had been added. C. A. Wagner, who bought the building for $5,000 in 1924, either demolished it to build what is there today, or else enlarged and renovated the original building; he sold it for $10,000 in 1926. A two-story hexagonal bay is visible from the Bellechasse side, and on the Ursulines side, tile awnings echo the red tile roof. At the ground level, a picture window allows a sightline into the business.

1908: 3222 Desoto Street Contracted by Ulysses Daussat, this two-story house and its neighbor at 3226 were erected in 1908 by Osborn & Darensbourg builders ($4,000 and $4,140). A bookkeeper at the Security Brewery, Daussat resided at 3222 Desoto with his wife, Anna Hauser, and daughter. Anna's parents occupied the house next door at 3226. Although the city directory indicates the Daussats still lived at

3222 in 1919, the 1920 census places them at 3226, living with Anna's widowed mother (George Hauser had died in 1911). By 1933 the city directory showed Daussat residing at 1215 North Hagan, but he returned to Desoto (3241) by 1960.

1908: 3226 Desoto Street The house at 3226 Desoto, constructed for Ulysses Daussat's father-in-law, George Jacob Hauser, a Frenchmen Street shoe merchant, is a mirror image of Daussat's residence at 3222, although varying paint colors and vegetation partially mask architectural similarities. Both houses have a bay on one side, galleries on the opposite, and two shingled roof gables: one over the main portion of the house, another over the bay. Abundant windows reflect the early twentieth-century preference for large, one-over-one windows. The wrap-around porch and many of the features described above suggest the Queen Anne style for both houses, even without traditional turrets. The dwellings have remained remarkably intact over the last 110 years.

3208 and 3210 Dumaine Street The 1896 Sanborn Map shows a house and store on this lot, but comparing the configuration of those buildings with the 1908 Sanborn Map suggests that the original buildings were razed and new structures built during the intervening years. The raised single shotgun at 3208 and the slab-on-grade structure at 3210 have always maintained independent addresses and have never been considered a "double." Until the current owners converted 3210 to a living space, it had served non-residential purposes—a store, a cleaner, an office. Perhaps its most notorious use was as headquarters of the National Party, where twenty-one-year-old David Duke and accomplices were arrested in 1972 for making fire bombs.

ca. 1932: 3300 Dumaine Street The building at Dumaine and North Hagan was built circa 1932 as a Sinclair Service Station, replacing an earlier double residence on the site as well as Munch's Garage, an automotive repair service. The station exemplified Sinclair's stylish 1930s designs, many incorporating elements of Art Deco and Mission styles. Here, the green barrel tiles refer to Mission revival. As operators of the gas station changed over the years, the name of the business changed to match. The building served other purposes, including a Disabled American Veterans Auxiliary until 2003, when artist Robert Guthrie converted it to his home and studio. He installed the vintage Sinclair sign on the cornice of the canopy.

3237 St. Philip Street The original structure at this address appears on the 1896 Sanborn Map as a narrow house with side gallery, hugging the corner of St. Philip and North Hagan. By 1908, however, the building shape and footprint changed to that of a larger residence (wider and longer), raised on six-foot piers and recessed from the sidewalk. An addition between that date and 1929 changed the footprint. The first commercial use of the new single-story space at the corner was as a drugstore, but the red and white stripes suggest that it has also served as a barbershop.

3323-25 St. Philip Street This double shotgun house is a shining architectural example of late nineteenth-/early twentieth-century Eastlake style. Its open frieze or grille of turned spindles and pierce-work panels between turned columns could well have been ordered locally or delivered from a Chicago- or Philadelphia-based general millwork catalog. A shingled gable featuring a Palladian-style attic window offers a less common artifact. Features include drop-lap siding, quoins, half-glass doors, six-over-nine walk-through windows, and cornices above all façade openings. Louvered shutters once fronted all openings. Additional changes include the likely loss of two columns and the replacement of wooden stairs with the current Queen Anne-style cement ones.

2741 Ursulines Avenue Exuberantly painted, this bracket-style double shotgun is set back from the sidewalk a significant distance, accommodating a front garden and full-width porch. The house has a hip-and-gable roofline, intricately patterned milled brackets, cast iron soffit vents, and two full-length windows that balance the half-glass doors. Cornices above the windows and doors, drop-lap siding, and quoins in the corner boards are typical of late nineteenth-century houses. The balustrade around the porch has newel posts embellished with applied diamond-shaped woodwork. Turned balusters connect to the posts and ring the porch. Decorative shingles fill the gable, where square attic vents flank an opening, now boarded, that likely once held a decorative attic window.

2824 Ursulines Avenue Shaded by spectacular branches of oak trees on Ursulines Avenue, this raised basement house is a high-style twentieth-century single-family residence. With its red tile roof over the main body of the house and barrel-vaulted portico in the center of the façade, the house makes a dramatic statement on the block. Clusters of wooden boxed columns support the weight of the barrel vault, and monumental boxed masonry columns support the corners of the roof. The front porch stretches the full width of the house. Retired from the sidewalk to make room for the monumental central stair, the house has plenty of space for a front garden.

3034 Ursulines Avenue It is very possible that John Minot, described in 1901 as "the well-known and popular contractor and builder," constructed this grand two-story house, for he constructed two others, one of which (at 3042) served as his office, in the same block. Also, it displays the repetitions so prevalent in the Eclectic style, for which he is well known. This deep frame porch, supported by three squared masonry columns, repeating brackets, and crowned with interlocking pantiles, recalled previous years. A wide entry stair is enhanced by verdant foliage and a wrought iron fence with decorative scrollwork gate, which encloses the property.

3114 Ursulines Avenue Among the characteristics of this side-hall frame residence, also possibly built by Minot, are grouped Ionic columns on masonry piers that support the second-story balcony, accentuated with Chippendale detailing, and a protruding bay. A prominent red tile roof caps the main body of the house as well as the front gable. Another feature is his placement of the house to a far side so that space for a garden and drive is available. In 1901 Minot advertised his ability to "furnish your house, whether a cottage or a palace," at low prices. He also advertised general contracting, able to construct public buildings, office buildings, and residences, and to furnish millwork.

3233 Ursulines Avenue Built in 1915, this raised-basement bungalow underwent a succession of owners before its purchase in 1924 by Henry Jacob Reuther (b.1893), known as one of New Orleans's "most esteemed bakers." He had married Sybella Elizabeth Leidenheimer in 1916 and still lived here in 1940. The house is distinguished by a hipped roof that extends over the front porch and is supported by a colonnade of Doric columns, along with Craftsman-style columns sheathed in mitered weatherboards. A gabled dormer, embellished with faux timbering, extends forward from the roof ridges. A horizontal band of square windows outfit the dormer. The red tile steps suggest that the home once featured a matching roof.

1315-17 Vignaud Street By virtue of the windows' stained glass upper sashes and their segmented fanlight transoms, this four-bay, hipped-roof double reflects an owner's individuality. Stained glass is repeated in the three dormer windows, each with a diamond-shaped center pane. The early twentieth-century cottage appears to have extra area on the property devoted to a late twentieth-century double garage. Brackets and door cornices of earlier style were still available at the time of construction through catalogs and secondhand stores. The monochromatic taupe-colored paint contrasts nicely with the vibrancy of the stained glass. The façade is fronted by a small garden flanked by masonry stoops.

716 White Street, North Located at the intersection of North White Street and Orleans Avenue, this building, an early twentieth-century raised basement structure, exemplifies one of the most prevalent two-level house types in every New Orleans neighborhood. Residences usually occupy the entire square footage, but this layout allows gracefully for commercial space below. Its asymmetrical façade features tiled, terraced steps that lead to a front porch, supported by Tuscan-style columns at the tiled edges. The porch roof—like that above the main living quarters—is hipped and is sheathed with red tile. A fan transom appears over the multi-component front door and the paired windows above the steps.

921-23 White Street, North The oldest house still standing on its block, this bracketed Italianate double shotgun was built between 1895 and 1908. It features an array of nineteenth-century elements, including drop-lap siding, half-glass doors with raised millwork panels, and louvered shutters over the full-length windows. Pre-ordered brackets, quoins, and fleur-de-lis verge board are enriched by the multi-colored coved shingles in the gable. Paint colors accentuate the various millwork elements from which the house derives its exuberant personality. Side windows adhere to the six-over-six pattern, and the shallow camelback is original. An additional unifier is the small garden between the brick sidewalk and the street.

937 White Street, North This house and its neighbors at 935 and 941 were built in the early decades of the twentieth century (after 1908), after earlier houses on the lots were demolished. Each house in the trio is distinguished by protruding gables that extend forward on the façade, forming a shallow roof overhang. Like the house on the right, this was originally a shotgun double. When converted to a single, it lost a front door and a stoop, making way for a small garden. Another conversion replaced the attic windows with vents. The façade of this house and of the house to the right sit flush with the property line, precluding a porch.

941 White Street, North Originally a shotgun double (as evidenced by the pair of windows and door casings), this house has a distinctive clipped gable roof. When converted to a single, the second door and its stoop were removed, even though the transom-topped door casing—infilled with boards arranged in a decorative herringbone pattern—remains. The entryway door is a replacement but its casing remains, as does its two-pane transom. Original chimneys pierce the roofline at intervals, and a double six-pane window fills the gable. Windows adhere to a four-over-four arrangement, which is a later iteration of the six-over-six pattern that was prevalent in the nineteenth century.

DEVELOPMENT IN THE TWENTIETH CENTURY

Dupre Street

1896-1908: 1127 Dupre Street, North This raised side-hall house dates from between 1896 and 1908, when it was outlined in its current configuration on the Sanborn Map of that year. An additional hipped-roof extension blends with the clapboard siding on the front. Changes in the floor plan of this house reflect years of differences, but the exterior architectural elements blend well to create a harmonious garden setting. Two full-length windows and a recessed, half-glass entry door comprise the openings. Four plain boxed columns support the roof over the front gallery.

Gayoso Street

934 Gayoso Street, North Painted a cheerful shade of turquoise with white trim with a raised salmon-colored front door, this Craftsman house is retired from the sidewalk behind a white picket fence. The single shotgun has expanded in the rear to include the addition of a camelback. It derives its style from exposed rafter tails, two angle-front brackets, and the oversized attic vent. A large, twenty-pane metal frame window is framed by two of the three flared boxed columns, atop masonry piers, which support the gable overhanging the porch. Despite the alterations, the home's Craftsman styling and vivid colors make it attractive.

1012 Gayoso Street, North This Craftsman-style house is barely visible behind abundant plantings. It exhibits the same general style as 934 Gayoso, with brick piers, recessed porch, and roof cornice vents. It differs by being built along the property line, with narrow side yards that barely accommodate a driveway. The small gold ball at the crest of the pitched roof is stylistically correct, as is the introduction of red tile cresting. The entire Bayou St. John neighborhood demonstrates outstanding individuality of plantings found at single residences and in small public spaces. Vegetation is a hallmark of the area and a unifying characteristic.

Grand Roure St. John

ca. 1900: 3213 Grand Route St. John Built about 1900 by Gustave Daniel Revol, this house replaced a much earlier one owned by Emile Torregrossa. Revol, a first-generation American whose career began as a blacksmith, continued as a carriage maker, and eventually led to wealth as owner of a Cadillac dealership, resided there in 1910 with his wife, Emma Duvic, and their five daughters. In 1927 Revol sold to W. H. Ennis, whose family lived there for nearly fifty years. Two stories tall, it stands on an immense lot, retired from the sidewalk. Distinctive features include a red tile roof, galleries at both levels, and a handsome Chippendale railing. The low, cast cement block wall is original.

Ursulines Avenue

ca. 1908: 2935 Ursulines Avenue First occupied by poultryman James L. Grosening, this Craftsman bungalow was built about 1908. Herman Hall, president of the New Orleans and Lower Coast Railway, purchased it and lived there from 1917 to 1922, when it became the home of Dr. Wallace Wood, dean of the Tulane School of Dentistry. Perfectly following the prescription for Craftsman bungalows, the house is low slung, with narrow, banded attic windows in the wide, shed-roofed dormer accenting the horizontal. Rafter tails are exposed, and short, battered columns atop piers support the roof over the porch. Knee brackets in the side gables and the top sash of the probably original windows are configured in a complex pattern.

1908-10: 3118 Ursulines Avenue The commanding two-story home at 3118 Ursulines was built between 1908 and 1910, likely for attorney Joseph Lautenschlaeger and his wife, the former Marie Virginia Jacob. Subsequent owners included clothier Maurice J. Garrot, then his daughter, Evelyn, and her husband, Dr. Henry F. Ader. Its eclectic early twentieth-century style borrows elements from various then-popular revival styles. Faux timbering and stucco in the larger gable refers to the Tudor revival, the stained-glass windows to the Neoclassical revival. Entirely original, however, are the elliptically arched openings on the front porch that extend downward to the porch decking and serve as columns.

ca. 1910-15: 929 Dupre Street, North Many owners cherish their lots in Faubourg St. John, even when their families have outgrown the lot's residential capacity. This lofty, two-story side-hall house dates from circa 1910-15, as indicated by its Edwardian-style dormer. Situated among single-level homes, its height and lot position make it stand out, as do the Doric capitals on the four boxed columns. Its three-bay frame design is found in every New Orleans neighborhood. The Lower Garden District and Esplanade Ridge particularly abound in this popular style. A builder's choice of style and floor plan often reflects an owner's selection.

3221-23 Grand Route St. John This two-story symmetrical double may look new, but a double residence stood here as long ago as 1896, according to the Sanborn Map. In the ensuing 120+ years, either the one-story original structure was demolished and a two-story dwelling built, or a second floor was added to the original house. In 2012 the owner removed the existing siding and replaced it with Hardie-Plank®, constructed a gallery on the second floor, replaced all the windows, and performed other changes. Sidewalk gardening effectively unifies a neighborhood proclivity toward façade planting.

3319 Grand Route St. John This two-level, single-family home is a twentieth-century addition to the property, placed to showcase a decorative façade and garden. The roofline follows a form commonly seen in these later versions of classic double-gallery, side-hall houses: a hipped roof over the main house and a front gable that extends slightly forward from the body to distinguish this modern house style. Grand Route St. John is a model street to the Bayou St. John neighborhood, as evidenced by this twentieth-century addition, which adds to the diversity of the historic community's architectural offerings.

1908-15: 3241 Ursulines Avenue This gleaming white two-story house with symmetrical façade, built between 1908 and 1915, originally had a much more pronounced Craftsman appearance, as shown in a 1924 photograph. The stout boxed columns that support the roof of the porch

were more rustic, consisting of upward-spiraling wooden bars, mimicked by newel posts on the second-floor porch. Rafter tails formerly extended outward beyond the second-floor porch to create a small arbor. The home retains its Craftsman character in its side-gable roof, knee brackets in the side gables, multi-paned top sash in the windows, and wide transom over the door. The Dutch-style gable adds an important vertical element in a composition that would otherwise be purely horizontal.

CONTRIBUTORS

Mary Louise Mossy Christovich (1928-2017)

Mary Lou Christovich was a veritable powerhouse in the preservation community of New Orleans—and the driving force behind *Gateway to New Orleans: Bayou St. John, 1708-2018*. A proud twelfth-generation New Orleanian, she embodied achievement. She was well known for contributions to architectural history and to cemetery and architectural preservation that reach across Louisiana and beyond, and as a prolific author and lecturer on subjects relating to her beloved city.

Throughout her life, Mary Lou exemplified volunteerism and leadership—with New Orleans as the major beneficiary of her dedication and enthusiasm. She was co-founder, board member, and president of the Friends of the Cabildo. In 1974 she founded the non-profit Save Our Cemeteries in response to the proposed demolition of wall vaults in historic St. Louis Cemetery No. 2. Active on its board for forty-four years, she raised funds, spearheaded restorations, and, most of all, elevated civic consciousness of the need to protect and preserve these priceless cities of the dead.

In 1972 Mary Lou was elected to the board of directors of the Kemper and Leila Williams Foundation, which oversees The Historic New Orleans Collection. She went on to serve with distinction as president and as chairman of the board until the last month of her life. She also served on the board of directors of the Felicity Street Redevelopment Association and as a board member of Newcomb College Alumnae and Tulane University, and on various Tulane School of Architecture committees. She was actively involved in the Preservation Resource Center of New Orleans, which she co-founded, and served on the Vieux Carré Commission. Mary Lou was a member of the State Review Committee for Historic Places and participated in the 1960s battle to defeat the Riverfront Expressway. As an avid supporter of the Louisiana Landmarks Society, she continued to encourage and strengthen historic preservation and to champion proper land use practices in the city of New Orleans.

One of her most notable contributions to New Orleans was co-authoring and editing the first six volumes of the *New Orleans Architecture* series (published by the Friends of the Cabildo, 1971–80), for which she earned the Alice Davis Hitchcock Award in 1977. These influential books were instrumental in educating the community regarding the uniqueness and significance of our historic neighborhoods and in helping to coalesce preservation efforts outside of the French Quarter. They sparked the impetus to form neighborhood associations and ultimately to create historic districts beyond the Vieux Carré, resulting in the establishment of the Historic District Landmarks Commission in 1976.

A talented writer, Mary Lou was the author of *Boyd Cruise* (1976), *New Orleans Interiors* (1980), and, most recently, the widely acclaimed *Garden Legacy* (2017, in collaboration with Roulhac Bunkley Toledano), all published by The Historic New Orleans Collection. *Gateway to New Orleans: Bayou St. John, 1708-2018* (Louisiana Landmarks Society, 2018), her final book, crowns a lifetime of research and commitment to architectural preservation. It commemorates the tricentennial of the city of New Orleans and demonstrates Mary Lou's unbounded love of the city that was her home.

In recognition of her commitment to preservation, education, and advocacy, Mary Lou received numerous awards, including the Louisiana Endowment for the Humanities Award for Lifetime Contribution to the Humanities (posthumously, 2018), Distinguished Alumna of Newcomb College (1982) and of Tulane University (1989), the Harnett T. Kane Award from the Louisiana Landmarks Society (1985), the Grace King Award from Save Our Cemeteries (1986), and the Louisiana Colonials Award from the Louisiana Association of Museums (2004).

Mary Lou's love of Louisiana's culture and architecture, and her dedication to preserving it, are evident in her writings, her history of volunteerism, and her leadership. Her accomplishments have etched her legacy, one that endures in the architectural richness throughout New Orleans, serving as the foundation for the future. She is deeply missed.

– Sandra L. Stokes, President
Louisiana Landmarks Society

Robert S. Brantley

Robert S. Brantley is a New Orleans-based architectural photographer, researcher, and writer. His work has appeared independently and with that of his late wife, Jan White Brantley, in numerous magazine articles and books on New Orleans and Louisiana. He is the author of the biography *Henry Howard, Louisiana's Architect*. Originally from Georgia, he has made New Orleans his home since 1977.

Jan White Brantley

Jan White Brantley received her MFA from Tulane University in May 1980. After teaching photography at the Newcomb Art Department of Tulane from 1980 to 1981, she headed the Photography Department at The Historic New Orleans Collection for over twenty-five years. Her work has been exhibited in Germany, New York, New Jersey, Louisiana, and Washington, D.C. She died in December 2008 after courageously fighting breast cancer for twenty-one years. She took many of the photographs in this volume, individually or in collaboration with her husband.

R. Stephanie Bruno

R. Stephanie Bruno is a lifelong New Orleanian and an author who writes about her city's architecture, streetscapes, and neighborhoods. She worked for a dozen years at the Preservation Resource Center, where she led projects to rehabilitate historic homes in Holy Cross and Faubourg Marengo, taught dozens of workshops, and wrote articles for *Preservation in Print*. After contributing weekly to the *Times-Picayune* for nine years, she has written about houses and gardens in the New Orleans *Advocate* for the past five years. She authored *New Orleans Streets: A Walker's Guide to Neighborhood Architecture* and, most recently, contributed to the anthology *New Orleans: The First Three Hundred Years*.

Hilary Somerville Irvin

A native of the Mississippi Delta hamlet of Minter City, Hilary Somerville Irvin moved to New Orleans in 1972 from Providence, Rhode Island, where she had the pleasure of working with the grand dame of preservation, Antoinette Downing, who whetted her appetite for urban preservation. Her formal training includes a BA in history from Hollins College, MA in history from the University of New Orleans, fellowships with the Attingham Trust for the Study of the Country House and the Victorian Society's Summer School in London, and Alumni Study Week in Glasgow, Scotland. From 1985 until retirement in 2013, she served as the principal architectural historian with the Vieux Carré Commission. Her research has resulted in numerous published articles and essays, several of which center around the city's French landscaping traditions. Now she works as an independent historical and architectural consultant.

Florence M. Jumonville

Florence M. Jumonville, a native New Orleanian, serves as archivist for the Touro Infirmary Foundation. In previous positions at The Historic New Orleans Collection and the Louisiana and Special Collections Department at the University of New Orleans Library, she has worked with Louisiana materials and special collections for over forty-five years. Florence holds four advanced degrees in library science, history, and education from Louisiana State University and the University of New Orleans. She has authored two books and more than fifty book chapters, articles, and conference papers, emphasizing the history of libraries, printing, and publishing in Louisiana.

S. Frederick Starr

S. Frederick Starr is the author of five books on New Orleans. He is a former vice president and provost of Tulane University, a founder of the Greater New Orleans Foundation, and co-leader since 1980 of the Louisiana Repertory Jazz Ensemble. Starr is the founding chairman of the Central Asia-Caucasus Institute in Washington and Stockholm.

Heather Veneziano

Heather Veneziano lives in New Orleans, where she owns and operates Gambrel & Peak, a multifaceted historic preservation consulting firm. She holds advanced degrees in studio-based craft from the University of the Arts and the University of Edinburgh, in addition to a Master of Preservation Studies from Tulane University. Heather has lectured nationally and internationally on her work and has authored numerous conference papers and articles focused on vernacular architecture, deathscapes, ritual, craft, and architectural/landscape preservation. She is a founding member of the Louisiana Chapter of the Association for Gravestone Studies and currently serves as co-chair.

ACKNOWLEDGMENTS

Hilary Somerville Irvin

I am grateful to my parents, who shared their enthusiasm for architecture with their four children. My brother-in-law, Henry Wiley Krotzer Jr., further piqued my curiosity in this city's built past before and after my move here. In the early 1970s, my good fortune aligned me, as a volunteer, with Mary Louise Christovich, Roulhac Toledano, and Sally Kittredge Evans (now Reeves), coauthors of the early volumes of the Friends of the Cabildo architectural series. And as a graduate student, I was pointed toward linking architectural trends with cultural ethnicity by the late Joseph Logsdon, esteemed professor of history at the University of New Orleans.

The city's archives are unrivalled in their resources, which would be worthless without their staffs. Over the past four decades, faces have changed but their cumulative knowledge and helpfulness have not. In working on *Gateway to New Orleans*, I would have been lost without the assistance of The Historic New Orleans Collection's Howard Margot, Rebecca Smith, and Mary Lou Eichhorn, who speedily answered my queries, always adding a few lagniappe tidbits of her own; Orleans Parish Notarial Research Center's Sally Sinor and Siva Blake, who pulled out volume after volume of acts and scanned image after image, as well as digging up new information; Tulane University's Southeastern Architectural Archive's Kevin Williams, who over the years has patiently answered my many queries; and Christina Bryant, head of the New Orleans Public Library's Louisiana Division. What a pleasure working with you all has been!

R. Stephanie Bruno

I first met Mary Lou Christovich in December of 2016 when I wrote about her Prytania Street home for the New Orleans *Advocate*. After hearing for years about this lion of a woman—a pillar of historic preservation and a fierce taskmaster—I didn't know what to make of the charming and gracious person before me. I was stunned by her beauty and musical voice and how she could weave a tale. When I left that day, she brought up a book on Faubourg St. John that she had researched twenty or more years ago but had never had time to write. "I think you could do that book," she said. "The research is done—all it needs is a writer."

I took the bait, but more than a year later, I can attest that it needed much more than a writer. It needed a real historian and researcher to tell the tale of the homes and families who lived in them (Hilary Irvin). It needed a superb photographer who could work hand in glove with Mary Lou making decisions about what to include, how the book should look, and so on (Robert Brantley); it required not one but two stellar essayists (Richard Campanella and Fred Starr); it required a trusted colleague to edit thousands of words of text (Florence Jumonville); and it needed the energy of someone from the new generation of preservationists to manage the project while researching an important piece of the bayou's history (Heather Veneziano).

For my part of the book, I am especially indebted to Erin Albritton and Liz Warner, two friends who both happen to be crackerjack historians and researchers. Without them, I (and therefore the reader) would never have learned about the fascinating and endlessly intriguing past of this neighborhood. What an amazing group of professionals came together to fulfill Mary Lou's vision—my hat is off to them all!

Heather Veneziano

In addition to the names mentioned in print as active contributors to the text and illustrations, there are many others, without whose support this book would not have been completed.

I am especially grateful for all of the help and enthusiasm displayed by members of The Historic New Orleans Collection (THNOC) staff. Jennifer Navarre, Heather Szafran, and Mary Lou Eichhorn guided me through the Christovich archives and always made my visits to the Williams Research Center a pleasure. Rebecca Smith and Robert Ticknor greatly helped in securing images from THNOC's collections for publication and assured me, when I asked them countless times if all of this was possible, that it was. I would also like to thank THNOC staff members Howard Margot and Albert Dumas Jr., Howard for always going above and beyond to help with projects and Albert for brightening my mood whenever I set foot in the door.

In addition, I would like to thank Clara B. Armstrong for her optimistic presence, even during the most difficult times. I am especially indebted to Florence M. Jumonville, whose calm demeanor and extraordinary work ethic is something that I shall always aspire to mirror. I would also like to mention my appreciation for having counted Mary Lou Christovich among my friends; her belief in the importance of this book was what kept me going through to the end of the project.

In closing, I would like to thank my parents for their unwavering support of all of my endeavors and Christopher for more than I would be able to ever put into words.

Robert S. Brantley

Books, specifically books such as this one, require assistance from many people. Their advice, expertise, and selflessness make it possible to complete a work more authoritatively and accurately than had it been done alone. Authors rely, therefore, on collaboration, and it is with sincere gratitude that I thank Alfred E. Lemmon, Howard Margot, and Mary Lou Eichhorn at The Historic New Orleans Collection: Alfred Lemmon, for his invaluable knowledge of Louisiana's colonial period and for his aid in locating documents and maps in Spanish archives; Howard Margot, for his assistance in navigating French archives; and Mary Lou Eichhorn, for finding answers to endless questions.

I thank my friend and colleague, Richard Vallon, for contributing his knowledge of and wizardry with Photoshop® and Lightroom. His proficiency, advice, and adroit skill at removing hundreds of power lines and other unwanted intrusions have made many images much better.

A very special thank you to Diana Lewis for allowing us to reproduce the portrait of Evariste Blanc and his son. To Adam Montegut of the New Orleans Tattoo Museum for his excellent artistic *interpretation* of Bienville and his many tattoos, based on written accounts of Henri de Tonti (1704) and the research of Jacob Laurence, curator of exhibits (2006-15), History Museum of Mobile, and included in the permanent exhibit at the Site of Fort Condé, Mobile, Alabama.

To Father Jonathan P. Hemelt of Our Lady of the Holy Rosary Catholic Church for his kind support and encouragement during the photographing of the church sanctuary.

I want to express my admiration, indebtedness, and gratitude to Clara B. Armstrong for her endless and delightful sense of humor during the many months of work on this volume, and for the wisdom and kindness she so freely gave, always with that special laugh.

IMAGE CREDITS

Archival drawings from the Plan Book Collection of the New Orleans Notarial Archives Research Center (hereafter NARC), identified below, appear in *Gateway to New Orleans* courtesy of Honorable Dale N. Atkins, Clerk of Civil District Court, Notarial Archives Division, Parish of Orleans.

Cover Image:
Vue de la Nouvelle Orléans en 1719, from R. Thomassy, *Géologie de la Louisiane*, 1860. The Historic New Orleans Collection (hereafter THNOC), The L. Kemper and Leila Moore Williams Founders Collection, 00.12 ii.

Endpapers:
Jean Antoine Bourgerol, Nov. 10, 1838. NARC, 056/002.

Front Matter:
i: Robert S. Brantley, *Pitot House, 1440 Moss Street, Gate*, 2017. Photograph; **ii:** Robert S. Brantley and Jan White Brantley, *Pitot House, 1440 Moss Street*, 1992. Photograph; **iv-v:** Jules Picou, July 24, 1857; detail. NARC, 024/022; **vi:** Robert S. Brantley, *Cut-glass door, 1308 Moss Street*, Aug. 9, 2017. Photograph; **vii:** Robert S. Brantley, *3111 St. Philip Street, Bracket*, Sept. 28, 2017. Photograph; **viii:** Robert S. Brantley, *Pitot House, 1440 Moss Street, Diagonal view*, Nov. 30, 2013. Photograph.

Preface:
x: *Carte du cours du fleuve St. Louis depuis dix lieues audessus de la Nouvelle Orleans jusqu'à son embouchure ou sont marquées les habitations formées, et les terrains concedez [i.e. concedes], auxquels on n'a pas travaille*, ca. 1732. Map; detail. Library of Congress; **xi:** William Henry Buck, *View of Bayou St. John*, 1880. Oil on canvas. Courtesy of Neal Auction Company; **xii top:** Charles F. Zimpel, *Topographical Map of New Orleans and its Vicinity*, 1834. Hand colored engraving; detail. THNOC, 1945.13 i-xix; **xii bottom**: *Along Bayou Saint John, New Orleans, La*. Detroit Publishing Co., 1910. Photograph. Library of Congress; **xiii:** *Aerial View to North toward Grounds and City Park*, image 1922, print 1979-1983. Gelatin silver print. The Charles L. Franck Studio Collection at THNOC, 1979.325.6430.

Historical Overview:
xiv: Antoine Joseph Vinache, *Plan de la Nouvelle Orleans et des environs*, 1803. Watercolor and ink. THNOC, 1987.65; **2:** Barthélémy Lafon, *Plan of Petites Coquilles*, 1814. Ink, pencil, and watercolor on paper. THNOC, 1970.2.14; **3:** Tomás Lopez de la Vargas Machuca, *La Luisiana*, 1762. Engraving. THNOC, 1955.20 i-iii; **4 top:** *Don Bernardo de Galvez*, Goupil and Company, 1903. Lithograph. THNOC, gift of Mr. Thomas N. Lennox, 1991.34.15; **4 bottom:** *Francisco Luis Hector, Baron de Carondelet*. Oil on canvas. Courtesy of the Collections of the Louisiana State Museum, #T0001.1967; **5:** Maxwell Ludlow, *A Map of the State of Louisiana with Part of the State of Mississippi and Alabama Territory*, ca.1820. Engraving. THNOC, 1939.2 i,ii; **6:** Louis Amedee Bringier, July 1, 1830; detail. NARC, 105/027; **7:** Willis J. Roussel, Feb. 12, 1911. NARC, 102/013; **8 top:** Theodore Lilienthal, *Old Basin*, 1867. Photograph. THNOC, courtesy of Fritz A. Grobien, T101116.10012; **8 bottom:** Charles Alexandre Lesueur. *Lac Pontchartrain avec ce phare de l'entrée du canal du Bayou St. Jean*, ca. 1830. Pencil on paper. Muséum d'Histoire Naturelle du Havre, Le Havre, France; **9 top:** Theodore Lilienthal, *Bayou St John*, 1867. Photograph. THNOC, courtesy of Fritz A. Grobien, T101116.10012; **9 middle:** Robert S. Brantley, 2017. Photograph; **9 bottom:** S. T. Blessing, *Old Basin*, ca. 1868. Photoprint mounted on board. THNOC, 1998.93.2 i,ii; **10:** Charles Alexandre Lesueur, *Untitled view of Bayou St. John*, May 16, 1830. Pencil on paper. Muséum d'Histoire Naturelle du Harve, Le Havre, France; **11:** Charles Alexandre Lesueur, *View of the Port on Bayou St. John*, May 28, 1830. Pencil on paper. Muséum d'Histoire Naturelle du Harve, Le Havre, France; **12:** Alexander Allison, *Schooners in tow*, ca. 1905–1915. Photograph. Louisiana Division/City Archives, New Orleans Public Library; **13 top:** W. Ridgeway, *New Orleans, La and Its Vicinity*, 1863. Watercolor engraving. THNOC, 1953.20; **13 bottom:** Claude Jules Allou d'Hémécourt and Barthélémy Lafon, *Plan de Fauxbourg St. Jean execute sur la propriete de Mr. D. Clark*, June 19, 1875. Ink on paper. THNOC, 1966.34.1; **14:** *Evening on Bayou St. John, New Orleans, La*. Detroit Publishing Co., between 1900 and 1906. Photograph. Library of Congress, Prints and Photographs Division. (https://www.loc.gov/item/det1994000692/PP, accessed Feb. 15, 2018); **15:** Robert S. Brantley, *Bayou St. John: Reflections*, Nov. 3, 2017. Photograph.

Exploration and Colonization:
16-17: *Carte de la Cote de la Louisiae depuis l'Embouchure du Mississipi jusqu'a la Baye de Pensacola*, from R. Thomassy, *Géologie de la Louisiane*, 1860. THNOC, The L. Kemper and Leila Moore Williams Founders Collection, 00.12 ii; **18:** Nicholas de Fer, *Les Costes aux Environs de la Riviere de Misisipi*, 1701. Watercolor engraving. THNOC, bequest of Richard Koch, 1971.34; **19:** *Jean-Baptiste le Moyne, sieur de Bienville*, ca. 1743-1753. Oil on canvas. THNOC, acquisition made possible by the Clarisse Claiborne Grima Fund, 1990.49; **20:** Antoine Simon Le Page du Pratz, *Crocodil / Serpent a Sonette / Serpent Verd*, from *Histoire de la Louisiane*, vol. II, 1758. Engraving. THNOC, The L. Kemper and Leila Moore Williams Founders Collection, 73-16-L; **20:** Adam Montegut, *Bienville with Tattoos*, 2017. Charcoal and pencil on paper. Courtesy of Adam Montegut, New Orleans Tattoo Museum; **21:** Alexander Debrunner, *Copy and Translation From the Original Spanish Plan*

[by Carlos Laveau Trudeau] *dated 1798, showing the City of New Orleans*, April 1875. Hand-colored lithograph. THNOC, gift of Irving Saal, 1959.81.2; **23:** François-Gérard Jollain, *Le Commerce que les Indiens du Mexique Font avec les François au Port de Missisipi*, between 1719 and 1721. Watercolor engraving. THNOC, 1952.3; **24 top:** *Vue de la Nouvelle Orléans en 1719*, from R. Thomassy, *Géologie de la Louisiane*, 1860. THNOC, The L. Kemper and Leila Moore Williams Founders Collection, 00.12 ii; **24 bottom:** Antoine Simon Le Page du Pratz, *Naturels en Hyver*, from *Histoire de la Louisiane*, vol. II. Engraving. THNOC, 1980.205.31; **25:** François Chéreau, *Le Missisipi ou la Louisiane Dans l'Amerique Septentrionale*, ca. 1720. Engraving with watercolor. THNOC, 1959.210.

A Glorious Village:
26-27: Richard Vallon and Robert S. Brantley, 2017. Photograph; **28:** William Henry Buck, *The Hotel at Spanish Fort on Bayou St. John*, 1879. Oil on canvas. Courtesy of Neal Auction Company; **29:** E. A. Robinson, *Atlas of the City of New Orleans and Environs*, plate 9, 1883. NARC; **30:** Robert S. Brantley, *738 Moss Street*, 2017. Photograph; **31:** Robert S. Brantley, *800 Moss Street*, 2017. Photograph; **32:** Charles Alexandre Lesueur, untitled view of Bayou St. John, May 16, 1830. Pencil on paper. Muséum d'Histoire Naturelle du Havre, Le Havre, France; **33:** Joseph Pilié, survey, 1826. Attached to Hugh Gordon, NP, Feb. 28, 1826. NARC; **34 top:** William Woodward, *Old Spanish House on Bayou St. John, New Orleans*, 1889. Oil on panel. Courtesy of Neal Auction Company; **34 bottom:** *Constance "Tiny" Corcoran Adorno*, ca. 1910. Photograph. Courtesy of Constance Adorno Barcza (granddaughter of Constance "Tiny" Corcoran Adorno); **35 top:** Robert S. Brantley, *924 Moss Street*, July 1, 2017. Photograph; **35 bottom:** George de Armas, *Surveyor Sketch Book #107*, page 78V, 1893-1894. THNOC, MSS 290.3.58; **36 top:** Jacques Amans (attributed), *Evariste Blanc with youngest son, James*. Courtesy of Diana Lewis; **36 bottom:** Charles F. Zimpel, *Topographical Map of New Orleans and its Vicinity*, 1834. Hand colored engraving; detail. THNOC, 1945.13 i-xix; **37:** Robert S. Brantley, *924 Moss Street, Rear elevation*, Sept. 12, 2017. Photograph; **38 top:** Robert S. Brantley, *924 Moss Street, First floor library*, Nov. 15, 2017. Photograph; **38 bottom:** Robert S. Brantley, *Iron latch from 924 Moss Street*; **39:** Robert S. Brantley, *924 Moss Street, Center hall*, Nov. 15, 2017. Photograph; **40 top left:** Robert S. Brantley, *928 Moss Street*, Sept. 8, 2017. Photograph; **40 top right:** Robert S. Brantley, *936 Moss Street*, Aug. 29, 2011. Photograph; **40 bottom:** Robert S. Brantley, *940 Moss Street*, Sept. 23, 2017. Photograph; **42:** Robert S. Brantley, *1218 Moss Street*, May 26, 1917. Photograph; **43 top left:** Robert S. Brantley, *1218 Moss Street, Interior*, June 14, 2011. Photograph; **43 top right:** Robert S. Brantley, *1218 Moss Street, Interior, entrance hall*, June 14, 2011. Photograph; **43 bottom:** Robert S. Brantley, *1218 Moss Street, Interior*, June 14, 2011. Photograph; **44 top:** Robert S. Brantley, *1256 Moss Street*, July 1, 2017. Photograph; **44 bottom:** Robert S. Brantley, *1200 Moss Street*, June 19, 2017. Photograph; **45 top:** Robert S. Brantley, *1260 Moss Street*, July 4, 2017. Photograph; **45 middle:** Robert S. Brantley, *3307-09 Grand Route St. John*, June 22, 2017. Photograph; **45 bottom:** Robert S. Brantley, *3301-03 Grand Route St. John*, June 22, 2017. Photograph; **46 top:** Jean Francois Aime Bercegeay, Feb. 23, 1870. NARC, 086/038; **46 bottom:** Theodore Lilienthal, *Bayou St John*, 1867. Photograph. bpk Bildagentur, Napoleon Museum, and Art Resource, NY; **47:** Charles Alexandre, Lesueur, *View of Bayou St. Jean from the house of Mr. Albin Michel at sunset*, ca. 1830. Pencil on paper. Muséum d'Histoire Naturelle du Havre, Le Havre, France; **48:** Robert S. Brantley, *Spanish Custom House*, Apr. 23, 2017. Photograph; **49 top:** Richard Koch, *Front—South West Elevation—Spanish Custom House, 1300 Moss Street, New Orleans, Orleans Parish, LA.*, 1934. Photograph, Historic American Engineering Record, National Park Service, U.S. Department of the Interior. Prints and Photographs Division, Library of Congress (HABS LA, 36-NEWOR,3--2; http://www.loc.gov/pictures/item/la0006.photos.072845p/resource/ accessed Jan. 1, 2018); **49 bottom:** Richard Koch, *Mantel—South Bedroom Wall—Spanish Custom House, 1300 Moss Street, New Orleans, Orleans Parish, LA*, 1934. Photograph, Historic American Engineering Record, National Park Service, U.S. Department of the Interior. Prints and Photographs Division, Library of Congress, HABS LA, 36-NEWOR,3--10; http://www.loc.gov/pictures/resource/hhh.la0006.photos.072853p/ accessed Jan. 1, 2018); **50:** Robert S. Brantley, *1308 Moss Street*, Sept. 9, 2017. Photograph; **51:** Robert S. Brantley, *Holy Rosary Rectory (1342 Moss Street)*, June 14, 2017. Photograph; **52:** *Residence, 1342 Moss Street*, image 1930s, print 1979-1983. Gelatin silver print. The Charles L. Franck Studio Collection at THNOC, 1979.325.1425; **53:** William Woodward, *Bayou St. John at end of Grand Route St. John*, 1887. Oil on canvas. THNOC, gift of Laura Simon Nelson, 2006.0430.15; **54:** Robert S. Brantley, *1318 Moss Street*, Sept. 8, 2017. Photograph; **55 top:** Robert S. Brantley, *1318 Moss Street, Mantel detail*, Dec. 21, 2017. Photograph; **55 bottom:** Robert S. Brantley, *Classical-style entrance, 1354 Moss Street*, Nov. 6, 2017. Photograph; **56:** Charles Alexandre Lesueur, Untitled view of the Michel-Pitot House, ca. 1830. Pencil on paper. Muséum d'Histoire Naturelle du Havre, Le Havre, France; **57 top:** Dan Leyrer, *Front Elevation, Overlooking Bayou St. John—Michel-Pitot House, 1370 Moss Street (moved to 1440 Moss Street), New Orleans, Orleans Parish, LA*, 1964. Photograph, Historic American Engineering Record, National Park Service, U.S. Department of the Interior. Prints and Photographs Division, Library of Congress, HABS LA,36-NEWOR,64—1; **57 bottom:** Marshall Dunham Photograph Album (Mss. 3241). Louisiana and Lower Mississippi Valley Collections, LSU Libraries, Baton Rouge, LA, USA; **58:** Robert S. Brantley and Jan White Brantley, *Pitot House, 1440 Moss Street*, 1992. Photograph; **59 top:** Robert S. Brantley and Jan White Brantley, *Pitot House, Parlor, second floor*, 1992. Photograph; **59 bottom:** Robert S. Brantley and Jan White Brantley, *Pitot House, Rear lower loggia*, 1992. Photograph; **60 top:** Robert S. Brantley, *Pitot House, Dining room*, 1992. Photograph; **60 bottom:** Robert S. Brantley and Jan White Brantley, *Pitot House, South bedroom, second floor*, 1992. Photograph; **61:** Robert S. Brantley, *Pitot House, Parlor detail, highly ornamented boxed mantel and chimney breast in the French manner*, Nov. 6, 2017; **62 top:** Dan Leyrer, *Front Elevation Overlooking Bayou St. John—Fernandez-Tissot House, 1400 Moss Street, New Orleans, Orleans Parish, LA*, 1964. Photograph, Historic American Engineering Record, National Park Service, U.S. Department of the Interior. From Prints and Photographs Division, Library of Congress, HABS LA, 36-NEWOR,65—1; **62 bottom:** F. Grage, J. H. Bohlke Jr., and M. Weil. *Fernandez-Tissot House, 1400 Moss Street, New Orleans, Orleans Parish, LA*, 1965. Measured drawing, Historic American Landscapes Survey, National Park Service, U.S. Department of the Interior. Prints and Photographs Division, Library of Congress, HABS LA,36-NEWOR,65-(sheet 4 of 4); **63:** Pietro Gualdi, May 6, 1854. NARC, 005/003; **64:** Theodore Lilienthal, *Bayou St John*, 1867. Photograph. THNOC, courtesy of Fritz A. Grobien, T101116.10012; **65 top:** Robert S. Brantley, *Magnolia Bridge*, Nov. 3, 2017. Photograph; **65 bottom:** John Norris Teunisson, *Bayou St. John*. Photograph. John Norris Teunisson Photographs, Courtesy of the Collections of the Louisiana State Mu-

seum, Accession #08482.160; **66:** Robert S. Brantley, *1454 Moss Street*, Sept. 11, 2017. Photograph; **67 top:** Robert S. Brantley, *1454 Moss Street*, Nov. 27, 2017. Photograph; **67 bottom:** Robert S. Brantley, *1454 Moss Street, Mantel*, Nov. 27, 2017. Photograph; **68:** Ellsworth Woodward, *Bayou St. John near City Park—Wilkinson House*, between 1890 and 1920. Pencil on paper adhered to board. THNOC, 2008.0203.3; **69 top:** Robert S. Brantley, *1492 Moss Street*, Apr. 23, 2017. Photograph; **69 bottom:** Robert S. Brantley, *1460 Moss Street*, Nov. 6, 2017. Photograph; **70:** Robert S. Brantley, *919 Moss Street*, Sept. 9, 2017. Photograph; **71 top:** Edgar Pilié, survey, 1909, attached to J. F. A. Hebel, NP, Oct. 15, 1909. NARC; **71 bottom:** Robert S. Brantley, *921 Moss Street*, Sept. 8, 2017. Photograph; **72:** Robert S. Brantley, *1031 Moss Street*, Sept. 8, 2017. Photograph; **73 top:** Robert S. Brantley, *1047 Moss Street*, Sept. 10, 2017. Photograph; **73 bottom:** Robert S. Brantley, *1335 Moss Street*, Sept. 8, 2017. Photograph; **74:** Robert S. Brantley, *1347 Moss Street*, Sept. 11, 2017. Photograph; **75:** Robert S. Brantley, *1411 Moss Street*, Sept. 8, 2017. Photograph; **76 top:** *Y.M.G.C. Rowing Club, New Orleans*, C. B. Mason, 1907. Picture postcard. THNOC, gift of Boyd Cruise, 1958.85.345; **76 middle:** John William Orr, *New Orleans Row Boat Club*, ca. 1873. Wood engraving. THNOC, 1951.41.33; **76 bottom:** St. John Rowing Club, *St. John Rowing Club ribbon*, between 1870 and 1903. Ink on silk. THNOC, 2005.0336.7; **77 top:** "St. John Rowing Club Heel and Toe Polka," L. Grunewald, 1880. Sheet music cover. William Ransom Hogan Jazz Archive, Howard-Tilton Memorial Library, Tulane University, Box 38 Folder 06; **77 bottom:** John Tibule Mendes, [*Southern Park by Bayou St. John*], ca. 1925. Gelatin dry plate negative. THNOC, gift of Waldemar S. Nelson, 2003.0182.545; **78 top:** Robert S. Brantley, *1415 Moss Street*, Sept. 8, 2017. Photograph; **78 bottom:** Jean Antoine Bourgerol, Nov. 10, 1838. NARC, 056/002; **79:** Robert S. Brantley, *1431-33 Moss Street*, Sept. 8, 2017. Photograph; **80:** Robert S. Brantley, *1417 Moss Street*, Sept. 8, 2017. Photograph; **81:** Robert S. Brantley, *1437 Moss Street*, Sept. 9, 2017. Photograph; **82 top:** Robert S. Brantley, *1451 Moss Street*, Sept. 8, 2017. Photograph; **82 bottom left:** Robert S. Brantley, *1451 Moss Street, Dining room*. Photograph; **82 bottom right:** Robert S. Brantley, *1451 Moss Street, Living room*. Photograph; **83 top:** Robert S. Brantley, *1455 Moss Street*, Sept. 8, 2017. Photograph; **83 bottom:** Robert S. Brantley, *1455 Moss Street, Entrance hall*. Photograph; **84 top:** Robert S. Brantley, *1459 Moss Street*, Sept. 8, 2017. Photograph; **84 bottom:** Robert S. Brantley, *1463 Moss Street*, Sept. 8, 2017. Photograph; **85:** "Mrs. Picheloup Shot to Death, and the tragedy is shrouded in Mystery." *Times-Picayune*, March 20, 1897; **86:** Robert S. Brantley, *2630 Bell Street*, Sept. 12, 2017. Photograph; **87:** Louis Amedee Bringier, Apr. 11, 1837. NARC, 022/020; **88 top:** Robert S. Brantley, *2734 Bell Street*, Sept. 1, 2017. Photograph; **88 bottom:** Robert S. Brantley, *2805 Bell Street*, Sept. 21, 2017. Photograph; **89:** Robert S. Brantley, *3017 Bell Street*, Nov. 7, 2017. Photograph; **90:** Robert S. Brantley, *1015 North Broad Street*, Sept. 10, 2017. Photograph; **91:** Robert S. Brantley, *2934 Desoto Street*, Aug. 31, 2017. Photograph; **92 top:** Robert S. Brantley, *3020 Desoto Street*, Sept. 23, 2017. Photograph; **92 bottom:** Robert S. Brantley, *3123 Desoto Street*, Sept. 18, 2017. Photograph; **93**: Robert S. Brantley, *3129 Desoto Street*, Nov. 7, 2017. Photograph; **94 top:** 1809 survey, attached to notarial act, A. J. Lewis, NP, Nov.8, 1872. NARC; **94 bottom**: Robert S. Brantley, *3139 Desoto Street*, Aug. 29, 2011. Photograph; **95:** Robert S. Brantley, *3212 Desoto Street*, Sept. 23, 2017. Photograph; **96:** Robert S. Brantley, *3217, 3219, and 3233 Desoto Street*, June 22, 2017. Photograph; **97:** Charles G. de L'Isle, Mar. 22, 1873. NARC, 074/026; **98-99:** Eugene Surgi, June 9, 1847. NARC, 044/004; **100 top:** Robert S. Brantley, *3238 Desoto Street*, Oct. 17, 2017. Photograph; **100 bottom:** Dany & Waddill, Survey, Apr. 24, 1907, attached to William J. Formento, NP, Mar. 27, 1912. NARC; **101:** Robert S. Brantley, *1141 North Dupre* Street, Aug. 31, 2017. Photograph; **102 top right:** Robert S. Brantley, *1239 North Dupre Street*, Aug. 31, 2017. Photograph; **102 bottom left:** Robert S. Brantley, *100 block North Dupre Street, Saints signs*, June 23, 2017. Photograph; **103:** Robert S. Brantley, *2936 Esplanade Avenue*, Sept. 11, 2017. Photograph; **104:** Robert S. Brantley, *3018 Esplanade Avenue*, Sept. 11, 2017. Photograph; **105 top**: *McDonogh #28 School*. Photograph. Louisiana Division/City Archives, New Orleans Public Library; **105 bottom:** Robert S. Brantley, *3102 Esplanade Avenue*, Sept. 12, 2017. Photograph; **106:** Robert S. Brantley, *3330 Esplanade Avenue*, Sept. 11, 2017. Photograph; **107 top:** Robert S. Brantley, *3336 Esplanade Avenue*, Oct. 4, 2017. Photograph; **107 bottom**: Robert S. Brantley, 3342 Esplanade Avenue, Sept. 11, 2017. Photograph; **108 top left and right:** Arthur de Armas, Survey, Aug. 29, 1887, attached to act of succession of Joseph Klar, Felix Dreyfous, NP, Sept. 1, 1887. NARC; **108 bottom:** Robert S. Brantley, *3243 Ponce de Leon Street*, Oct. 4, 2017. Photograph; **109:** Robert S. Brantley, *3356 Esplanade Avenue*, Oct. 17, 2017. Photograph; **110:** Robert S. Brantley, *3368 Esplanade Avenue, Our Lady of the Holy Rosary*, 2009. Photograph; **111 top:** Robert S. Brantley, *Sanctuary of Our Lady of the Rosary*, Oct. 18, 2017. Photograph; **111 bottom:** *Sacred Heart Orphanage, Esplanade Ave. New Orleans, LA*, C. B. Mason, ca. 1907. Picture postcard. THNOC, 1981.350.48; **112 top:** Robert S. Brantley, *823-25 North Gayoso Street*, Sept. 9, 2017. Photograph; **112 bottom:** Robert S. Brantley, *1302 North Gayoso Street*, Oct. 5, 2017. Photograph; **113:** Robert S. Brantley, *3216 Grand Route St. John*, Oct. 10, 2017. Photograph; **114 left:** Claude Jules Allou d'Hémécourt. *Plan of a Portion of Faubourg Saint Jean*, 1870s, copy of a plan by Jacques Tanesse, 1809. Ink on paper. THNOC, 1966.34.16; **114 right:** Robert S. Brantley, *1868 Grand Route St. John, Fire hydrant*, June 22, 2017. Photograph; **115:** Robert S. Brantley, *700 block (odd) North Hagan Avenue*, Sept. 28, 2017. Photograph; **116:** Robert S. Brantley, *923-29 North Lopez Street, Columns*, Sept. 9, 2017. Photograph; **117 top:** Robert S. Brantley, *1219 North Lopez Street*, June 30, 2017. Photograph; **117 bottom:** Robert S. Brantley, *1219 North Lopez Street, Entrance*, Sept. 9, 2017. Photograph; **118:** Robert S. Brantley, *1325 North Lopez Street*, Sept. 18, 2017. Photograph; **119 top:** Robert S. Brantley, *2775 Orchid Street*, Sept. 23, 2017. Photograph; **119 bottom:** Robert S. Brantley, *2765 Orchid Street*, Sept. 23, 2017. Photograph; **120 top:** George Francois Mugnier, *McDonogh #31 School*, ca. 1908. Photograph. Louisiana Division/City Archives, New Orleans Public Library, **120 bottom:** Robert S. Brantley, *800 North Rendon Street, Entry door*, Sept. 23, 2017. Photograph; **121 top:** Robert S. Brantley, *1320 North Rendon Street*, June 22, 2017. Photograph; **121 bottom:** Robert S. Brantley, *716, 722, and 724 North Salcedo Street*, June 23, 2017. Photograph; **122 left:** Robert S. Brantley, *2821 St. Ann quoins*, September 16, 2017. Photograph; **122 center:** Robert S. Brantley, *3009 St. Ann quoins*, September 16, 2017. Photograph; **122 right:** Robert S. Brantley, *2824, 2820, 2816, and 2812 St. Ann Street*, June 28, 2017. Photograph; **123 top:** Robert S. Brantley, *2739, 2743, 2747, and 2753 St. Philip Street*, June 23, 2017. Photograph; **123 bottom:** D. Seghers, Survey, July 22, 1902, attached to A. Doriocourt, NP, Oct. 13, 1902. NARC; **124:** Robert S. Brantley, *2815, 2821, and 2823 St. Philip Street*, Aug. 31, 2017. Photograph; **125:** Robert S. Brantley, *3039 St. Philip Street*, Sept. 22, 2017. Photograph; **126:** Robert S. Brantley, *2731 Ursulines Avenue*, Sept. 18, 2017. Photograph; **127:** Robert S. Brantley, *2834 Ursulines Avenue*, Sept. 18, 2017. Photograph; **128:** Henry L. Zander, Survey, 1905, attached to Roger Meunier, NP, Jan.

24, 1925. NARC; **129:** Robert S. Brantley, *2924-36 Ursulines Avenue*, Sept. 18, 2017. Photograph; **130 top:** Robert S. Brantley, *3042 Ursulines Avenue*, June 30, 2017. Photograph; **130 bottom:** Robert S. Brantley, *3036 Ursulines Avenue*, June 30, 2017. Photograph; **131:** Robert S. Brantley, *3100 Ursulines Avenue*, June 30, 2017. Photograph; **132:** Robert S. Brantley, *3200 Ursulines Avenue*, June 30, 2017. Photograph; **133 top:** Robert S. Brantley, *1206 North White Street*, June 19, 2017. Photograph; **133 bottom:** Robert S. Brantley, *1206 North White Street, Cornstalk and sunflower cast iron fence detail*, Aug. 23, 2011. Photograph.

Photo Index:
135: Robert S. Brantley, *2909 St. Ann Street, Garden gate*, Sept. 8, 2017. Photograph; **136 top left:** Robert S. Brantley, *2608-10 Bell Street*, Sept. 1, 2017. Photograph; **136 top center:** Robert S. Brantley, *2721 Bell Street*, Nov. 7, 2017. Photograph; **136 top right:** Robert S. Brantley, *3001-03 Bell Street*, June 23, 2017. Photograph; **136 bottom left:** Robert S. Brantley, *3135 Bell Street*, Sept. 23, 2017. Photograph; **136 bottom center:** Robert S. Brantley, *2901 Desoto Street*, Aug. 23, 2017. Photograph; **136 bottom right:** Robert S. Brantley, *3200 Desoto Street*, Sept. 23, 2017. Photograph; **137 top left:** Robert S. Brantley, *3201 Desoto Street*, Sept. 23, 2017. Photograph; **137 top center:** Robert S. Brantley, *2800 block (even) Dumaine Street*, June 28, 2017. Photograph; **137 top right:** Robert S. Brantley, *2822-24 Dumaine Street*, Sept. 12, 2017. Photograph; **137 bottom left:** Robert S. Brantley, *2826-28 Dumaine Street*, June 28, 2017. Photograph; **137 bottom center:** Robert S. Brantley, *2830-32 Dumaine Street*, June 28, 2017. Photograph; **137 bottom right:** Robert S. Brantley, *2834 Dumaine Street*, June 28, 2017. Photograph; **138 top:** Robert S. Brantley, *1034-36 Crete Street*, June 23, 2017. Photograph; **138 center:** Robert S. Brantley, *3115 Desoto Street*, Sept. 18, 2017. Photograph; **138 bottom left:** Robert S. Brantley, *2900 block (odd) Dumaine Street*, Aug. 31, 2017. Photograph; **138 bottom right:** Robert S. Brantley, *3019 Dumaine Street*, Sept. 22, 2017. Photograph; **139 top:** Robert S. Brantley, *3245 Desoto Street*, Oct. 4, 2017. Photograph; **139 bottom left:** Robert S. Brantley, *3029 Dumaine Street*, Sept. 22, 2017. Photograph; **139 bottom right:** Robert S. Brantley, *3037 Dumaine Street*, Sept. 22, 2017. Photograph; **140 top left:** Robert S. Brantley, *2837 Dumaine Street*, July 2, 2017. Photograph; **140 top center:** Robert S. Brantley, *3041 Dumaine Street*, Nov. 13, 2017. Photograph; **140 top right:** Robert S. Brantley, *3138 Dumaine Street*, June 30, 2017. Photograph; **140 bottom left:** Robert S. Brantley, *3343-45 Dumaine Street*, Aug. 31, 2017. Photograph; **140 bottom center:** Robert S. Brantley, *2700 Esplanade Avenue*, Sept. 12, 2017. Photograph; **140 bottom right:** Robert S. Brantley, *2826 Esplanade Avenue*, Sept. 11, 2017. Photograph; **141 top left:** Robert S. Brantley, *2914 Esplanade Avenue*, Sept. 12, 2017. Photograph; **141 top center:** Robert S. Brantley, *2918 Esplanade Avenue*, Sept. 12, 2017. Photograph; **141 top right:** Robert S. Brantley, *3322-24 Esplanade Avenue*, Sept. 11, 2017. Photograph; **141 bottom left:** Robert S. Brantley, *3118-20 Grand Route St. John*, Sept. 1, 2017. Photograph; **141 bottom center:** Robert S. Brantley, *3208-10 Grand Route St. John*, Sept. 1, 2017. Photograph; **141 bottom right:** Robert S. Brantley, *3209 Grand Route St. John*, June 22, 2017. Photograph; **142 top right:** Robert S. Brantley, *3058 Dumaine Street*, Sept. 23, 2017. Photograph; **142 top left:** Robert S. Brantley, *935 North Dupre Street*, June 28, 2017. Photograph; **142 bottom right:** Robert S. Brantley, *917 North Gayoso Street*, Sept. 18, 2017. Photograph; **142 bottom left:** Robert S. Brantley, *3027 Orleans Avenue*, Sept. 22, 2017. Photograph; **143 top:** Robert S. Brantley, *3238-40 Dumaine Street*, June 30, 2017. Photograph; **143 bottom:** Robert S. Brantley, *1014 North Gayoso Street*, June 19, 2017. Photograph; **144 top left:** Robert S. Brantley, *3301-03 Grand Route St. John*, June 22, 2017. Photograph; **144 top center:** Robert S. Brantley, *3307-09 Grand Route St. John*, June 22, 2017. Photograph; **144 top right:** Robert S. Brantley, *1215 North Hagan Street*, Sept. 23, 2017. Photograph; **144 bottom left:** Robert S. Brantley, *1221 North Hagan Street*, Sept. 23, 2017. Photograph; **144 bottom center:** Robert S. Brantley, *1235 North Hagan Street*, Sept. 23, 2017. Photograph; **144 bottom right:** Robert S. Brantley, *1249 North Hagan Street*, Sept. 23, 2017. Photograph; **145 top left:** Robert S. Brantley, *1100 North Lopez Street*, Aug. 29, 2017. Photograph; **145 top center:** Robert S. Brantley, *1204 North Lopez Street*, Sept. 21, 2017. Photograph; **145 top right:** Robert S. Brantley, *1205 North Lopez Street*, June 30, 2017. Photograph; **145 bottom left:** Robert S. Brantley, *1303-05 Mystery Street*, Aug. 31, 2017. Photograph; **145 bottom center:** Robert S. Brantley, *1307-09 Mystery Street*, Aug. 31, 2017. Photograph; **145 bottom right:** Robert S. Brantley, *3121 Orleans Avenue*, Nov. 13, 2017. Photograph; **146 top left:** Robert S. Brantley, *1019 North Rendon Street*, Sept. 21, 2017. Photograph; **146 top right:** Robert S. Brantley, *2801 St. Ann Street*, June 19, 2017. Photograph; **146 bottom left:** Robert S. Brantley, *2711 Ursulines Avenue*, Nov. 13, 2017. Photograph; **146 bottom right:** Robert S. Brantley, *824 North White Street*, June 19, 2017. Photograph; **147 top:** Robert S. Brantley, *3311 St. Ann Street*, Sept. 9, 2017. Photograph; **147 center:** Robert S. Brantley, *2803 Ursulines Avenue*, June 23, 2017. Photograph; **147 bottom:** Robert S. Brantley, *1115-1123 North White Street*, Sept. 23, 2017. Photograph; **148 top left:** Robert S. Brantley, *3127 Orleans Avenue*, Nov. 13, 2017. Photograph; **148 top center:** Robert S. Brantley, *3137 Orleans Avenue*, Nov. 13, 2017. Photograph; **148 top right:** Robert S. Brantley, *3237-39 Orleans Avenue*, Sept. 22, 2017. Photograph; **148 bottom left:** Robert S. Brantley, *1219 North Rendon Street*, Aug. 31, 2017. Photograph; **148 bottom center:** Robert S. Brantley, *1227 North Rendon Street*, Sept. 23, 2017. Photograph; **148 bottom right:** Robert S. Brantley, *716 North Salcedo Street*, June 23, 2017. Photograph; **149 top left:** Robert S. Brantley, *925-27 North Salcedo Street*, Sept. 9, 2017. Photograph; **149 top center:** Robert S. Brantley, *2820 St. Ann Street*, Sept. 11, 2017. Photograph; **149 top right:** Robert S. Brantley, *2901-03 St. Ann Street*, Sept. 22, 2017. Photograph; **149 bottom left:** Robert S. Brantley, *2909 St. Ann Street*, Sept. 8, 2017. Photograph; **149 bottom center:** Robert S. Brantley, *3325-27 St. Ann Street*, Sept. 9, 2017. Photograph; **149 bottom right:** Robert S. Brantley, *3223-25 St. Philip Street*, Sept. 22, 2017. Photograph; **150 top left:** Robert S. Brantley, *1001 North Broad Street, Crescent City Steaks*, Sept. 28, 2017. Photograph; **150 center left:** Robert S. Brantley, *3019-21 Desoto Street*, Sept. 23, 2017. Photograph; **150 center right:** Robert S. Brantley, *3100 Desoto Street*, June 30, 2017. Photograph; **150 bottom left:** Robert S. Brantley, *3063 Dumaine Street*, June 22, 2017. Photograph; **150 bottom right:** Robert S. Brantley, *3200 Dumaine Street*, June 30, 2017. Photograph; **151 top:** Robert S. Brantley, *1101 North Broad Street*, Sept. 1, 2017. Photograph; **151 center left:** Robert S. Brantley, *3222 Desoto Street*, June 22, 2017. Photograph; **151 center right:** Robert S. Brantley, *3226 Desoto Street*, Sept. 1, 2017. Photograph; **151 bottom left:** Robert S. Brantley, *3208 and 3210 Dumaine Street*, June 30, 2017. Photograph; **151 bottom right:** Robert S. Brantley, *3300 Dumaine Street*, June 30, 2017. Photograph; **152 top left:** Robert S. Brantley, *3237 St. Philip Street*, June 23, 2017. Photograph; **152 top center:** Robert S. Brantley, *3323-25 St. Philip Street*, Nov. 13, 2017. Photograph; **152**

top right: Robert S. Brantley, *2741 Ursulines Avenue,* June 26, 2017. Photograph; **152 bottom left:** Robert S. Brantley, *2824 Ursulines Avenue,* Sept. 18, 2017. Photograph; **152 bottom center:** Robert S. Brantley, *3034 Ursulines Avenue,* June 30, 2017. Photograph; **152 bottom right:** Robert S. Brantley, *3114 Ursulines Avenue,* June 30, 2017. Photograph; **153 top left:** Robert S. Brantley, *3233 Ursulines Avenue,* June 26, 2017. Photograph; **153 top center:** Robert S. Brantley, *1315-17 Vignaud Street,* Sept. 1, 2017. Photograph; **153 top right:** Robert S. Brantley, *716 North White Street,* June 19, 2017. Photograph; **153 bottom left:** Robert S. Brantley, *921-23 North White Street,* June 28, 2017. Photograph; **153 bottom center:** Robert S. Brantley, *937 North White Street,* June 28, 2017. Photograph; **153 bottom right:** Robert S. Brantley, *941 North White Street,* June 28, 2017. Photograph; **154 top right:** Robert S. Brantley, *1127 North Dupre Street,* Aug. 31, 2017. Photograph; **154 top left:** Robert S. Brantley, *934 North Gayoso Street,* June 22, 2017. Photograph; **154 center left:** Robert S. Brantley, *3213 Grand Route St. John,* June 22, 2017. Photograph; **154 center right:** Robert S. Brantley, *3221-23 Grand Route St. John,* June 22, 2017. Photograph; **154 bottom:** Robert S. Brantley, *2935 Ursulines Avenue,* June 26, 2017. Photograph; **155 top right:** Robert S. Brantley, *929 North Dupre Street,* June 28, 2017. Photograph; **155 center left:** Robert S. Brantley, *1012 North Gayoso Street,* June 19, 2017. Photograph; **155 center right:** Robert S. Brantley, *3319 Grand Route St. John,* June 22, 2017. Photograph; **155 bottom left:** Robert S. Brantley, *3118 Ursulines Avenue,* June 30, 2017. Photograph; **155 bottom right:** Robert S. Brantley, *3241 Ursulines Avenue,* June 23, 2017. Photograph; **158-59:** Robert S. Brantley, *1325 North Lopez Street, Detail,* Sept. 21, 2017. Photograph; **160:** Robert S. Brantley, *1206 White Street, Cornstalk fence,* Aug. 23, 2011. Photograph; **166:** Robert S. Brantley, *2909 St. Ann Street,* Sept. 8, 2017. Photograph; **174:** Robert S. Brantley, *Ursulines pottery street sign,* Sept. 9, 2017. Photograph.

NOTES

HISTORICAL OVERVIEW

1. James Pitot, *Observations on the Colony of Louisiana, from 1796 to 1802* (Baton Rouge: Published for The Historic New Orleans Collection by Louisiana State University Press, 1979), 13.

2. Pitot, *Observations*, 112.

EXPLORATION AND COLONIZATION

1. Pierre Le Moyne, Sieur d'Iberville, *Iberville's Gulf Journals*, trans. and ed. Richebourg Gaillard McWilliams (University, AL: University of Alabama Press, 1981). Translation of Le Moyne d'Iberville's journals of three voyages to the Mississippi between December 31, 1698, and April 27, 1702.

2. Le Moyne, *Iberville's Gulf Journals*, 111-12.

3. Gordon M. Sayre, *Les Sauvages Américains: Representations of Native Americans in French and English Colonial Literature* (Chapel Hill: University of North Carolina Press, 1997), 170.

4. Jean-François Bertet de la Clue Sabran, *A Voyage to Dauphin Island in 1720: The Journal of Bertet de la Clue*, trans. and ed. Francis Escoffier and Jay Higginbotham (Mobile, AL: Museum of the City of Mobile, 1974), 63–64.

5. Marcel Giraud, *A History of French Louisiana*, vol. 1: *The Reign of Louis XIV, 1698-1715* (Baton Rouge: Louisiana State University Press, 1974), 79.

6. Jay Higginbotham, *Old Mobile: Fort Louis de la Louisiane, 1702-1711* (Mobile, AL: Museum of the City of Mobile, 1977), 346; Concessions, box 6, folder 168, Mary Louise Christovich Papers (MSS 565), The Historic New Orleans Collection, New Orleans (hereafter THNOC).

7. Giraud, *French Louisiana*, 190.

8. Higginbotham, *Old Mobile*, 345.

9. Giraud, *French Louisiana*, 217.

10. Ibid., 216.

11. Edna B. Freiberg, *Bayou St. John in Colonial Louisiana, 1699-1803* (New Orleans: Harvey Press, 1980), 33.

12. Giraud, *French Louisiana*, 249-50.

13. R. Christopher Goodwin & Associates, Inc., "Results of Phase II Testing and Evaluation Excavations at Site 16OR19" (Baton Rouge, LA: FEMA/Louisiana Office of Cultural Development, 2013), 299.

14. Giraud, *French Louisiana*, 216.

15. Antoine Simon Le Page du Pratz, *The History of Louisiana* (2 vols.; London: Printed for T. Becket and P. A. De Hondt, 1763), 93.

16. Richard Campanella, *Bienville's Dilemma: A Historical Geography of Louisiana* (Lafayette: Center for Louisiana Studies, University of Louisiana at Lafayette, 2008), 109.

17. Freiberg, *Bayou St. John*, 39.

18. Ibid., 41.

19. Le Page du Pratz, *History of Louisiana*, 18.

20. Freiberg, *Bayou St. John*, 41.

A GLORIOUS VILLAGE—MOSS STREET: EAST BANK

1. F. J. Dreyfous, NP, December 31, 1907, New Orleans Notarial Archives Research Center (hereafter NARC).

2. F. D. Charbonnet, NP, September 26, 1927, NARC.

3. 1880 Federal United States Census; *Times-Picayune*, March 30, 1930.

4. Oscar Droit, NP, December 22, 1881, NARC; *Times-Picayune*, March 5, 1893.

5. Succession of Firmin Lavaseur, April 25, 1892, no. 35662, Orleans Parish Civil District Court.

6. *Times-Picayune*, February 18, 1889; *New York Times*, February 19, 1889; *Times-Democrat*, June 19, 1895.

7. Frank Macheca, NP, Building contract between owner Sidonie and Nina Palates and Saputo and Governali, contractors, $8,600, December 14, 1938, NARC.

8. Samuel Wilson Jr., *The Pitot House on Bayou St. John* (New Orleans: Louisiana Landmarks Society, 1992).

9. In records from 1894 until at least the 1950s, the short block of Moss between St. Philip and Bell was designated the 1000 block. Current records inexplicably divide the block, consisting of only two structures, as both the 1000 and 1100 block.

10. Edna B. Freiberg, *Bayou St. John in Colonial Louisiana, 1699-1803* (New Orleans: Harvey Press, 1980), 276-277; François Broutin, NP, André Almonester y Rojas to Louis Blanc, January 1, 1793, NARC.

11. John Lynd, NP, February 4, 1813, NARC.

12. Narcisse Broutin, NP, April 30, 1816, NARC.

13. Michel de Armas, October 22, 1822, NARC.

14. Evariste Blanc, July 1834, box 5, folder 100, Mary Louise Christovich Papers (MSS 565), The Historic New Orleans Collection, New Orleans.

15. Felix de Armas, NP, September 26, 1834, NARC.

16. Felix Grima, NP, November 4, 1834, NARC.

17. Joseph Cuvillier, NP, August 5, 1836 and August 5, 1849, NARC.

18. Thomas F. Army Jr., *Engineering Victory: How Technology Won the Civil War* (Baltimore, MD: Johns Hopkins University Press, 2016); William Arba Ellis, comp. and ed., *Norwich University, 1819-1911: Her History, Her Graduates, Her Roll of Honor* (3 vols.; Montpelier, VT: Capital City Press, 1911); *The National Cyclopædia of American Biography: Being the History of the United States*, vol. 17 (New York: James T. White Co.), 1920.

19. Selim Magner, NP, October 31, 1859, NARC.

20. Selim Magner, NP, May 23, 1864; Joseph Cohn, NP, November 6, 1876, both NARC; E. Robinson, comp., *Atlas of the City of New Orleans* (New York: E. Robinson, 1883).

21. Robert Legier, NP, June 20, 1904, NARC.

22. S. Farrar, NP, December 3, 1925, NARC; *New Orleans States*, May 9, 1916; *Times-Picayune*, May 22, 1925; *Times-Picayune*, May 9, 1926; *Times-Picayune*, May 12, 1926; Dufour Bayle, NP, January 30, 1930, NARC. Although the 1926 contract did not name an architect, Moise Goldstein or one of his associates may have been involved with the project. The Moise Goldstein Office Records at Tulane University Libraries' Southeastern Architectural Archive (collection no. 4) formerly included photocopied drawings for the "Bernhard Residence, 924 Moss" (folder 10, 1926). The drawings no longer can be located, however, and the empty folder was removed from the collection in 2017.

23. *Times-Picayune*, July 18, 1950; *Times-Picayune*, July 10, 1963; *Times-Picayune*, August 31, 1965; A. P. Schiro III, NP, December 16, 1972, NARC.

24. *Times-Picayune*, November 17, 1951.

25. Theodore Guyol, NP, December 28, 1848 and January 18, 1849, NARC.

26. Leocarde, f.w.c., v. Cammack, administrator of Blanc, No. 2889, Third District Court of New Orleans, May 7, 1850; Judith Kelleher Schafer, *Becoming Free, Remaining Free: Manumission and Enslavement in New Orleans, 1846–1862* (Baton Rouge: Louisiana State University Press, 2003), 49.

27. No. 40927, Second District Court of New Orleans, April 22, 1879.

28. Felix Grima, NP, May 10, 1879 and April 23, 1879, NARC.

29. Freiberg, *Bayou St. John*, 325-326.

30. *Soards' New Orleans City Directory, for 1878* (New Orleans: L. Soards, [1878].

31. J. C. Wenck, NP, January 3, 1900, with attached 1898 survey, NARC; 1900 United States Federal Census.

32. *Times-Picayune*, February 19, 1914 and September 21, 1920.

33. *Times-Picayune*, February 20, 1982.

34. The Petit succession and real estate holdings are discussed in following sections.

35. Felix J. Puig, NP, November 4, 1905, NARC.

36. Edward B. Ellis, NP, July 14, 1934, NARC.

37. Succession of Victor Petit, June 14, 1892, no. 36061, Orleans Parish Civil District Court. Although Petit died in 1892, legal entanglements among heirs and debtors delayed partitioning his estate for a decade.

38. Antoine Doriocourt, NP, March 30, 1889, NARC.

39. Pierre Courdain, NP, May 16, 1866, NARC.

40. *Edwards' Annual Directory to the Inhabitants, Institutions, Incorporated Companies, Manufacturing Establishments, Business, Business Firms, Etc., Etc., in the City of New Orleans, 1872* (New Orleans: Southern Publishing Co., [1872]); Isaac Magendie estate sale, *New Orleans Republic*, February 27, 1875.

41. Freiberg, *Bayou St. John*, 217, 308, 314.

42. *Orleans Gazette and Commercial Advertiser*, July 26, 1806.

43. *Times-Picayune*, May 6, 1866.

44. Freiberg, *Bayou St. John*, 365.

45. Samuel Wilson Jr., *The Architecture of Colonial Louisiana: Collected Essays of Samuel Wilson, Jr., F.A.I.A.*, ed. Jean M. Farnsworth and Ann M. Masson (Lafayette: Center for Louisiana Studies, University of Southwestern Louisiana, 1987), 374-79.

46. N. Broutin, NP, October 19, 1816; F. Dreyfous, NP, July 13, 1901, NARC.

47. Wilson, *Colonial Louisiana*, 376,

48. Ibid., 377.

49. Historic American Buildings Survey, "Spanish Custom House, 1300 Moss Street, New Orleans, Louisiana," 1933.

50. Amedee Ducatel, NP, Succession of Widow Evariste Blanc, March 27, 1876; T. Guyol, NP, Succession of Evariste Blanc, November 29, 1853, NARC.

51. Amedee Ducatel, NP, Estate of Widow E. Blanc, May 31, 1876, NARC.

52. Felix Grima, NP, November 4, 1834; M. de Armas, NP, January 3, 1811, NARC.

53. F. J. Puig, NP, 1905, NARC.

54. Roger Baudier, *Golden Jubilee: Our Lady of the Holy Rosary Parish* ([New Orleans: Southern Printing Co.], 1958), box 11, folder 435, Christovich Papers.

55. G. William Nott, "Blanc Mansion Survival of Old Days When Hospitality Went with Home Life," *Times-Picayune*, August 20, 1922.

56. *Times-Picayune*, August 7, 1904.

57. *Times-Picayune*, August 2, 1936.

58. *New Orleans Picayune*, December 8, 1897.

59. George M. Barnett, NP, April 17, 1917, NARC.

60. Louisiana Landmarks Society, Articles of Incorporation, 1953, Louisiana Landmarks Society Records and Collection (collection 38), box 12, folder 148, Tulane University Libraries, Southeastern Architectural Archive.

61. Historic American Buildings Survey, "Michel-Pitot House, 1370 Moss Street, HABS No. LA-1116, New Orleans, La.," 1964.

62. James Wade, *The Pitot House: A Landmark on Bayou St. John* (Gretna, LA: Pelican Publishing Co., 2014), 31-39.

63. Wade, 54.

64. Alex Bonneval vs. Felix Ducayet, July 15, 1857, no. 11832, Second District Court of New Orleans.

65. Historic American Buildings Survey, "The Fernandez-Tissot House, 1400 Moss Street, HABS No. LA-1117, New Orleans, La.," 1965.

66. *Le Télégraphe, et le Commercial Advertiser,* August 23, 1806.

67. Thomas Ashe, *Travels in America, Performed in 1806* (London: R. Phillips, 1808), Letter XLIII, https://archive.org.

68. Felix de Armas, NP, March 2, 1825 and January 2, 1826; G. R. Stringer, [act destroyed; executed between 1843 and 1849], NARC.

69. Felix de Armas, NP, October 7, 1831 and April 25, 1832, NARC.

70. J. Cuvillier, NP, June 8, 1849, NARC.

71. Jules F. Meunier, NP, June 6, 1903, NARC.

72. *Times-Picayune,* June 19, 1868.

73. *Times-Picayune,* October 10, 1867.

74. *Times-Picayune,* July 8, 1908; *New Orleans Item,* October 22, 1908.

75. Christovich Papers, box 15, folder 630.

76. *Times-Picayune,* February 6, 1882; *New Orleans Item,* January 15, 1908; Succession of Widow Dominique (Maria) Cefalu, January 20, 1908, no. 84855, Civil District Court of New Orleans.

77. F. J. Dreyfous, NP, August 8, 1908; Succession of Luther D. Ott, 1924, no. 155295, Civil District Court of New Orleans.

78. *Times-Picayune,* January 25, May 9, and May 21, 1926.

79. Southeastern Architectural Archive Blog, March 11, 2014, http://southeasternarchitecture.blogspot.com/2014/03/.

80. Alan Biery, NP, September 7, 1912, contract between Dixie Homestead and Paul Mazzi, builder, $4,385, NARC.

81. *Times-Picayune,* April 4, 1916.

82. *Times-Picayune,* February 3, 1977.

A GLORIOUS VILLAGE—MOSS STREET: WEST BANK

1. In 1995 the Parkview National Register District was named for the area between Orleans Avenue, West Moss Street, and North Carrollton Avenue.

2. *Times Picayune,* August 30, 1947.

3. G. M. Barnett, NP, May 9, 1900, NARC.

4. *Times-Picayune,* August 7, 1947.

5. *Times-Picayune,* August 31, 1919.

6. *Times-Picayune,* September 23, 1923.

7. C. J. Theard, NP, June 17, 1907, NARC.

8. Amedee Ducatel, NP, May 7, 1847, NARC.

9. *Times-Picayune,* April 5, 1885; E. M. Stafford, NP, October 18, 1904, NARC.

10. *Times-Picayune,* April 5, 1885.

11. R. Stephanie Bruno and Liz Warner, "1347 Moss" (unpublished report, 2015).

12. *New Orleans Times,* July 4, 1865.

13. *Times-Picayune,* May 20, 1897.

14. James Fahey, NP, April 25, 1883, NARC. The Merz family also founded Dixie Brewery.

15. C. T. Soniat, NP, April 3, 1909, NARC.

16. David Ritchey, "Robert de Lapouyade: The Last of the Louisiana Scene Painters," *Louisiana History* 14, no. 1 (Winter 1973), 5-20.

17. Harnett T. Kane, "Studio on Bayou St. John Relic of Days When City Basked in Film Glory," *Times-Picayune,* March 6, 1938.

18. P. Lacoste, NP, August 7, 1850; J. G. Eustis, NP, October 7, 1886, NARC.

19. *Times-Picayune,* June 1, 1913, June 1, 1916, October 5, 1919.

20. *Times-Picayune,* May 23, 1897.

21. *Times-Picayune,* February 14, 1912.

22. *Times-Picayune,* September 4, 1921; U.S. Federal Censuses, 1900, 1910, and 1930.

23. *New Orleans States,* April 17, 1934.

24. *Times-Picayune,* March 25 and 26, 1922; *New Orleans Item,* April 13, 1922.

25. M. S. Dreifous, NP, March 22, 1922, NARC.

26. *Times-Picayune,* March 20, 1897.

27. *Times-Picayune,* February 28, 1937.

28. Lyle Saxon, *The Story of La Louisiane* ([New Orleans, 1932]); *Times-Picayune,* October 7, 1928.

A GLORIOUS VILLAGE—OTHER STREETS

1. Writ of Seizure and Sale, P. Canton versus Joseph Girard, July 1, 1878, Conveyance Book 111/folio 581, Civil District Court for the Parish of Orleans, Land Records Division.

2. Abel Dreyfous, NP, January 14, 1881, NARC.

3. Louis Amedee Bringier, Plan book 22, plan 20, April 1, 1837, NARC.

4. For a detailed discussion of the expansion of Esplanade Avenue into the Faubourg St. John, see Mary Louise Christovich et al., *New Orleans Architecture,* vol. 5, *The Esplanade Ridge* (Gretna, LA: Pelican, 1977).

5. Theodore Tureaud, NP, December 28, 1843, NARC.

6. Hilary B. Cenas, NP, February 21, 1854, NARC.

7. *Times-Picayune,* April 1 and June 10, 1904.

8. *Times-Picayune,* July 15, 1908.

9. Agreement for construction was entered into under a private contract and mortgage released June 1, 1906, as noted by E. M. Stafford, NP, act of April 24, 1912.

10. C. J. Theard, NP, June 28, 1893.

11. Succession of Fidele Kellar, June 8, 1875, no. 38046, NARC.

12. Joseph Cohn, NP, July 3, 1862, NARC.

13. A. J. Lewis, NP, November 8, 1872, NARC.

14. P. E. Laresche, NP, June 15, 1847, NARC.

15. J. F. Meunier, NP, October 12, 1907, NARC.

16. W. J. Formento, NP, March 27, 1912, NARC.

17. F. D. Charbonnet, NP, July 17, 1908, NARC.

18. F. D. Charbonnet, NP, December 15, 1911.

19. Christovich, *Esplanade Ridge*, 164 notes the decorative use of architectural firm of Toledano and Wogan's trademark shield motif in this building. A blog spot created by the current owner discusses finding, during renovation, evidence in the attic of an earlier structure (slimbolala.blogspot.com).

20. G. Le Gardeur Jr., NP, February 24, 1906 and August 15, 1907, NARC.

21. M. S. Dreifous, NP, August 14, 1917, NARC.

22. H. Pedesclaux, NP, May 15, 1834, NARC. In 1838 Joseph sold a portion of these lots to his brother, Jean, but regained ownership after the latter's death in 1873.

23. A. Dreyfous, NP, November 11, 1873, NARC.

24. P. Coudrain, NP, May 17, 1865, NARC.

25. C. J. Theard, NP, November 3, 1894, NARC.

26. Louis A. Hubert, NP, September 17, 1902, NARC.

27. A. E. Bienvenu, NP, June 3, 1878, NARC; Succession of Alexandre Seruntine, September 9, 1920, no. 132055, Civil District Court for the Parish of Orleans.

28. Claude d'Hémécourt, copy of an 1809 plan originally surveyed by Jacques Tanesse, depicting the subdivision of a number of blocks into lots within the Bourg Pontchartrain, THNOC, 1966.34.16.

29. B. Lafon, plan showing the rope walk dividing the Faubourgs St. John and Pontchartrain, June 1, 1809, attached to A. J. Lewis, NP, November 8, 1872.

30. *New Orleans Item*, August 5, 1906.

31. *Baltimore Sun*, March 1, 1917.

32. Frank J. Stich, NP, January 3, 1939, NARC.

33. Succession of Victor Petit, June 14, 1892, no. 36061, Orleans Parish Civil District Court.

34. Antoine Doriocourt, NP, October 13, 1902, NARC.

35. F. J. Dreyfous, NP, December 19, 1906.

36. George Montgomery, NP, February 24, 1920, NARC.

37. *Times-Picayune*, July 10, 1904.

38. Jules F. Meunier, NP, September 3, 1903; William V. Seeber, NP, August 16, 1905, NARC.

39. Joseph Duvigneaud, NP, April 7, 1888, NARC. Attached survey shows properties offered for sale by Mrs. Rodney A. Ford.

40. W. J. Hennessey, NP, December 22, 1903; John Wagner, NP, August 3, 1906, NARC.

41. Joseph Cuvillier, NP, July 28, 1848, NARC.

42. N. B. Trist, NP, April 24, 1878, NARC.

43. George Montgomery, NP, September 27, 1906, NARC.

44. Robert S. Brantley with Victor McGee, *Henry Howard, Louisiana's Architect* (New Orleans: The Historic New Orleans Collection; New York: Princeton Architectural Press, 2015).

BIBLIOGRAPHY

Archival Collections

Christovich, Mary Louise Mossy. Papers (Mss 565). The Historic New Orleans Collection.

Conveyance Records. Notarial Archives Research Center, Orleans Parish Civil District Court, New Orleans.

Goldstein, Moise, Office Records (Collection 4). Southeastern Architectural Archive, Tulane University Libraries.

Gulledge, Dorothy Violet, Photograph Collection. Louisiana Division/City Archives, New Orleans Public Library.

Louisiana Image Collection, 1850-1990 (LaRC/Manuscripts Collection 1081), Louisiana Research Collection, Tulane University Libraries.

Louisiana Landmarks Society Records and Collection (Collection 38). Southeastern Architectural Archive, Tulane University Libraries.

Louque, Charles. Papers (Mss. 1473). Louisiana and Lower Mississippi Valley Collections, LSU Libraries, Baton Rouge, LA.

Notarial Records. Notarial Archives Research Center, Civil District Court, New Orleans.

Plan Book Drawings. Notarial Archives Research Center, Civil District Court, New Orleans.

Real Estate Records. Real Estate & Records Office, City of New Orleans.

Surveyors' Sketch Book Collection, 1830-1929 (MSS 290). The Historic New Orleans Collection.

United States Federal Census, 1850-1930.

Published Sources

Army, Thomas F., Jr. *Engineering Victory: How Technology Won the Civil War*. Baltimore: Johns Hopkins University Press, 2016.

Ashe, Thomas. *Travels in America, Performed in 1806*. London: R. Phillips, 1808. Letter XLIII, https://archive.org

Baudier, Roger. *Golden Jubilee: Our Lady of the Holy Rosary Parish*. [New Orleans: Southern Printing Co.], 1958.

Bertet de la Clue Sabran, Jean-François. *A Voyage to Dauphin Island in 1720: The Journal of Bertet de la Clue*. Trans. and ed. Francis Escoffier and Jay Higginbotham. Mobile, AL: Museum of the City of Mobile, 1974.

Brantley, Robert S., with Victor McGee. *Henry Howard, Louisiana's Architect*. New Orleans: The Historic New Orleans Collection; New York: Princeton Architectural Press, 2015.

Campanella, Catherine. *New Orleans City Park*. Charleston, SC: Arcadia, 2011.

Campanella, Richard. *Bienville's Dilemma: A Historical Geography of New Orleans*. Lafayette: Center for Louisiana Studies, University of Louisiana at Lafayette, 2008.

Christovich, Mary Louise, Sally Kittredge Evans, and Roulhac Toledano. *New Orleans Architecture*, vol. V: *The Esplanade Ridge*. Gretna, LA: Pelican, 1977.

Cullison, William R. *The Louisiana Landmarks Society: The First Thirty Years.* New Orleans: Louisiana Landmarks Society, 1980.

Curtis, Nathaniel Cortlandt. *New Orleans, Its Old Houses, Shops and Public Buildings.* Philadelphia: Lippincott, 1933.

E. L. Roberts & Co. *Roberts' Illustrated Millwork Catalog: A Sourcebook of Turn-of-the-Century Architectural Millwork.* New York: Dover, 1988.

Edwards' Annual Directory to the Inhabitants, Institutions, Incorporated Companies, Manufacturing Establishments, Business, Business Firms, Etc., Etc., in the City of New Orleans, 1872. New Orleans: Southern Publishing Co., [1872].

Ellis, William Arba, comp. and ed. *Norwich University, 1819-1911: Her History, Her Graduates, Her Role of Honor.* Montpelier, VT: Capital City Press, 1911.

Freiberg, Edna B. *Bayou St. John in Colonial Louisiana, 1699-1803.* New Orleans: Harvey Press, 1980.

Giraud, Marcel. *A History of French Louisiana,* vol. 1: *The Reign of Louis XIV, 1698-1715.* Baton Rouge: Louisiana State University Press, 1974.

Gitlin, Jay. *The Bourgeois Frontier: French Towns, French Traders, and American Expansion.* New Haven: Yale University Press, 2009.

Higginbotham, Jay. *Old Mobile: Fort Louis de la Louisiane, 1702-1711.* Mobile, AL: Museum of the City of Mobile, 1977.

Historic American Buildings Survey. *The Fernandez-Tissot House, 1400 Moss Street, New Orleans, Louisiana.* HABS No. LA-1117. [Washington: U.S. Department of Interior], 1968.

Historic American Buildings Survey. *Michel-Pitot House, 1370 Moss Street, New Orleans, Louisiana.* HABS No. LA-1116. [Washington: U.S. Department of Interior], 1965.

Historic American Buildings Survey. *Spanish Custom House,* 1300 *Moss Street, New Orleans, Louisiana.* HABS No. LA-18-3. [Washington: U.S. Department of Interior], 1934.

Huber, Leonard V. *Landmarks of New Orleans.* New Orleans: Louisiana Landmarks Society : Orleans Parish Landmarks Commission, 1984.

Kendall, John Smith. *History of New Orleans.* 3 vols. Chicago: Lewis Publishing Co., 1922.

King, Grace. *Creole Families of New Orleans.* New York: Macmillan, 1921.

Le Moyne, Pierre, Sieur d'Iberville. *Iberville's Gulf Journals.* Trans. and ed. Richebourg Gaillard McWilliams. University, AL: University of Alabama Press, 1981.

Le Page du Pratz, Antoine Simon. *The History of Louisiana.* 2 vols. London: Printed for T. Becket and P. A. De Hondt, 1763.

The National Cyclopædia of American Biography: Being the History of the United States, Volume 17. New York: James T. White Co., 1920.

O'Connor, Thomas. *History of the Fire Department of New Orleans.* New Orleans, 1895. Electronic reproduction. New York, NY: Columbia University Libraries, 2011.

Pitot, Henry Clement. *James Pitot, 1761-1831: A Documentary Study.* New Orleans: Bocage Books, 1968.

Pitot, James. *Observations on the Colony of Louisiana, from 1796 to 1802.* Baton Rouge: Published for The Historic New Orleans Collection by Louisiana State University Press, 1979.

Polk's New Orleans City Directory. New Orleans: R. L. Polk, 1938-1956.

R. Christopher Goodwin & Associates, Inc. "Results of Phase II Testing and Evaluation Excavations at Site 16OR19." Baton Rouge, LA: FEMA/Louisiana Office of Cultural Development, 2013.

Ritchey, David. "Robert de Lapouyade: The Last of the Louisiana Scene Painters." *Louisiana History* 14, no. 1 (Winter 1973), 5-20.

Robinson, Elisha, and R.H. Pidgeon, comp. *Atlas of the City of New Orleans, Louisiana: Based upon Surveys Furnished by John F. Braun*. New York: E. Robinson, 1883.

Sanborn Map Company. *Sanborn Fire Insurance Maps of New Orleans, Louisiana*. New York: Sanborn Map Publishing Co., 1885-1940.

Sayre, Gordon M. *Les Sauvages Américains: Representations of Native Americans in French and English Colonial Literature*. Chapel Hill: University of North Carolina Press, 1997.

Schafer, Judith Kelleher. *Becoming Free, Remaining Free: Manumission and Enslavement in New Orleans, 1846– 1862*. Baton Rouge: Louisiana State University Press, 2003.

Seebold, Herman de Bachelle. *Old Louisiana Plantation Homes and Family Trees*. 2 vols. [New Orleans]: Privately published, 1941.

Soards' New Orleans City Directory. New Orleans: L. Soards, 1878-1935.

Somers, Dale A. *The Rise of Sports in New Orleans, 1850-1900*. Baton Rouge: Louisiana State University Press, 1972.

Van Zante, Gary A. *New Orleans 1867: Photographs by Theodore Lilienthal*. New York: Merrell, 2008.

Villiers du Terrage, Marc de. "A History of the Foundation of New Orleans (1717-1722)." *Louisiana Historical Quarterly* 3, no. 2 (April 1920): 157-251.

Wade, James. *The Pitot House: A Landmark on Bayou St. John*. Gretna, LA: Pelican, 2014.

Whiffen, Marcus. *American Architecture Since 1780: A Guide to the Styles*. Cambridge, MA: MIT Press, 1969.

Wilson, Samuel, Jr. *The Architecture of Colonial Louisiana: Collected Essays of Samuel Wilson, Jr., F.A.I.A.* Ed. Jean M. Farnsworth and Ann M. Masson. Lafayette: Center for Louisiana Studies, University of Southwestern Louisiana, 1987.

Wilson, Samuel, Jr. *The Pitot House on Bayou St. John*. New Orleans: Louisiana Landmarks Society, 1992.

INDEX

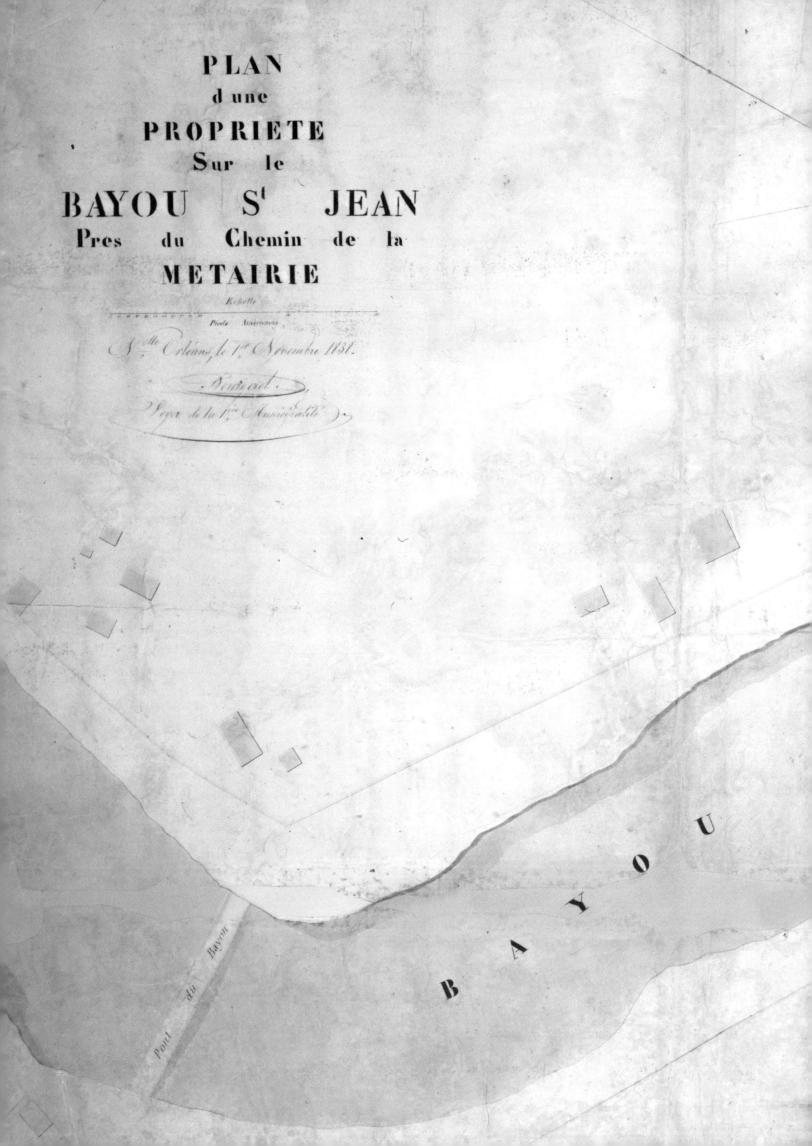

PLAN
d'une
PROPRIETE
Sur le
BAYOU St JEAN
Pres du Chemin de la
METAIRIE

Echelle

Pieds Américains

N.lle Orléans, le 1er. Novembre 1838.

Benejacet.

Voyer de la 1re. Municipalité.

Pont du Bayou

B A Y O U